The Humanitarian Enterprise

'The Humanitarian Enterprise,

DILEMMAS —AND— DISCOVERIES

LARRY MINEAR

Kumarian
Press, Inc.

The Humanitarian Enterprise: Dilemmas and Discoveries
Published 2002 in the United States of America by Kumarian Press, Inc.
1294 Blue Hills Avenue, Bloomfield, CT 06002 USA.

Copyediting, proofreading, and indexing by Bob Land.
Production and design by ediType.

The text of this book is set in ten-point Adobe Sabon.

Printed in the United States of America on acid-free paper by Thomson-Shore, Inc.
Text printed with vegetable oil–based ink.

∞ The paper used in this publication meets the minimum requirements of the American National Standard for Information Sciences—Permanence of Paper for Printed Library Materials, ANSI Z39.48-1984.

Library of Congress Cataloging-in-Publication Data

Minear, Larry, 1936-
    The humanitarian enterprise : dilemmas and discoveries / Larry Minear.
        p.   cm.
    Includes bibliographical references and index.
    ISBN 1-56549-149-1 (pbk. : alk. paper) – ISBN 1-56549-150-5 (alk. paper)
    1. War relief. 2. Humanitarian assistance. 3. Humanitarianism and War Project.
I. Title.
HV639 .M557 2002
361.2′6 – dc21

                                                                                    2002005658

---

11 10 09 08 07 06 05 04 03 02   10 9 8 7 6 5 4 3 2 1   First Printing 2002

To my parents
Paul and Gladys Minear

Contents

Foreword

Larry Minear has been a practitioner, publisher, and advocate of human-itarianism since long before humanitarian studies and practice came into vogue. From his days of advocacy work for Church World Service and Lu-theran World Relief in Washington, D.C., in the mid-1970s to his ten-plus years with the Humanitarianism and War Project in Providence and Bos-ton, Larry has been a consistent voice for understanding complex situations and tailoring practice to those realities, for professionalization of the hu-manitarian field, for action based on research and analysis, and for honest discussion of the issues facing the humanitarian community.

As director of the Humanitarianism and War Project, Larry has been a leader in the field, respected in European capitals, among international NGOs, and by international and U.S. government agencies. The Humanitar-ianism and War Project, cofounded and codirected by Larry and Thomas G. Weiss, who assumed other responsibilities in the fall of 1998, has had no equal over the last eleven years. It has been the most prolific and important publisher in the United States of materials on humanitarianism and has been a leader in bringing together practitioners to discuss its findings.

The project has published books and monographs on everything from the Iraq crisis and the wars in Central America early in the 1990s to the challenge of capacity building in complex emergencies late in the decade. The project has led NGO policy dialogues and other debriefings in numerous countries on its work. After its founding in 1991 by the Watson Institute for International Studies at Brown University and the Refugee Policy Group in Washington and a stretch of productive years in Providence from 1994 to 2000, the project moved to Tufts University in 2000, where it continues its innovative and practical work. Working closely with Larry and the project has been my pleasure.

This book is a thoughtful analysis of data that the project has amassed from thousands of interviews and discussions. Rather than summarizing its findings, the volume offers an innovative look at the key issues that have preoccupied humanitarian practitioners during the past decade. No pulling together of old materials, this book is instead an attempt to be guided by the lessons identified in the research and to see what has been done, what has changed, and what is to come in the field of humanitarianism.

Larry resists the temptation to trash the field or to focus on its many problems and missed opportunities. Some analysts choose to dwell on humanitarian organizations as big business, as driven by fund-raising and the media, as callous to local capacities, and as political Pollyannas that fail to understand how and when they are being manipulated or are manipulating others. Understanding the limitations of the current system, Larry's conclusions are quite critical, pointing to needed improvements. They are critical, however, within his basic premise that the system, with all its flaws, works and that it has — grudgingly and all too slowly and fitfully — changed during the past decade.

This study should be of particular interest to people seeking to improve the field craft of humanitarian agencies, which in recent years has paid more attention to standards for operations, professionalization of staff, and the need for contextual analysis. Larry acknowledges these positive changes, but he challenges the agencies and individuals who make up the humanitarian network to do much, much more. His chapter on coordination indicts the lack of progress in this crucial area. Agencies continue to go it alone and continue to resist coordination and effective joint work. Larry identifies serious unfinished business in other areas he reviews as well.

This study should also be of special interest to universities such as Tufts, where in recent years the development of new degree programs has underscored the heightened profile of humanitarian issues.

Although fair-minded, Larry is not a dispassionate analyst. At the end of the day, all his publications, and certainly this one, continue to advocate for change from within the system. In this study he wrestles thoughtfully and sympathetically with the crucial issues facing humanitarians and their institutions. The book will have succeeded if it leads others not only to reflect upon these issues but to accelerate the pace and depth of change.

DR. JOHN C. HAMMOCK
Director, Feinstein International Famine Center

Medford, Massachusetts
August 2001

INTRODUCTION

Humanitarian Action 1991–2001

Ambassador Jan Eliasson

Ten years have passed since the founding of the Department of Humanitarian Affairs at the United Nations and, coincidentally, of the Humanitarianism and War Project. As vice president of the UN Economic and Social Council (ECOSOC) and as Sweden's ambassador to the UN, I chaired the General Assembly Working Group on Emergency Relief and afterward served as the UN's first under-secretary-general for humanitarian affairs.

During the summer and fall of 1991, the international debate on humanitarian action was intense. Paradoxically, the end of the Cold War in the late 1980s had led to more civil wars and internal strife both in the Balkans and in Africa. Conflict resolution turned out to be more complicated and civilian casualties more extensive than earlier. Dealing with conflicts inside nations triggered fundamental questions of sovereignty.

Bernard Kouchner of France carried the torch of *ingérence humanitaire,* humanitarian intervention, which many developing nations viewed with strong suspicion and criticism. Was this not in fact a humanitarian Trojan Horse, hiding political schemes for overturning distasteful governments in the developing world?

This concern clearly influenced the negotiated text of UN Resolution 46/182, the resolution establishing the UN Department of Humanitarian Affairs (DHA), which stressed the responsibilities of sovereign states, underlined the need in principle for consent, and limited UN action to clearly specified humanitarian crises and natural disasters. No one during these negotiations in 1991 used the term "humanitarian intervention" or dared speak about intervening against grave human rights violations.

How much has changed since 1991? No doubt, awareness of humanitarian issues has progressed. Placing the human being at the center has been a positive result of the end of the Cold War. Nations are no longer seen as pawns in geopolitical chess games — they are societies, composed of individuals with rights and needs. In standing up for the individual's dignity, UN Secretary-General Kofi Annan has played a crucial role in moving the positions forward on humanitarian action and has contributed more than anyone else to dispelling the notion that humanitarian action, or even intervention, is a North/South issue.

Awareness of the urgent need for prevention and preventive diplomacy has grown tangibly in the last decade. During my years at the UN, particularly dealing with the crisis in Somalia during 1992 and 1993, I felt a growing frustration, anger, and despair over late responses, neglect of early warning signs, and passivity in facing emerging crises. Our aid workers were like firemen who were on day shifts as well as night shifts and who, all too often, came to houses that had already burnt down.

Inside the United Nations, among governments, and in the important NGO community, the advocacy for prevention was impressive in the 1990s. The Swedish government adopted an Action Plan for Prevention in 1999. The European Union established a similar program in 2001. In the UN, the General Assembly, the Security Council, and the secretary-general have all underlined the need for early action, coordination, and comprehensive approaches, but we still have a long way to go.

Enhanced awareness is always an essential first step, but concrete and rapid action must follow, along with adapting the responses to the need for coordinated action. Coordination in today's world means close cooperation not only within the UN and the Bretton Woods institutions but also between other international organizations, governments, and NGOs. Progress is being made, but not enough.

We are now seeing an impressive mobilization to deal with the humanitarian challenges in Afghanistan where, by the way, DHA in earlier days helped establish one of the first demining operations. The UN Office for the Coordination of Humanitarian Affairs (OCHA) and the World Food Program are doing a solid job. The UN system and other international actors are laying the foundation for long-term rehabilitation, which must start at the same time as relief efforts — another conceptual step forward since Resolution 46/182, which stressed a "continuum from relief to rehabilitation and development."

To draw the right lessons from the Afghanistan crisis, we should now urgently identify other nations and places where conditions are such that not only humanitarian disasters but also political extremism can evolve. Somalia is a case in point. A massive effort in dealing with the Somali humanitarian crisis could mean not only the difference between life and death for hundreds of thousands of people but also the difference between peace and war as well as between economic development and political disintegration.

Although "placing the human being at the center" is an increasingly accepted formulation and norm, I cannot hide my deep disappointment over the rampant disregard of human life when it comes both to civilian populations and to aid workers in armed conflicts today. Far too often, we see breaches of international law, including of the neutrality of humanitarian action. Far too often we see civilians and humanitarian workers become hostages or victims in political or military crossfires. World leaders and public opinion must rise against these unacceptable violations of international law and human dignity.

One of the more hopeful developments is the acknowledgment that effective action requires a coordinated and global response. Even hard-core critics of multilateralism agree that no one can fight terrorism, money laundering, and organized crime alone. There has to be effective international cooperation.

This change of attitude, brought home by the September 11 tragedy, could and should spread to other areas such as migration and refugee issues, health and development, arms control, and the environment. Indeed, we may have a historic opportunity to make international cooperation a natural reflex of enlightened self-interest. Yet we have to make sure that an institutional structure is in place that is strong and flexible enough to deal with the complex issues facing us. Furthermore, we must develop a political framework which gives the institutional structure — with the UN in the center — the mandate and authority to act quickly and decisively in early stages of conflict. Governments and NGOs have important roles here. Political acceptance of substantial, far-reaching, multilateral cooperation is sorely needed.

Concerted and early international action must be our goal in both the humanitarian and political arenas. In order to develop the best machinery for such action, we must listen to people who have "walked the walk," both in practice and in analysis.

Through the years, I have gained great respect for the Humanitarianism and War Project that Larry Minear has led. We need critical, independent studies like the project's on how the system is performing if we are to succeed in reforming it, and succeed we must.

The worst-case scenario after September 11 is so terrifying that we simply have no choice but to mobilize political will and all resources to make the best-case scenario a reality — and to do it with a combination of passion and compassion.

Washington, D.C.
January 2002

1

The Setting and the Research

This first chapter provides an overview of the volume, introduces the Humanitarianism and War Project and its methodology, and presents the organization of the book.

The First Post–Cold War Decade

The first decade of the post–Cold War era, corresponding roughly to the final decade of the twentieth century, was a time of unusually high visibility for international humanitarian issues. Earlier decades in the century are associated with wars hot and cold, decolonization, and the creation of the United Nations. Unforgettable images include the battles and battlefields of the two world wars and the Korean and Vietnam conflicts, German concentration camps and the detonation of the atomic bomb, and international conferences designed to bring wars to an end and establish an enduring set of global political and financial institutions.

The final decade of the millennium is remembered for a series of conflicts, each with a prominent humanitarian dimension. The Persian Gulf War and its human displacement is etched in memory by U.S. missile attacks against Baghdad and hordes of fleeing Iraqis pressed up against the Turkish border. The civil strife in Somalia is remembered by the bloody interclan bloodshed, banditry, and looting that imperiled the civilian population, as well as by the image of a U.S. serviceman being dragged through the jeering streets of Mogadishu. The shelling of Dubrovnik and the deadly targeting of civilians in Snipers' Alley in Sarajevo call to mind the breakup of the former Yugoslavia, driven by ethnic cleansing and political ideology.

Wars and their casualties also included the genocide in Rwanda and, at decade's end, the mass exodus of ethnic Albanians from Kosovo and the bloodletting in East Timor. High-profile coverage of such events throughout the decade made "humanitarian" a household word. In 2001, one Internet search engine, checking the term "humanitarianism," generated over fifteen thousand references. Appendix 1 provides a time line of seminal events from these years.

Without doubt, the humanitarian enterprise during the 1990s confronted

1

a new and often more perilous landscape for humanitarian action. Humanitarian organizations are now forced to contend with insurgencies as well as recognized political authorities, many of them operating without reference to international law and even unfamiliar with its existence or their obligations to uphold it. Humanitarian activities, personnel, and emblems are no longer sacrosanct. The number of individual emergency relief and human rights agencies — private and public, multilateral and bilateral — has burgeoned. Nongovernmental organizations (NGOs) have proliferated, bringing more energy but also more disarray to what are appropriately called crisis "theaters."

International military forces have been pressed into service, sometimes to good effect but often complicating and sometimes even undercutting the overall humanitarian response. Diplomats and politicians have discovered that responding to human need can contribute to international peace and security, but may also serve as a convenient subterfuge for failure to address the underlying causes of misery and oppression. The international media has become a more active player in the humanitarian sphere, not only dramatizing human need and spurring responses but also stampeding action and contributing to the application of Band-Aids rather than systemic solutions.

According to conventional wisdom, the post–Cold War era represents a radical departure from the years that preceded it. The past decade is said to have harbored more conflicts waged more viciously affecting more people and requiring greater amounts of humanitarian assistance. Our own research, drawing on the work of other institutes that have done more detailed studies, suggests a rather different reality.[1]

Without question, significant political-military changes in the past decade have had a direct bearing on the humanitarian enterprise. The defusing of East-West tensions has been a positive development, with the geopolitical jockeying of superpowers now less of a factor in local conflicts. Some of those conflicts they had tamped down while others they had financed. Without question, too, the number of internal actors and "an increased blurring and blending of various forms of violence, whether political, . . . communal, . . . [or] criminal" have proliferated.[2]

Violence by belligerents, warlords, and criminals clearly increases the difficulties that humanitarian organizations face as they ply their trade. Aid workers who were occasionally caught in the crossfire are now sometimes pinpointed in the crosshairs. Civilians needing international succor find themselves more often dislocated within their own countries than strangers in exile outside. Their vulnerable and dispossessed status within their own nations draws international relief and rights organizations more directly into the conflicts that produce displacement.

Such changes in the landscape for humanitarian organizations, however fundamental, should not be allowed to obscure basic continuities with earlier eras. Indeed, a close reading of the record suggests that "Continuities . . . may well outnumber discontinuities."[3] The number of conflicts has actually been declining since the early 1990s.[4] Although conflicts are nowadays more likely to erupt from internal grievances than from threats, that phenomenon itself is not recent. The intranational origins of conflicts "have been a distinguishing feature of the decades since World War II,"[5] with internal conflicts outnumbering interstate ones since the early 1960s. The critical new element is not ethnic tension but rather the fanning of such tension by unscrupulous politicians and private actors operating in broader and more permissive environments.

Even the truism that civilians are increasingly the victims of today's conflicts needs nuancing. The oft-cited statistic that the casualties of war have transitioned from 90 percent military to 90 percent civilian applies not to the past decade but to the past century. Significant peril to civilians was a fact of life during the Cold War years, as the inhumanity of the strife in places such as Ethiopia, Mozambique, and Angola and, earlier still, in Biafra and Algeria suggests. Although the greater availability of modern weapons has loosened traditional social restraints on violence, countries during the Cold War stocked local arsenals with the small weapons and land mines that are now wreaking widespread havoc.

What of the apparent upsurge in the need among civilian populations for relief and protection? The availability of data from previously inaccessible areas — the states of the former Soviet Union and individual countries such as Iran come to mind — is a major contributing factor to the perceived increase in need. Yet the perception of a quantum leap in the need for international assistance is more likely a function of expanded humanitarian access and better information than of an absolute increase in persons affected. The difference, it turns out, may well be in the eye of the international beholder. That said, however, the amount of funding provided for humanitarian assistance has increased by more than a factor of five during the 1990s to $4.365 billion in 1999.[6]

Understanding the changing humanitarian landscape and increasing the effectiveness of international efforts to assist and protect vulnerable populations spurred the creation of the Humanitarianism and War Project in 1991. The evolving understanding of the humanitarian challenge during the post–Cold War period represents the subject matter of this volume. While the study draws on research that the project has conducted over the past decade, the focus is not on what one particular research team produced but rather on what the wider humanitarian family has learned and the issues of continuing contention and disagreement.

Why does the historical setting matter? Why not respond to civilian need in Somalia in the 1990s as in Biafra in the 1960s, in Azerbaijan in the 1990s as in Angola in the 1980s? Effective humanitarian strategies need a basis in accurate contextual analysis. Overstating the novelty of the post–Cold War landscape limits the important lessons that earlier experience can teach and narrows the ability to discern the early warning signs of pending crises. "If action is to move beyond current political and organizational limitations, humanitarian agencies will need to contextualize their activities more knowledgeably in the post–Cold War environment. That will require making analytical links where appropriate to Cold War precedents while responding to newer post–Cold War dynamics as well."[7]

Conventional wisdom also holds that every conflict is unique. Indeed, our 1992–93 case studies on the Persian Gulf, Central America, Cambodia, Somalia, and the former Yugoslavia underscored our impression from an earlier review of the Sudan that each major post–Cold War crisis was highly idiosyncratic. Each had its own underlying causes, political dynamics, and socioeconomic impacts. Yet our country research later in the decade into new crises — such as in Haiti, Afghanistan, western and southern Africa, and the Caucasus — confirmed the recurrence of common challenges and constraints. An analysis prepared for a UN conference in February 1997 provided an opportunity to struggle with the tensions between country-specific idiosyncrasies and broader commonalities exemplified in the dozen case studies conducted up to that point.

Somewhat to our surprise, our data suggested that "each crisis pits the same institutions (the United Nations, governments, NGOs, the Red Cross and Red Crescent Movement) against the same protagonists (government and insurgent groups, civilian and military officials) in a continuing effort to find solutions to recurring problems (the obstruction of humanitarian access, the manipulation of relief, inequitable economic relationships, the absence of viable and accountable local structures)."[8] Our more recent work has confirmed such recurrent patterns as well.

Indeed, no crisis is unique. The particularities of context, essential to understanding a given conflict, should not be allowed to overshadow the issues and actors that recur from place to place. Emphasizing the idiosyncratic can undermine savvy programming. For example, "the UN tendency — shared by other institutions as well — to approach each crisis as unique" limits the possibility of realizing potential synergies between humanitarian and peacekeeping activities. Understanding the commonalities also has important practical consequences. "As long as every crisis is perceived as wholly without precedent or parallel, there will be little scope for institutional learning. The price of reinventing the wheel with each new crisis is the repetition of mistakes and the obscuring of possible lessons."[9]

The humanitarian enterprise is comprised of four major international sets of actors: the United Nations and other intergovernmental organizations, governments, NGOs, and members of the International Red Cross and Red Crescent movement. The enterprise includes indigenous agencies in crisis areas as well, although the focus of this volume is on the international actors. The humanitarian function is defined broadly to include both assistance to persons in need and protection of fundamental human rights. Also highlighted is the ongoing interaction between humanitarian actors and an array of other officials with political, diplomatic, military, and media portfolios who influence the landscape on which humanitarian action takes place.

In our early study of humanitarian action in Nicaragua, El Salvador, and Guatemala during the years 1981–93, we proposed the concept of "humanitarian space" to describe the area — political as well as geographical — within which assistance and protection activities are undertaken. Reviewing the experience of the region, we suggested that the concept be viewed in dynamic and elastic terms, expanding or contracting according to circumstances. Humanitarian space "may be circumscribed — or expanded — by the actions of political and military authorities; it also may be enlarged — or contracted — by humanitarian actors themselves." Indeed, "Access reflected not only the constraints imposed on humanitarian actors but also their own ingenuity and resolve in mobilizing and managing humanitarian resources."[10]

Toward the end of the decade, we examined the inroads of politicization on humanitarian space at regional and international, as well as local, levels.[11] The growing priority and energy accorded to advocacy efforts by humanitarian organizations had succeeded in expanding available humanitarian space: witness the role advocacy played in the successful adoption of an international convention to ban land mines. Once again, however, advocacy was found to be anything but an exclusively post–Cold War phenomenon. Humanitarian agencies at the Hague Peace Conference of 1899 had been energetic and successful promoters of the ban on dumdum bullets.[12]

The 1990s created a significant amount of new political space for humanitarian initiatives. Reviewing in 1992 the challenges of famine relief in the Sudan, Francis M. Deng and I had sensed the beginnings of a change. The acceptance of horrendous conflict-related suffering and death in the Sudan in 1986–88 contrasted sharply with the more assertive international move to wrest agreement from the belligerents to accept Operation Lifeline Sudan in 1989. With a hopeful eye to the future, we noted that "Rising moral expectations that now influence international responses to such tragedies and the increasing globalization of humanitarian action mean that suffering which might have been ignored in the past can no longer be tolerated today."[13]

Evolution in the direction of greater space for humanitarian action, however, has remained uneven and fragile. Without doubt, the overall trend is positive. "[A]s the world moves from the Cold War to the post–Cold War era, sovereignty as traditionally understood is no longer sacrosanct. The age-old balance between state assertions of sovereignty and international expressions of solidarity with those who suffer has begun to shift perceptibly in favor of those in need."[14] At this writing in 2001, however, the task of situating humanitarian action more firmly in its broadest possible historical context has received new urgency. Recurrent tensions suggest that the death certificate for the Cold War may have been written prematurely. Some residual problems are specific to East-West relations; others reflect the more generic problem of positioning humanitarian values within a broader political/security framework.

One news report in April 2001 noted the growing perception in Europe that the newly installed U.S. administration of President George W. Bush had, in effect, rekindled the Cold War. "'U.S. criticism of other countries on human rights grounds,' an analyst was quoted as saying, 'is being held in some suspicion in Europe because they feel that it's part of a return to cold war politics, in which human rights are really an instrument of something else.'"[15] In June 2001, one journalist, observing the lack of concern about the ongoing war in Chechnya, anticipated the dynamics of the first meeting between President George W. Bush and Vladimir Putin. "This week Bush will restore the central tenet of Cold War diplomacy: that it is Moscow's strategic cooperation, and not its treatment of its own people, that really matters."[16] By September 2001, the administration's highly selective support of multilateral institutions and arrangements in the security and human rights field had fueled concern about the viability of cooperative international problem-solving on humanitarian issues.

Some of the resurgence of Cold War geopolitical tensions may stem from a retrogression in U.S. policies and approaches. In a broader sense, however, to have expected the Cold War years to have been followed by an era of principled multilateralism and a new sense of humanity seems historically naïve.[17] In retrospect, in era after era and within the panoply of competing objectives, humanitarian values have often been the bridesmaid but rarely the bride. Against this more extended backdrop, lessons from the Cold War and earlier have ongoing relevance to the charting of humanitarian action in the new millennium.

This volume, written during the first eight months of 2001, was on its way to the publisher for review at the time of the September 11 terrorist attacks against the United States. Those events, and the response of the United States and the community of nations to them, have had a profound impact upon the humanitarian enterprise and the future of international cooperation on issues of global poverty alleviation, nation-building, justice, and peace: that is, on the broader human security agenda. Some analysts have been even more categorical, seeing the post–Cold War era giving way to the post–post–Cold War era, a radically new period in which political and economic alliances have shifted in an attempt to respond to the reality of global-reach terrorism.

Once again, however, we find important commonalities between the post–

September 11 period and the realities of politics and humanitarian action during the Cold War and first post–Cold War decades. In fact, the terrorist attacks against the United States and the diplomatic, military, and humanitarian response to them highlight many of the dilemmas that form the subject of this volume. The wider — and, in my view, foreboding — implications of the Afghanistan crisis and response for the humanitarian enterprise itself are the subject of an epilogue to this volume, written at the end of 2001, some four months into the newfound preoccupation with global terrorism. References to Afghanistan are also found throughout the volume, although, in the interest of historical balance and perspective, the individual chapters themselves have not been rewritten to encompass the post–September 11 experience.

The heightened prominence of the humanitarian dimension in the first post–Cold War decade, reinforced now in the early stages of the Afghanistan crisis itself, has spurred international institutions, many of them founded earlier in the century or even before, to change their traditional ways of functioning. In order to alleviate human suffering more effectively and to protect fundamental human rights more adequately, many institutions have rethought their basic missions and reexamined their traditional ways of doing business. Among the positive accomplishments are

- the appreciation by humanitarian actors of the political dynamics and dimensions of their involvement in emergencies;
- greater attention to the legitimacy of and need for advocacy on issues with humanitarian implications;
- the introduction of safeguards to address the insecurity of humanitarian operations and personnel and to frame appropriate collaborative uses of military assets;
- augmented assistance and protection for internally displaced persons;
- greater collaboration between relief and rights agencies as integral parts of a common humanitarian task;
- more nuanced interaction with the media on humanitarian concerns; and
- growing attention to issues of effectiveness and accountability.

Sorely tested by the situations encountered and constrained by culture and tradition, however, humanitarian organizations' adaptation to the new realities has been for the most part lethargic and phlegmatic. Institutional reform among humanitarian actors has not kept pace with the changing political-military landscape. This lag is in part a function of the reality that the key features of the present humanitarian enterprise were well established at the end of the Cold War. In fact, with the exception of the International

Committee of the Red Cross (ICRC) and some venerable NGOs, "Today's constellation of humanitarian institutions is largely a product of the Cold War."[18] Indeed, the depth of its roots helps explain why the humanitarian apparatus has changed so little. Numerous structural and institutional problems illuminated by inadequate responses to first-decade crises remain to be addressed. The changes made, and the agenda for future action, are the subject of this book.

The Humanitarianism and War Project

Paralleling the upsurge in humanitarian activities and interest has come an increase in research on humanitarian matters. Unlike the 1970s and 1980s, which witnessed few major studies of humanitarian action, emergency aid efforts in the 1990s operated under detailed scrutiny, both from relief and rights agencies and outsiders. The best-established international repository of evaluations contains only four published during the years 1986–90, followed by a steep increase during the balance of the 1990s, culminating in forty-nine published in 2000.[19]

Case studies have become a virtual cottage industry, with new and old research groups weighing in on the act. On the aid agency side, many organizations have become more conscious of the need to review policies and practice. On the academic side, the field of humanitarian studies is taking shape as a scholarly discipline and teaching area in its own right, appropriating into its own evolving framework insights from economics, politics, international organizations, area studies, anthropology, demography, development, gender and peace studies, and other established social sciences.

One of the research initiatives that has both reflected and prefigured the upsurge in interest in humanitarian action is the Humanitarianism and War (H & W) Project. Founded in late 1991, the project was based at the Refugee Policy Group in Washington, D.C., and in Providence, Rhode Island, at Brown University's Watson Institute for International Studies. At Brown during the years 1994–2000, the project then moved in September 2000 to the Feinstein International Famine Center in the Friedman School of Nutrition Science and Policy at Tufts University in Medford, Massachusetts. The project combines an independent academic and analytical base with a constituency of practitioner organizations that provides financial support and substantive input for its work and makes use of its findings and recommendations.

The Humanitarian Enterprise: Dilemmas and Discoveries examines the evolution in the thinking and practice of humanitarian organizations regarding certain central challenges. In doing so, this book offers something of an annotated roadmap through ten years–plus of studies and discussions, highlighting our most essential and provocative contributions to the broader debate. The H & W Project had its origins in a study of Operation Lifeline Sudan (OLS) conducted in 1990 by a team of seven researchers, an idea that originated with an Ethiopian peace activist and aid worker, Abdul Mohammed. He realized early on that OLS embodied important innovations in the humanitarian enterprise, foremost among them the negotiation with the two belligerents of international access to Sudanese civilians caught in an active civil war. Supported by UNICEF and other humanitarian organizations, our team interviewed more than two hundred persons in the region and beyond, preparing a report that became the subject of a series of debriefings to the agencies as well as a book for more general consumption.[20]

THE HUMANITARIANISM AND WAR PROJECT AT A GLANCE

Founded: 1991 by Brown University's Watson Institute for International Studies (Providence, R.I.) and the Refugee Policy Group (Washington, D.C.)

Supporters to date: Sixty governments, UN and other intergovernmental organizations, NGOs, and foundations

Books: Twelve

Occasional Papers: Twenty-four

Current location: Feinstein International Famine Center, Gerald J. and Dorothy R. Friedman School of Nutrition Science and Policy, Tufts University, Medford, Mass.

E-mail contact: hwproject@tufts.ed

Web site: hwproject.tufts.edu

Our Sudan work received an enthusiastic reception. Because some of our recommendations had implications ranging well beyond the Sudan, the agencies encouraged us to do additional case studies on other internal armed conflicts to generate data to use as the basis for systemwide action. The H & W Project was then launched, underwritten by funds from organizations that had contributed to the Sudan study, joined by other practitioner agencies and, later, by several foundations. (See appendix 3.)

In June 1992, the first H & W case study reviewed the international humanitarian response to the crisis in the Persian Gulf. True to later form, our review represented the first such report on the Gulf crisis by any group. Humanitarian in focus but contextualized in its broader political setting, the study drew on visits by a five-person team to Baghdad, Amman, Teheran, Damascus, Ankara, and Kuwait City, as well as Geneva, New York, and Washington. More than two hundred persons were interviewed while events were still fresh in mind and officials still at their posts.

As of September 2000, the H & W Project entered its fourth phase. Earlier years featured a series of country-specific case studies in conflict situations such as Cambodia, Central America, the Balkans, Rwanda, and the Caucasus. Beginning with phase 2 in 1994, we launched a number of thematic reviews of issues such as the humanitarian roles of international military forces and the media and the humanitarian impacts of economic sanctions. During phase 3 from 1997 through 2000, our focus was on the dynamics of learning and change among humanitarian agencies, with particular attention to the ethical dilemmas and the human rights dimensions of humanitarian action, including gender. Phase 4 involves some new research, along with greater attention to disseminating our earlier and current work.

The Sudan study was important in establishing features of the H & W Project that over the years have come to distinguish it from other similar undertakings. First, the research uses an *inductive methodology*, relying heavily on interviews with the staff of humanitarian organizations and associated institutions, including the belligerents in internal armed conflicts, governments, the media, local civil society, and the affected persons themselves. Each study casts the interview net as widely as possible. To date, the project has conducted more than five thousand interviews. To encourage frank expression of views, people are interviewed off the record, with statements attributed to individuals only with their specific permission.

Interview data forms the starting point of our analysis and lends specificity to our findings and recommendations. Unlike other research groups, which approach humanitarian action within a theoretical framework drawn from the fields of political science, international organizations, or international law, we draw from those fields in examining how the humanitarian enterprise functions and how its activities shed light on evolving international institutions and norms. We seek to provide a rubric for understanding humanitarian action that is derivative from and reflective of the experience of practitioners. The book's chapters begin with vignettes drawn from the project's research and designed to convey the immediacy of the issues and the experiential nature of our approach.

Second, our *primary stakeholders* are humanitarian practitioner organizations. These include fourteen UN and other intergovernmental agencies, eight governments, and twenty-eight NGOs and members of the International Red Cross and Red Crescent movement. Major underwriting has also come from nine foundations. While the practitioner share of our overall budget declined and the foundation share increased during the course of the decade, the contributions of humanitarian organizations themselves remain practically as well as symbolically important.

Third, we are committed to *widespread dissemination* of our work. We hold debriefings as new research is published. For example,

- *The Landmine Ban: A Case Study in Humanitarian Advocacy,* published in late 2000, was the subject of workshops in Geneva, New York, London, and Nairobi, engaging UN officials, NGOs, government representatives, and academics. The study's author also brought his findings to bear on issues the International Action Network on Small Arms (IANSA) faced as it strategized in preparation for the July 2001 UN Conference on the Illicit Trade in Small Arms and later reviewed its next steps.[21]

- Even before its publication in mid-2001, *Patronage or Partnership: Local Capacity Building in Humanitarian Crises* had been the subject of a workshop on Parliament Hill in Ottawa and in our twice-yearly NGO policy dialogue series in New York.

- Published in 1998, *Humanitarian Action in the Caucasus: A Guide for Practitioners* reflected input received during a series of five roundtable meetings for aid agencies in the north and south Caucasus in 1997, followed by another eight strategy sessions with aid groups in 1998. Aid agencies and consortia in the region and international and regional conferences on the issues have used the *Guide* widely.[22]

Efforts to engage practitioners and policy makers set the project apart from institutions that do research largely on and about humanitarian activities rather than with and for the humanitarian enterprise. Phase 4 gives still higher priority to dissemination, with the present volume an example of that effort. In 2002, we will have available on a CD-ROM most of our corpus of publications, designed to meet the needs of field personnel without reliable Internet access and of agencies training field personnel.

Fourth, the composition of the Sudan team, which included two Ethiopians, a Kenyan, a Sudanese, and three Americans, prefigured what has become the project's *international and interdisciplinary approach.* Team members had backgrounds in history, development economics, geography, communications, political science, international organizations, and humanitarian policy and program management. Subsequent teams have paired persons with knowledge of humanitarian institutions and praxis with those having expertise in the countries and regions under review. This approach mirrors our conviction that effective humanitarian action requires contextual savvy as well as technical competence.

The project, which has only a small core staff, has to date employed some seventy consultants and others drawn from a variety of academic and national backgrounds. This volume presents our research and analysis generally without reference in the narrative to the authors of individual studies. Their names are identified in the endnotes, in appendix 4, and on our Web site at *hwproject.tufts.edu*.

Fifth, the H & W Project is *international* in character. While on occasion we have been criticized for reflecting an "American" perspective on the issues or a U.S. foreign policy stance on humanitarian affairs, we have cultivated an international approach through our selection of issues, choice of constituency, mobilization of resources, and use of consultants. All of our publications have appeared in English. Our *Handbook for Practitioners* is available in French and Spanish, our *Guide for Practitioners in the Caucasus* in Russian, our studies of Haiti and of the military and local capacity building in French, and our three-country Central America review in Spanish.

Sixth, we have focused on *complex humanitarian emergencies:* crises with major political and military dimensions that are related to armed conflict, whether between countries or, more typically these days, within countries. The project has not examined the international response to so-called natural disasters, events that can themselves be complex in their origins and often bear a heavy element of human causality. However, a 1992 study by Francis Deng and myself notes the extent to which the same generic challenges the humanitarian enterprise faces in natural disasters are heightened in complex humanitarian emergencies.[23]

Finally, animating our work is a spirit of *constructive criticism*. The decade has seen many "slash and burn" exposés of bungled humanitarian responses to crises. We do not hesitate to be critical, sharing some of the frustrations of the practitioners interviewed. Yet we highlight success stories and frame criticism so as to encourage remedial action. Our collaborative approach has not deterred us from making the occasional far-reaching proposal, sometimes to the consternation of aid agencies. Like relief and rights workers, we are committed to the humanitarian enterprise and its improvement. We have what might be called a "lover's quarrel" with the humanitarian apparatus.

Mindful that every methodology has its limitations, we have built in safeguards to protect the quality, independence, and credibility of our work. We share with our stakeholder agencies in draft form the proposed terms of reference for each study. We frame individual studies as "policy reviews" rather than evaluations in the hope of conveying a less quantitative and more wideranging approach. While we may seek special funding from a given agency for a particular study, each undertaking draws resources from our wider family of contributors. As a rule, reports are not shared in draft form with organizations in advance of publication, an unusual policy that has occasioned some objection. We balance extensive use of consultants from a mix of national backgrounds and sectoral specializations with our own active engagement with them to test and refine their findings.

In a book that highlights the recurrent dilemmas that humanitarian practitioners face, we also identify the dilemmas we face as a research group. First, the practitioner-oriented approach lends special concreteness that more theoretical studies lack. In fact, one of the rewards of our research lies in seeing recurrent patterns emerge from the data generated in widely different conflicts. Still, too great a fixation on individual trees can blur the shape of the forest. Examples from this or that conflict must ultimately take their place within an analytical framework and contribute to a necessary level of abstraction. The inductive methodology places a burden on ourselves as social scientists to weigh the data and frame such broader conclusions and recommendations carefully.

Second, financial contributions from our stakeholders give us a comparative advantage as "inside outsiders" while our independent university base and support from foundations underscore our status as "outside insiders." The access that we enjoy to aid agencies and personnel and the relationships cultivated over time, however, place a burden on us that others more detached from the humanitarian enterprise do not share. Given the constraints of such relationships, we acknowledge the need for exposés from others who from time to time offer more categorical critiques that generate greater public reaction. While we have yet to encounter, or to develop, data on the subject, we suspect that the institutional change produced by both types of reviews — the exposés and the more nuanced critiques such as our own — is probably modest at best.

Out of the project's activity has emerged what we call the "H & W optic." By this we mean the approach just outlined: inductive rather than theoretical, bringing to bear insights from the social sciences on the vexing challenges facing humanitarian practitioners, committed to improving the functioning of the enterprise. This optic was elaborated in our formative years in dialogue between the two codirectors of the project, Thomas G. Weiss and myself, and with our consultants. The approach has evolved over time, reflecting the accumulation of data and experience.

The H & W optic does not represent a uniform "humanitarian worldview" that encompasses and reflects all of what we have produced, offering a set of prescriptions for any and all settings. In fact, the array of researchers has been so diverse and the conflicts examined so disparate as to ensure a wide variety of perceptions, conclusions, and recommendations. We have often seriously disagreed on specific issues: for example, on the extent to which coordination requires a command element (chapter 2), on whether humanitarian action can and should be neutral (chapter 5), and on the appropriate roles of the military in the humanitarian sphere (chapter 6). Divergent perspectives, energetically articulated in the course of our research and analysis, have strengthened our work and identified policy issues requiring further research and reflection.

In this volume the pronoun "we" refers to statements of recurrent findings and conclusions that have emerged from our research and publications. The occasional "I" refers to judgments of Larry Minear as project director, which my colleagues may or may not share. The text thus presents our general consensus where it exists, noting points of difference as well. An earlier draft downplayed such disagreements but reduced the presentation to a "lowest common denominator" approach, thus denying the reader much of the intellectual struggle that has infused our work. Despite differences on this issue or that, however, the project's work as a whole, and its individual publications as well, are viewed through a broadly consistent optic that acknowledges humanitarian action in its rich and variable interplay with politics and conflicts.

To facilitate presentation, the narrative quotes amply from project publications, referenced in endnotes to indicate the author or authors of the particular research cited. When use is made of material from nonproject sources, the origins are described in the narrative itself. All quotations appearing in the narrative without other attribution originate with the project. The fact that the majority of the endnotes reference the project's own publications may raise some academic eyebrows, yet each of the earlier studies made ample use of the perspectives of other researchers and analysts.

The present volume does not offer a comprehensive review of responses to all of the major post–Cold War emergencies: we did not do studies of East Timor or North Korea, for example. Nor is this book intended as an all-purpose guide to the full range of issues of humanitarian policy and operations: we have not carried out cross-country comparisons of emergency food programs or refugee resettlement, undertaken in-depth studies of individual UN agencies or NGOs, or joined the debate about standards and accountability. Confined to the project's work to date, the present review should still be valuable for identifying trends and issues, conclusions and recommendations.

This introduction is geared to identifying the project for readers not familiar with our work and to locating it in relation to the wider process of reflection on humanitarian action and the work of other research groups. Further information is available at our Web site, *hwproject.tufts.edu*. In addition to making available most of our publications in their entirety, the site includes critical commentary from users and journal reviews and is linked to thematically related sites. We encourage readers of the present study to share their reactions with us by e-mail at *h&w@tufts.edu*.

Organization of the Volume

The remainder of the volume contains eight chapters, each reviewing a particular aspect of the humanitarian enterprise, and an epilogue. The first three chapters examine major challenges that the humanitarian enterprise faces within its own ranks. Chapter 2 analyzes the experience of coordinating the work of humanitarian agencies. Chapter 3 unpacks some of the tensions between the delivery of assistance and the protection of basic human rights. Chapter 4 reviews the record of humanitarian actors in strengthening the capacity of local institutions and individuals.

Chapters 5 and 6 examine the challenges faced by the humanitarian enterprise in its dealings with a wider array of political and military actors. Chapter 5 addresses tensions between the would-be neutrality of humanitarian activities and the politicized arenas in which they take place. The chapter examines the different approaches taken by various agencies to their inevitable interactions with the political realm and its changing understanding of sovereignty. Chapter 6 analyzes the attitudes of humanitarian actors toward the use of military and economic force and, more specifically, their terms of engagement in settings where international troops and/or economic sanctions have been imposed.

Both among humanitarian organizations themselves and in their relationships with political-military actors, progress is evident in clarifying the issues and in adapting the frameworks of collaboration. At the same time, residual structural problems remain in serious need of attention. Chapter 7 sketches the outlines of an architecture that would be more suited to both the internal and the external sets of challenges. Chapter 8 discusses the process of equipping the enterprise to function more effectively, especially in complex contexts too little understood and amid conflicts to which agencies may inadvertently contribute. Chapter 9 examines the dynamics of institutional change and some reflections on the contribution of the Humanitarianism and War Project. The epilogue reviews the impacts of terrorism and antiterrorism, with specific reference to Afghanistan, on the humanitarian enterprise, revisiting in sequence the themes of chapters 1 through 9.

The volume contains appendixes providing a time line of selected seminal events (appendix 1); lists of Project publications (appendix 2); financial contributors (appendix 3); consultants, authors, coauthors, and staff (appendix 4); abbreviations used in the text, and brief biographical information about the author and other contributors to this volume.

The subtitle of the volume, "Dilemmas and Discoveries," reflects a leitmotiv of the project's research and analysis. We use the term "dilemmas" to describe the vexing choices faced by practitioners who are often forced to choose between alternatives, each of which is likely to have serious negative consequences. Each chapter identifies dilemmas that the humanitarian enterprise has encountered and discoveries made regarding their effective management.

Within the humanitarian community, trade-offs occur between the clear-cut delegation of authority that well-orchestrated operations require and the relative autonomy that individual agencies prefer (chapter 2); between embracing a "rights framework" and adopting a studied posture of concentrating on the delivery of emergency assistance to meet survival needs (chapter 3); and between a hard-charging international aid emergency apparatus and the slower and longer-term process of nurturing indigenous institutions and leadership (chapter 4).

The humanitarian enterprise also faces the dilemma of whether to approach humanitarian action as an element in a political framework that includes conflict prevention and conflict resolution, or to isolate humanitarian action from such broader political agendas (chapters 5 and 6). Perhaps the most overarching reality is that political, diplomatic, and military institutions have a significant bearing on the success of the humanitarian enterprise, even though humanitarian interests themselves have at best limited influence on them.

Our research suggests that understanding and managing such dilemmas contribute to more effective humanitarian action. We are heartened that humanitarian organizations are making progress in identifying the policy options and in anticipating the likely consequences of each. Their current approach contrasts starkly with Cold War–era humanitarian action, when they largely denied the political context within which they functioned and its implications for relief and rights work. The enterprise does well to confront rather than ignore such dilemmas and to chart a course that reflects past experience and embraces the inevitable uncertainty of the future.

We would like to express appreciation to the many individuals and institutions who have assisted in the work of the project over the years and in the preparation of this volume. Thomas G. Weiss, cofounder of the project in 1991 and its codirector until 1998, played a formative role early on and, more recently, as a consultant, has provided input and encouragement. In addition to their earlier research and writing for the project, a number of consultants have made detailed comments on the manuscript: Greg Hansen, Steve Lubkemann, S. Neil MacFarlane, Julie Mertus, Marc Sommers, and Ted van Baarda. I am indebted to colleagues at the Fletcher School of Law and Diplomacy, Peter Uvin, Karen Jacobsen, Ian Johnstone, and Ellen Lutz, for their comments on chapter 3. That chapter also draws on research and reflection by William O'Neill.

Within the Feinstein International Famine Center at Tufts University's School of Nutrition Science and Policy, extensive research assistance from John Patten and energetic administrative support from Jennifer Gatto is also gratefully acknowledged. Peter Hoffman, a student at the Graduate Center of the City University of New York, has also been helpful.

Special thanks go to John Hammock, director of the Feinstein International Famine Center, who has encouraged the writing of this volume and commented on its various drafts. Thanks go as well to the institutional contributors to the Humanitarianism and War Project over the years (appendix 3). They have made possible not only the project itself but also this review of the issues of the decade. The earlier institutional homes of the project have also played important roles: the Refugee Policy Group in Washington, D.C., and the Thomas J. Watson Institute at Brown University.

The author's standard disclaimer is perhaps more necessary and appropriate in this instance than in other volumes. While I have made extensive use of the work of many colleagues, I take full responsibility for the presentation of the work of the project and for any errors in fact or interpretation.

2

Coordination

Visiting Kigali in September 1994 during our case study on Rwanda, I attended an impressive coordination meeting convened by the UN Rwanda Emergency Operation (UNREO). The meeting brought together representatives of the international humanitarian enterprise, including the UN agencies, nongovernmental groups, the Red Cross movement, and donor governments. The Rwandan government sent its coordinator of humanitarian assistance as well. Shifting back and forth from English to French, UNREO coordinator Charles Petrie led the group of about sixty in a brisk and businesslike exchange.

The agenda included information on human needs around the country and their coverage by one agency or another; reports on the situation in the camps for Hutu refugees across the Rwandan border in Zaire and Tanzania; problems encountered by, and with, the largely Tutsi Rwandan government (then about two months in office); and security concerns regarding civilians and aid workers. The inhumane condition of prisoners in government jails, soon to become an explosive issue, was also flagged. A session later the same week briefed the first visiting head of state, Mary Robinson, then president of Ireland and later UN High Commissioner for Human Rights, on the situation.

Everyone associated with the humanitarian enterprise touts the value of coordination. Donors want resources used cost-effectively. Aid agencies seek an efficient division of labor and fear media exposure of unseemly rivalries. Political authorities receiving aid expect coherence among the many actors that descend upon them in times of crisis. The public has had enough experience with multi-ring humanitarian "circuses" to expect the worst.[1] Yet coordination is easier to advocate than to achieve. The political economy of the humanitarian enterprise — that is, the perceived institutional needs of donors and operational agencies and the power-based dynamics of their interaction — work against it.

This chapter reviews the elements involved in coordination and the obstacles it faces in the form of power, profile, cost, structures, and leadership. The chapter also identifies discoveries made regarding the effective manage-

19

ment of the various dilemmas involved. At issue are an understanding of the various facets of the coordination task, the importance of clear authority to coordinate, the necessity for both individual and institutional leadership, and the need to moderate the competitiveness of the humanitarian marketplace. In my judgment, the continuing absence of effective coordination structures remains the soft underbelly of the humanitarian enterprise.

The Elements

In our first case study of a major post–Cold War conflict, the international response to the crisis in the Persian Gulf in 1990–92, our research group offered a definition of coordination that reflected data gathered from interviews around the region and at UN headquarters in New York and Geneva. Coordination, we suggested, is a multifunctional activity involving

> the systematic use of policy instruments to deliver humanitarian assistance in a cohesive and effective manner. Such instruments include: (1) strategic planning; (2) gathering data and managing information; (3) mobilizing resources and assuring accountability; (4) orchestrating a functional division of labor in the field; (5) negotiating and maintaining a serviceable framework with host political authorities; and (6) providing leadership.[2]

In the decade that followed, we confirmed and refined that definition as a result of individual studies of the former Yugoslavia and Georgia. Comparative reviews of coordination mechanisms in Afghanistan, Mozambique, and Rwanda[3] and in Sierra Leone and Tanzania offered corroborating evidence.[4] Coordination has formed a leitmotiv throughout our work.[5]

Coordination is also multilayered, involving the orchestration of relationships not only at headquarters but also at the regional, national, and field levels. In fact, many of the six functions require activities at multiple levels. Planning, information management, and leadership take place in New York and Geneva as well as in Mogadishu and San Salvador, in Brussels and Washington as well as in Goma and Sarajevo. Even functions with a predominantly field orientation such as arranging a division of labor among organizations or negotiating arrangements with host political authorities may require outside reinforcement.

The multilayered aspect of coordination also exists within individual countries. The international response to the emergency in Sierra Leone involved multiple sets of coordinating structures: Freetown-based policy and technical bodies at the national level and also technical committees at regional levels throughout the country. Some of the most effective coordination took place in technical committees with responsibilities for a given

programming sector — no fewer than ten existed. The food aid committee was particularly innovative. An organization chart of the coordination
apparatus within the country, featuring consultative forums at each level,
identifies some twenty-five separate committees and platforms.[6] At the most
local level, the tribal chiefs' court committees and local community-based
organizations themselves involved multiple players.

Coordination involves responding to life-and-death emergencies that take
unexpected twists and turns. "Coordination is a messy, dynamic, and evolving process," observed our comparative study of Tanzania and Sierra Leone.
"[T]he crises that created the humanitarian emergencies in the first place ensure that this will be true."[7] In December 1996, the Tanzanian government
rescinded UNHCR's role as refugee coordinator and launched an operation
to force Rwandans back across the border. In Sierra Leone, a military coup
in May 1997 forced the regime of President Kabbah into exile, changing
the political and humanitarian situation dramatically. "Humanitarian actors were sometimes equal to the challenge, but on other occasions failed to
keep pace with — much less to anticipate — changes in the political, military,
and humanitarian situation on the ground."[8]

Crises thrust individuals as well as agencies into key decision-making
roles. Sometimes staff take charge and rise to the occasion, filling an institutional vacuum and forging an effective response. On other occasions, they
are overwhelmed by events. Sometimes staff members have the necessary
institutional authority to function effectively but fail to do so. On other
occasions, they lack the authority but still manage to bring international
resources to bear effectively on the crisis. The interplay between individual
humanitarian officials and the agendas of their respective institutions, each
avowedly committed to coordination, may also play a make-or-break role
in coordination efforts.

The Obstacles

The decade has seen undeniable progress in meeting the coordination challenge. The quantifiable indicators are positive: the number of persons with
portfolios that include coordination responsibilities, the number of inter-
agency coordination meetings held, the amount and real-time nature of the
information shared, prenegotiated memoranda of agreement among agencies, and the now-standard funding appeals that place requests for a given
country within a common rubric and requests for each country within a
common global framework.[9]

Yet serious constraints remain. Five are examined here: issues of competing power and authority, the desire for agency profile, the costs of
achieving effective coordination, problems in devising appropriate structural
arrangements, and a lack of leadership.

Power

Coordination is about power. What agency or individual, if any, has the authority to orchestrate the activities of the diffuse and far-flung humanitarian community in a given emergency? What is the source of that authority? What accountabilities are involved, and to whom? Who, in short, pulls the entire operation together?

Different models have been tried in various settings with varying results. *The Politics of Mercy: UN Coordination in Afghanistan, Mozambique, and Rwanda* offered a tripartite typology as an analytical device:

> *Coordination-by-command,* involving clearly defined leadership authority reinforced by appropriate carrots and sticks. Prince Sadruddin Aga Khan functioned as commander-in-chief of humanitarian operations in Afghanistan under Operation Salam, beginning in 1988.[10]

> *Coordination-by-consensus,* which embodies less authority vested in a single organization and requires greater persuasion. The Rwanda response provides a case in point.

> *Coordination-by-default,* which, lacking clear structures for orchestrating concerted action, takes its chances on what a given situation may produce. The Mozambique response largely took this approach.

The data suggest that success is a function of the command element involved. That is, coordination-by-consensus is more effective than coordination-by-default, and, in turn, coordination-by-command more effective than coordination-by-consensus. In Afghanistan, significant amounts of resources placed at the disposal of the UN coordinating office in the late 1980s produced more concerted humanitarian programs. The office was able to function better administratively and to influence the spending of the funds it provided to other agencies. In Mozambique and Rwanda, UN coordinators without resources to dispense were forced to "rely solely on personalities, goodwill, and intellectual leadership," with disappointing results. The fundamental lesson from the experience in the three countries is that if humanitarian programs are to succeed, "more rather than less coordination is required."[11]

The utility of a command element is confirmed in other country case studies. One major factor in the success of the program for Rwandan refugees in Ngara, Tanzania, in 1994–96 was UNHCR's ability to limit the number of NGOs working in its camps. The Tanzanian government reinforced the authority it granted UNHCR by issuing entry visas only to NGOs that UNHCR designated, eliminating the freewheeling agencies that often flock to such emergencies. An innovative in-house arrangement also allowed UNHCR — on the spot in the field — to fund its chosen NGOs, short-circuiting the more laborious process of Geneva-based review, approval of grant proposals, and issuance of checks.

The existence of clear authority from the Tanzanian government and the creation of expedited procedures within UNHCR contrasted sharply with the situation in Sierra Leone, where a similar multitude of NGOs sought to establish operational presence. Neither the UN's Humanitarian Assistance Coordination Office (HACU) nor the UNDP office, which was formally in charge of coordination, received Ngara-esque authority from the Sierra Leonean government or had donor funds at its disposal. The chaotic result suggests the desirability of limiting the number of NGOs operational in a given emergency. Imposing controls on agency involvement, of course, runs against the live-and-let-live spirit of humanitarian response. Yet the cause of coordination would be better served with fewer players and more clearly delegated authority over them. For their part, individual NGOs might take the lead by working in coalitions rather than individually and by opting not to engage in certain emergencies.

Entrenched resistance to a greater command element comes from several quarters. The same donors that criticize lack of coordination complicate the task of achieving it by imposing conditions, earmarking resources, and injecting political and other agendas that often work against the coordination they profess to want. The German government insisted that the food aid it allocated to the UN World Food Program for Kosovo be distributed exclusively within the area under control of the German military for use in bakeries operated by German troops for bread distribution among Kosovar civilians served by German NGOs. What seemed eminently logical to government officials in Berlin, however, made little sense to multilateral program managers in Kosovo, whose responsibility was to advance countrywide objectives in a cost-effective manner with food aid contributed by numerous donors.[12]

Donors can play a constructive role too. "No single set of humanitarian actors has more power to influence coordination positively than donors," the experience in Sierra Leone and Tanzania suggested. "They sculpt humanitarian action."[13] Such was clearly the result of joint insistence by two major aid underwriters — the U.S. government's Office of Foreign Disaster Assistance (OFDA) and the European Community's Humanitarian Office (ECHO) — that all agencies receiving food aid in Sierra Leone have their activities coordinated by the Freetown-based Committee on Food Aid. In Tanzania, the channeling of U.S. government resources through UNHCR strengthened the UN's hand in its dealing with NGO implementing agents.

Resistance to more assertive coordination also comes from aid agencies themselves, which have little patience with the reduced power and authority that coordination-by-command necessitates. "The simple reality is that within the diverse UN family," concluded one independent study of the

1996–98 Rwanda response commissioned by the Inter-Agency Standing Committee (IASC), "no element has adequate authority to command, coerce or compel any other element to do anything."[14] Such authority is lacking in large part because of the resistance of operational agencies to lodging coordination responsibility in a single entity, as discussed below. Priding themselves on their autonomy and flexibility, NGOs, too, resist ceding authority to a coordinating entity, even one that is nongovernmental in nature.

Many practitioners question the coordination-by-command approach that we and some other analysts believe is essential. Some hold that, given the institutional politics involved, a command approach is so unlikely to be adopted that even examining its pros and cons is a waste of time. Others have a more substantive objection: that a process built upon consensus has a better chance of producing coordination than one relying on imposed authority. In this view, the contribution made by personalities, goodwill, and intellectual leadership can help avoid the reluctance and resistance that coerced coordination may engender. Coordination is thought to be most effective when it relies not on financial or institutional carrots or sticks but on persuasiveness and the demonstrable benefits in improved individual agency effectiveness.

Our research suggests, however, that the persuasiveness of coordination vehicles is limited in the absence of authoritative institutional reinforcement. As a result, a UN entity needs to be clearly tasked with coordination responsibility and held accountable for achieving it. The fear of operational agencies — that a coordinating agency will itself become operational — is answerable through carefully delimited terms of reference. Vesting a "lead agency" with coordinating responsibilities in addition to its own operational tasks has created considerable confusion in the past.

The comparison of coordination efforts in Afghanistan, Rwanda, and Mozambique also identifies an illuminating paradox: "effective coordination obeys the law of diminishing returns." When agencies see themselves needing coordination, they will tolerate more of it and underwrite its costs. The perceived need tends to be greatest at the peak of a given crisis, with structures established at that time becoming less essential as the crisis is brought under control. The three-country experience confirms that coordination needs to evolve to keep pace with changes in a given crisis, the circumstances of the civilian population, and the institutional array of agencies on hand.[15] Some of the problems identified in the earlier study of Afghanistan, from the 1980s through the mid-1990s, have recurred in the international response to the most recent Afghanistan crisis, as discussed in the epilogue.

Whatever the disposition of power between and among UN agencies, interaction between humanitarian actors and other centers of power is indispensable for successful coordination. The international response to the conflict in Nagorno-Karabakh offers an interesting perspective on the relative power of the actors involved. In Armenia, the presence of three strong sets of actors — the host government, the UN, and NGOs — made for effective coordination. In Azerbaijan, the government was less dynamic and committed, the UN less coherent in its approach, and NGOs more hobbled by donor restrictions. The wider lesson from the Karabakh response is that effective programming requires shared responsibilities among the multiple players involved, with each playing a key role.[16]

In settings of civil strife in which the central authorities are under duress and insurgents are interlocutors in the humanitarian dialogue, host authorities have the power and authority to cooperate with — but also to trump — the best efforts of the humanitarian enterprise. In some situations such as Tanzania and the Sudan, those authorities facilitated coordination. In other settings such as Sierra Leone and Azerbaijan and, later, in the course of relief operations in Tanzania and the Sudan, authorities frustrated coordination. While short-term advantages may accrue to international agencies in having the host authorities less involved, sooner or later those authorities need to assume a well-defined and recognized coordination role.

Profile

Coordination is also about visibility — that is, the orchestration of agency profile. The Goma experience stands as a dramatic recent example of agencies responding helter-skelter to a major crisis. The massive exodus of Rwandans into neighboring Zaire in July 1994 following genocide in their homeland led to a displaced population of upward of 1 million people. Their plight, soon complicated by the outbreak of cholera in hastily erected camps, attracted an array of humanitarian agencies and of military contingents with humanitarian tasks, all operating with little evident coordination. What some have cynically called the "gold rush" was soon on.

Coordination meetings were held on a regular basis during the Rwanda crisis, in Kigali (as recalled in the opening vignette) and in neighboring countries, yet coordination was widely perceived as a threat to agency autonomy and media access. NGOs jockeyed to be interviewed and become identified back home with the relief effort. "In disasters, each agency faces a conflict between operational objectives, which require good inter-agency cooperation, and management needs, which require good publicity for that agency," observes the International Federation of Red Cross and Red Crescent Societies (IFRC). "In Rwanda, at least at the start, the management need for publicity and funds overwhelmed operational objectives."[17]

Even agencies that are traditionally collaborative become nervous when collegiality threatens to compromise profile. They view identification with a given crisis — whether on television or in printed news accounts — as essential to mobilizing resources for their work. Moreover, as the media has come into its own as an influential actor in the humanitarian theater, agencies attach even greater importance to cultivating and retaining indepen-dent access.[18] Coordination is perceived as reducing the profile of individual aid groups, be they NGOs or bilateral or multilateral aid entities. Trade-offs clearly exist between supporting the common effort and maintaining independent visibility.

A comparison of the humanitarian response to the Kosovo crisis with the earlier disarray in Goma is instructive. In Tirana, Albania, the government constituted an emergency management group that functioned as a venue for discussions among governmental and intergovernmental actors. Later in Pristina, Kosovo, the UN played a more active coordination role. UNHCR helped underwrite an information center that provided a forum for NGOs to interact, share information, and plan joint activities. While more humanitar-ian organizations were involved in the Kosovo theater than in the Rwanda crisis — one participant in both puts the number at five hundred and two hundred respectively — the coordinating structures devised in Kosovo were generally more adequate to the task. The fact that key individuals who or-chestrated collaboration in Pristina had collaborated earlier in Tirana and Skopje and in other major crises suggested that lessons were being learned and improvements made. OCHA personnel with coordination-by-consensus mandates deployed not only in Pristina but elsewhere around the region.

While jockeying for position is often viewed as an NGO phenomenon, UN organizations, too, are anxious to be identified with a given crisis re-sponse. In Afghanistan in the mid-1990s, UN agencies responded quite differently to the challenges of the Taliban authorities. Following its takeover of Kabul in December 1996, the Taliban imposed an ultraconservative brand of Islam on the areas it controlled. Its edicts forbade women from working outside the home and circumscribed their access to health services, employ-ment, education, and training as well. Participation of women and girls in aid agency activities outside the home was limited, as were the terms of access of international personnel to them. The agencies faced a catch-22 situation, recalled a WFP official after the Taliban had been ousted from power. "[O]nly female staff could consult Afghan women on their needs, but the agency was allowed to employ only men."[19]

Individual UN agencies sought to chart their own courses of action in their respective areas of activity. UNICEF refused to support schools for boys as long as girls were barred from attending classes in those facilities. WFP pressed the authorities to ensure that women would benefit from its food-for-work programs, both as recipients and as employees.[20] WHO, by contrast, "positioned itself as fully cooperative with the authorities, par-ticularly the health ministry." While the embarrassing disarray among UN agencies triggered numerous UN missions from headquarters, interagency agreement on strategy proved elusive.[21]

How serious a problem is the welter of agencies that flock to emergencies, each with its own agendas and needs? "While as much as 75 percent of all global NGO humanitarian funding is handled by 10 to 15 international organizations," noted a review commissioned by the Inter-Agency Standing Committee (IASC), "dozens, and sometimes hundreds of smaller NGOs rush to the scene of an emergency, all wanting to assist — many of them aided and abetted by bilateral and multilateral donor agencies." The IASC study notes that "This can create a massive coordination problem on the ground and . . . confusion in the minds of donors in the North. It can also create problems of quality."[22]

Practitioners themselves are divided about the seriousness of the coordination problem. "Sometimes the problem seems worse than it really is," comments one NGO veteran of many emergencies and innumerable coordination meetings. "In Kosovo, for example, despite the highly publicized 200–300 NGOs present, there were really only a dozen or so serious players, all of whom were highly coordinated."[23] The fact that in many emergencies a few large international NGO families or federations control most of the resources is doubtless a more salient fact than the specific number of agencies on the ground at a given time.[24] Indeed, "without NGOs, many bilateral and multilateral agencies would be unable to deliver the bulk of their emergency assistance as fast, as well, or perhaps at all."[25]

Yet obstacles to coordination that the multiple moving parts represented should not be understated. UN agencies are generally more united in opposing greater coordinating authority than they are in harmonizing in-country activities and budgetary requests. Moreover, while the larger NGOs may join together in their own coordinating bodies and in negotiations with a given UN agency on overhead costs and reporting requirements, they may also go their separate ways in programming for this crisis or that. Smaller NGOs also have disproportionate power to affect the overall aid effort. When the Taliban authorities in August 2001 arrested eight expatriates and sixteen Afghan aid workers employed by the German-based NGO Shelter International, the entire humanitarian apparatus was affected. The Taliban specifically charged that the UN World Food Program and other aid agencies were attempting to convert Afghan Muslims to Christianity.[26]

Costs

Coordination is an expensive proposition. It involves salaries and travel costs for people who sit at coordination tables, whether in New York or Geneva, at operational command centers in a given country, or in meeting rooms at the province or district level in a given emergency. To carry out its global coordinating mandate, the UN's Executive Committee for Humanitarian Affairs (ECHA) meets quarterly at the technical level and biannually at the level of heads of UN agencies. The IASC, which includes representation from

NGOs and the ICRC as well as major UN organizations, meets for a full day every quarter.

In addition to countless internal meetings, the UN Office for the Coordination of Humanitarian Affairs (OCHA) meets monthly with NGOs to discuss country-specific challenges. The small New York staff of the Geneva-based UN High Commissioner for Human Rights is hard-pressed to attend, much less to prepare for and to follow up on, the meetings in New York of the four executive committees on which the high commissioner serves.[27] Governments also have their own interagency coordination mechanisms and associated costs, both within various ministries and among donor governments.

NGOs have numerous regular meetings of their own coordinating bodies: at the international level, the International Council of Voluntary Agencies and the Steering Committee for Humanitarian Response, both based in Geneva, and other bodies such as Voluntary Organisations in Cooperation in Emergencies (VOICE) in Brussels and InterAction in Washington. In addition to regularly scheduled meetings among humanitarian actors, special sessions are convened at the headquarters and in the field as a crisis escalates. During the peak of an emergency, coordination meetings in one or another forum may take place daily, with key actors patched in by telephone from distant locations. Were the direct costs of coordination tallied, the agencies as well as the public would doubtless be surprised.

Coordination also involves indirect costs, including the time, travel, and support of field and headquarters personnel to prepare reports for coordinating meetings and to follow up on them. The computer revolution, reinforced by external pressures aimed at harmonizing disparate aid efforts, has vastly increased the flow of information. Also increased is the cost of preparing and updating such data and of digesting and analyzing it. Needless to say, joint reports prepared by a coordination body and vetted with its members are more time-consuming and expensive than individual agency reports.

During the November–December 2001 period of the Afghan crisis, dispatches from OCHA's Integrated Regional Information Network (IRIN) averaged at least half a dozen per day, most of them including multiple (and sometimes contradictory) news stories and agency reports. Aid staff were hard-pressed to keep up with or attend international meetings held in quick succession in Islamabad, Bonn, Berlin, Brussels, and Tokyo convened and attended by the United Nations, the World Bank, the Afghan Support Group of governments, other donor governments, and NGOs.

Beyond direct and indirect outlays, opportunity costs are also involved in such coordination efforts. Resources invested in coordination are not available for the more direct relief of suffering. Staff people attending an interagency coordination meeting are not available to bolster agency operations. Participation in meetings involves detailed preparation on late-breaking events in the field and follow-up with headquarters and field staff. The real-time detail that makes the information shared at such meetings valuable require continuous checking and updating.

Paying for costs in their various forms is handled differently by various agencies. Some attribute costs of "interagency liaison" and information management to operational programs. For others, coordination constitutes a separate "administrative" function in a culture that seeks to keep overhead expenditures to a minimum. Rare is the public appeal that requests funds to help underwrite the coordination machinery needed to ensure greater cost-effectiveness of contributed funds. Instead, appeals typically stress the agency's low-overhead track record. UN consolidated appeals often have difficulty raising funds for administrative, as distinct from program, functions. Larger organizations, with more staff and more ample budgets, are better able to place their people at coordination tables and to exercise leadership in their respective areas. Smaller agencies have fewer resources and less flexibility, whatever their views on the importance of coordination.

Structures

Efforts to devise effective coordination structures, whether global or crisis-specific, have floundered because of uncertainty and lack of consensus about how they should be designed.[28] The problems have been most pronounced within the United Nations, where the arrangements tried during the past decade have met with generally unsatisfactory results. The UN's operational agencies have a well-documented history of resisting attempts to provide a central body with greater coordinating authority.

The concern of donor governments over the lack of coordination in the crisis in northern Iraq in 1990–91 led to the creation in December 1991 of the UN Department of Humanitarian Affairs (DHA). Yet the actual authority exercised by its head, the emergency relief coordinator, was strictly limited. In facing its most difficult challenge, the Rwandan genocide and its aftermath, DHA encountered great difficulty orchestrating systemwide action, despite the value of meetings such as the one described above that it convened in Kigali. The multidonor evaluation of the Rwanda response used the concept of a "hollow core" to convey "the weakness of DHA in relation to WFP, UNHCR, and UNICEF."[29]

The replacement of the *Department* of Humanitarian Affairs in 1997 with the *Office* for the Coordination of Humanitarian Affairs (OCHA) upgraded the status of its head to that of under-secretary-general but reduced its staff and budget and circumscribed its authority. At the same time, four executive committees were set up with broad coordination mandates over various aspects of the UN's work, including the Executive Committee for Humanitarian Affairs (ECHA).

The creation of an OCHA with higher-level status but reduced authority represented the defeat of a more radical proposal that the UN's coordinating nexus be given greater authority and more staff. UN agencies' tooth-and-nail resistance confirms the obstacles that lie in wait for eminently rational changes in organigrams. A similar fate met a U.S. suggestion in 1999 that UNHCR be made the focus of systemwide responsibility for internally displaced persons (IDPs). Agencies fought the idea that a single operational agency be granted lead responsibility for the displaced, whose needs many separate agencies sought to service. Resistance came from within UNHCR (on grounds that additional resources would not be provided to underwrite the agency's expanded mandate) as well as from outside (from organizations that feared growth in UNHCR's operational preeminence). After an extended period of back-and-forth, OCHA became the focal point for much lower profile UN IDP efforts.

The UN has also struggled to fashion productive coordination structures for individual emergencies. The function is sometimes entrusted to a specially designated "humanitarian coordinator" and sometimes to an official already serving as "resident coordinator" for all UN activities.[30] In addition to reporting to their respective headquarters (OCHA or UNDP, as the case may be), these designees often report to a special representative of the secretary-general (SRSG) for a given crisis. After lengthy interagency vetting, Secretary-General Kofi Annan in late 2000 issued a note of guidance clarifying such relationships, which stopped short of vesting augmented coordinating authority in any one individual or structure.[31]

Throughout the decade, various coordination arrangements have been tried in one crisis or another. In some settings, the major UN operational institution — UNICEF in the Sudan, UNHCR in Bosnia, WFP in North Korea — has been appointed "lead agency." The choice has reflected the nature of the problem (for example, population displacement or food shortages) and relative agency strengths on the ground. While a certain additional authority and profile result from "lead" status, the success on individual lead agencies as coordinating vehicles has proved uneven. A given agency often experiences difficulty functioning as an impartial broker vis-á-vis the interests of other operational entities. UNHCR as lead agency in Bosnia was seen as giving priority to its own needs over those of other agencies in assigning limited space on military aircraft.[32]

The most recent chapter in the checkered history of UN coordination discussions involves a review commissioned by the IASC in late 2000. The study was said to be necessary because of the need to "summarize the existing and considerable literature on the subject, examine the most recent efforts at humanitarian coordination, and make recommendations for the best ways forward."[33] Major changes proposed in the so-called Brahimi Report for the organization of the UN Department of Peace-keeping Operations had raised issues of coordination with humanitarian activities in such theaters.[34] Yet at this writing, the new IASC study, informative and constructive in its own right, has yet to be taken seriously by the agencies. Humanitarian agencies are better at commissioning studies than acting on their recommendations.

Government donors and NGOs are no more willing than UN agencies to accept direction. In fact, the IASC's recent review of global aid trends flags the anomaly of "increasing bilateralisation of humanitarian assistance in the face of calls [by governments themselves] for planned, integrated, coherent, global responses."[35] In a decade in which humanitarian assistance flows doubled, the share controlled by multilateral organizations fell from a half to a quarter.[36] Complicating the picture further, the two major bilateral aid donors, the United States and the European Union (EU) — together the source of about 75 percent of the resources in most crises — frequently take quite different positions on key humanitarian issues.[37] Moreover, differences of vantage point occur even *within* the U.S. government and *among* EU members.

U.S. State Department officials, seeking to promote resolution of the conflict between Armenia and Azerbaijan over Nagorno-Karabakh, sought greater flexibility in the application of U.S. restrictions on assistance to the government of Azerbaijan than AID officials were prepared to exercise, or congressional proponents of Armenia were willing to allow.[38] At one point in the long ordeal of Sierra Leone in the late 1990s, Netherlands aid officials, faced with the extremity of Sierra Leoneans trapped by the insurgents in Freetown, wanted to rush emergency assistance to the scene. The British government, however, at the time holding the rotating EU presidency, believed that more could be gained from withholding such aid.

Coordinating NGOs is often compared with herding cats. While NGOs themselves are uneasy with the chaos that prevails in the early phases of many emergencies, their heterogeneous and freewheeling nature resists efforts to impose greater discipline and accountability. A discussion in 1999 among several dozen North American NGOs of their experiences in the Kosovo crisis earlier that year offers a view in microcosm of the state of dialogue on coordination.[39]

Representatives of many NGOs agreed that the presence of hundreds of relief and rights organizations created problems for the overall enterprise. Yet assessments of the seriousness of the problem varied widely. Some saw the multiplicity of agencies as a sign of vitality, believing that the smaller and crisis-specific groups embodied humanitarian impulses and communicated a sense of solidarity that more established agencies had difficulty conveying. Others viewed the terrain as altogether too perilous for small, crisis-specific aid groups, which they saw as adding to the existing confusion and undercutting the ability of the NGO community to speak with a common voice.

Yet broad agreement existed on the notion that closer collaboration is needed among aid groups, and even some support for the exercise by donor governments of greater selectivity in granting funds. Some donors are now insisting that NGOs subscribe to the Sphere standards or meet other basic requirements as preconditions for funding.[40] The fact that the smaller number of aid agencies involved in responding to the extended but little-publicized famine in North Korea have achieved ostensibly better coordination than exists in the more high-profile emergencies provides food for thought.

Leadership

A recurrent finding throughout the decade's research has been the importance of leadership to successful coordination. In study after study, the indispensability of strong leadership has been confirmed. *The Dynamics of Coordination* highlighted not only the need for strong individual leadership but also the need for institutional support and reinforcement for those leaders. Its examination of coordination in Tanzania and Sierra Leone used three different optics: institutional, functional, and programmatic, seeking to identify "the relative importance of institutional structures, on the one hand, and leadership by key humanitarian officials, on the other."[41]

In both locations, coordination was in the hands of dynamic, take-charge individuals. Maureen Connelly headed UNHCR's office in Ngara, while Elizabeth Lwanga of UNDP functioned as humanitarian coordinator and the UN system's resident coordinator in Sierra Leone. Connelly benefited from authority granted by the government and by her own agency, allowing her to conclude agreements and provide funds directly to the NGOs of her choice, as noted earlier.

Lwanga's responsibilities to UNDP and the UN system required her to cooperate with and strengthen the government authorities, while her humanitarian mandate, reinforced by the OCHA-related Humanitarian Assistance Coordination Unit (HACU), required negotiating access with the insurgents and meeting emergency needs in the areas that the government no longer controlled. Tugged in both directions, Lwanga became the subject of sharp attacks from a number of NGOs, who in essence "personalized an institutional problem." At root, the difficulty was structural rather than personal: "UNDP's presence at the coordination helm proved to be a bad fit."[42]

Our coordination study reached a troubling if useful conclusion: that "humanitarian officials tend to overstate the role personalities play in bringing about effective coordination and to underemphasize the significance of well-structured institutional relationships and clearly delineated coordination systems."[43] Indeed, even the most creative and energetic individuals often cannot overcome serious structural problems. Experience elsewhere confirms that the leadership of individuals, however indispensable, requires institutional support in order to realize its full potential. In sum, no substitute is available for fundamental changes in the ways in which humanitarian agencies relate to each other.

Dilemmas and Discoveries

Major strides have occurred during the decade in meeting the coordination challenge. In terms of the six key elements identified in our 1992 study of the Gulf crisis, the greatest progress has been made in information sharing, planning, and leadership.

The amount of detail available on specific humanitarian crises today has grown exponentially. New coordinating structures are now in place and meet regularly, helping to orchestrate a more efficient division of labor in the field. The scale of financial and personnel resources committed to coordination activities, direct and indirect, is significant. Steps have been taken through the UN's consolidated appeal process to mobilize funding in more concerted form. A number of the officials entrusted with humanitarian responsibilities in the decade's most recent crises have become more seasoned, with a better sense of the benefits that accrue from effective coordination. Often they have been involved in a series of earlier crises, often with some of the same counterparts from the same agencies.

Indeed, the situation has changed considerably since the Rwanda crisis in 1994. We noted then that the UN Rwanda Emergency Operation had been forced to improvise in "the absence of a rule book, covering such basic administrative tasks as hiring and deploying staff, the management of funds, reporting requirements, and simple office procedures." The rule book has now been written, and the day of "dedicated but amateurish staff" has largely passed.[44]

Yet the coordination agenda remains replete with unfinished business. Few changes have been made in the underlying structures of power and authority or in the felt needs of individual agencies for special profile. The humanitarian community still struggles with the challenges of negotiating effectively with host political authorities and planning strategically for responding in volatile and rapidly evolving situations. While the value of individual leadership has been demonstrated, agency policies and resources frequently do not back up the creative and energetic field staff. Interagency rivalries abound, undercutting institutional and individual performance alike. Despite early efforts to seize the opportunity in Afghanistan in 2001–2 to achieve more effective systemwide coordination than in other crises, the results were disappointing, as recounted in the epilogue.

Dilemmas occur and recur. The constraints on the ground and the political economy of the humanitarian enterprise guarantee that however sensible the rationale for coordination, humanitarian action will prove difficult to orchestrate. Individual agencies, even with an eye to improving their own performance, remain reluctant to sacrifice their own power, authority, and profile or to pay the price of coordination in terms of increased outlays and changes in policies and procedures. Perhaps one missing link, countless studies notwithstanding, involves more compelling evidence to confirm the benefits of coordination: that reduced autonomy by individual agencies is more than offset by increases in agency effectiveness.

A consensus approach to coordination generates shared ownership, enlisting the entire community in the humanitarian effort. Yet that approach also requires time and energy to hammer out common approaches and mutually satisfactory arrangements. By contrast, the insertion or imposition of a command element provides clearer lines of authority and accountability and generates faster-paced action, sometimes sacrificing a sense of participation. The solution is not to devise a middle option but to choose one or the other and work to offset its inherent disadvantages. We have recommended pairing a stronger command element with the maximum collegiality feasible within such arrangements. Others prefer a consensus orientation, paired with an effort to act as decisively as possible within the constraints of consensus.

With respect to the UN system in particular, a humanitarian coordinator charged with managing relationships with the host political authorities brings a focused agenda and an urgent mandate to the table. Such a person, though, may lack knowledge of the government bureaucracy in question or the longer-term perspective needed when mounting relief activities. By contrast, a resident coordinator, whose relationships with the authorities are far broader than the particular crisis, brings a more comprehensive but also more deliberative and often less urgent approach to the table. We recommend the former route, deputizing an official with humanitarian-only responsibilities but encouraging the person to connect with other national and international actors with longer-term agendas.

In its response to a series of crises in the Caucasus, the UN has tended to appoint to positions involving management of humanitarian activities "excellent politicians and diplomats whose humanitarian credentials and track records have been questionable at best. As a result, opportunities for pressing the humanitarian imperative, as well as for forceful advocacy on behalf of humanitarian principles, have fallen victim to a culture of humanitarian *realpolitik*." We thus prefer the alternative approach: "to recruit tried and tested humanitarians with good political and diplomatic skills."[45] Experience confirms better results when a person with humanitarian credentials and sensitivity takes on a diplomatic portfolio rather than the reverse.

Dilemmas also involve the matter of individual agency profile. Organizations have a stake in being an identifiable part of a given humanitarian response. Although association with a flawed effort can represent a liability, agencies that hide their logos under a bushel risk losing out in the competitive humanitarian marketplace. Conversely, however, high-profile involvement requires the investment of staff time and resources and the development of expertise that will bear up under increasing public scrutiny. Here, too, individual agencies must chart their own course. An overemphasis on profile undercuts effective collaboration and joint results, yet collaboration, poorly orchestrated, can result in inaction.

Coordination is not exclusively or even primarily a technical task of matching available resources with existing needs. The coordination process requires dynamic leadership in settings that are naturally fluid and interactive. Thus while the six elements of coordination identified earlier recur with each new crisis, the particular mix of needs and resources, relationships and constraints, may vary considerably, requiring discerning judgment and adaptation of earlier experience.

Assertive and creative individuals bring a sense of direction and order to the frenetic world of emergency responses. Such leadership needs the reinforcement of supportive agency policies and resources. Individuals without institutional backup soon burn out, while agencies without imaginative leadership fail to lend their institutional weight to the coordination challenge. Agencies can have the best of both worlds by making in-house management and personnel policies more responsive to needs on the field, retaining experienced people on the front lines and empowering them to make the difficult decisions. In fact, late in the decade a number of UN organizations broke new ground by assigning senior people to spearhead their frontline efforts in emergencies.

Effective coordination is clearly a desideratum of every well-managed crisis response and, more broadly, of the humanitarian enterprise as a whole. Accordingly, one criterion of success is that agencies move in concert to accomplish the six identified functions of coordination. Yet in some civil war situations a tightly orchestrated approach encompassing all agencies inhibits the creativity and outreach of the effort as a whole. Indeed, although the purpose of coordination is to improve aid programs, more tightly coordinated activities may in some such settings have the effect of reducing the flexibility of the humanitarian community to reach those in need.

In the Sudan, the presence of relatively freewheeling and autonomous agencies had distinct advantages, not only for the nonconformists but also for the aid enterprise itself. Memoranda of agreement that Operation Lifeline Sudan had signed, on the insistence of both the government and the insurgents, rendered the entire UN-led humanitarian enterprise more susceptible to the political straitjackets imposed by the belligerents.[46] In Sierra Leone and Tanzania, "some humanitarian actors viewed coordinated action as restrictive and even counter to fundamental humanitarian principles."[47] In short, coordination needs to be viewed as a means to achieving greater effectiveness, not as an end in itself.

In this dilemma, too, structuring arrangements that allow for the best of both worlds is difficult. Yet humanitarian initiatives can certainly find ways and means to be both better coordinated and more respectful of seasoned organizations that, for appropriate reasons of policy and for legitimate concerns of effectiveness, choose to go their own ways. As with the other challenges faced by the humanitarian enterprise, the task of coordination involves understanding the dilemmas, weighing the options, choosing the best alternative in the circumstances, and monitoring the results, making course corrections along the way as needed.

3

Human Rights

With famine in Ethiopia deepening in 1984 and news reports about its severity beginning to circulate on Capitol Hill, a congressional committee called a hearing to review the situation. My office prepared testimony for two U.S.-based NGOs, Church World Service and Lutheran World Relief; a number of other NGOs also offered statements. Concerned about immediate relief of the suffering, most of us stressed the drought-related nature of the crisis. Based on interviews with refugees and its own analysis, Cultural Survival, a human rights NGO, focused instead on the economic, social, and human rights policies of the Communist government of President Mengistu Haile Meriam.

Most aid groups, my own included, probably never made conscious decisions to sidestep the human rights issues, yet we viewed Ethiopian policies, politics, and rights abuses as a quagmire that would derail life-saving efforts. The famine largely came and went without clearly established linkages being made by many aid groups to the underlying political issues. As for our fear that the Reagan administration would use the status of the Ethiopian government as a Cold War adversary to deprive needy Ethiopians of emergency assistance, an energetic NGO lobbying campaign helped produce the policy that "a hungry child knows no politics." The U.S. government eventually provided substantial emergency aid.[1]

The changed environment in the post–Cold War period has brought into sharp focus the need to protect the fundamental human rights of civilian populations. The 1990s witnessed growing awareness that within the humanitarian enterprise, protection activities must loom far larger and be related far more dynamically to life-saving assistance efforts. Some analysts have gone even farther, holding that after more than fifty years of developing international norms to protect civilians, "it is time to reconsider the overall assumptions that have directed previous efforts."[2]

Our research itself has reflected — and contributed to — the clarification of conceptual and programmatic issues at the interface between the delivery of emergency assistance and the protection of human rights. For one and all, wrestling with the interface has brought key dilemmas into sharper focus and produced some major discoveries, resulting in significant changes in how agencies conceive and conduct humanitarian operations.

Conceptual Issues

What is the relation between the humanitarian enterprise and fundamental human rights? Is life-saving assistance in the form of emergency food, medicine, and shelter a basic human right, with aid activities situated squarely within a rights framework, or are human rights a major component of an overarching humanitarian imperative?

"Humanitarian" and "human rights" organizations have traditionally defined themselves in contradistinction to each other, emphasizing differing mandates and embracing different strategies. Until recently, many aid workers have been reticent to tackle, or even to discuss, the basic human rights of civilian populations and the need to prevent abuses. Rights advocates, too, have taken a parochial view. At one international conference in March 1999, Pierre Sané, the secretary-general of Amnesty International, spoke disparagingly of relief operations as capers by idealistic aid workers who simply threw food off the backs of trucks indiscriminately in total ignorance of political context.[3]

However grotesque his caricature of emergency assistance and those providing it — which proved inflammatory at the meeting — his point was not completely without merit. The approach that many relief agencies took regarding the Ethiopian famine, described in the foregoing vignette, was characteristic of the aid mentality not only in the heyday of the Cold War but even after the thaw in East-West relations.

During the Cold War, international aid activities concentrated on populations that had fled Communist regimes in countries such as Angola and Mozambique, Afghanistan and Nicaragua. Assistance to the victims of Communist repression was perceived as converging with support for democratic, free-market values. Emergency assistance during the Cold War followed primarily the U.S. flag but, in a broader sense, the flag of democratic values. The main venue for international humanitarian action was among refugees of left-wing regimes gathered in camps in countries of first asylum. Resistance from the authorities in power ensured that assistance to persons before they fled their native countries was rarely undertaken. State sovereignty was sacrosanct, with governments that abused their populations brooking no interference in what were then considered their internal affairs. The UN Security Council adamantly refused to take up human rights issues.

A series of discussions among U.S. NGOs during the years 1985–87 demonstrated the prevailing reluctance of the aid enterprise to take East-West tensions into account in framing assistance activities. At the time, many American agencies were loath to acknowledge the political context in which they functioned, whether as institutions based in a superpower or as organizations using funds provided by the U.S. government. As a community, they rarely requested meetings with State Department officials to press for assistance to persons in unpopular countries or to request other changes in U.S. policy. Reflecting their unease with their own naiveté, however, one of the outcomes of their discussions was an articulation of their sense that American agencies should "become at one and the same time more scrupulously apolitical and more politically astute."[4]

Yet in the early post–Cold War years, the "don't ask, don't tell" approach of many aid agencies to matters political continued. The humanitarian enterprise viewed its task as delivery of emergency aid to needy populations, a full-time job in its own right in an environment of collapsing states and fight-to-the-death insurgencies. Picking up the cudgels for human rights, agencies feared, might jeopardize hard-won access to those in need, which depended on the cooperation, or at least the acquiescence, of the political authorities. As the 1990s proceeded, however, humanitarian organizations proved less and less able to keep their avowed distance from political issues in general and from human rights matters in particular. In a positive development, both NGOs and bilateral and multilateral aid officials over time became more aware of the political dimensions of their activities and more comfortable addressing rights concerns.

The evolution in approach reflected a number of developments, including new geopolitical realities. During the last decade, borders have become more porous, sovereignty less sacrosanct, forced migration a more prevalent political-military strategy, and humanitarianism more assertive.[5] International actors have begun to assist populations in the very places where rights are being violated. The creation in 1993 of the UN Office of the High Commissioner for Human Rights raised the profile of human rights and represented an acknowledgment that a state's treatment of its citizens is a legitimate item of international concern. Human rights became important in their own terms, not simply as an extension of an East-West agenda. The new context made the wish expressed by one of the pillars of the post–World War II American NGO community, Leo Cherne, seem dated: that he be remembered, beyond his work on refugees and human rights, for being "a cold warrior."[6]

Changes in the geopolitical universe, many of them positive from a humanitarian viewpoint, have represented major challenges to the humanitarian enterprise. Aid workers have been less able to sequester themselves from human rights abuses targeted against their clients. Taking up positions on the front lines of conflicts, aid workers are often present when human rights are violated. Earlier, they had waited to swing into action until the victims reached the relative safety of neighboring countries. Indeed, aid activities may function as a magnet for rights violations. In Haiti during the military regime following the coup against President Aristide, aid activities had to be suspended out of concern for the safety of civilians and aid workers.[7] Relief groups are increasingly hard-pressed to profess concern for the material welfare of distressed populations while ignoring blatant rights abuses that figure prominently in their distress.

Aid agencies are also more and more in the dock of public opinion for providing assistance that seems to perpetuate conflict and suffering.[8] Critics have implicated aid workers in the "well-fed dead" scenario: the view that their ministrations serve to keep vulnerable civilian populations alive only to have them brutalized by human rights violations, ongoing conflicts, and other forms of abuse. Aid officials are now more willing to concede the limited utility of sustaining life only to have it jeopardized by repressive governments or renegade nonstate actors. The imperative to assist, framed in isolation from the concomitant commitment to protect, is now understood to produce threadbare humanitarian action.

Human rights groups, for their part, have become more willing, as part of a broad rethinking of their own terms of reference, to acknowledge the contribution of international assistance in giving practical meaning to economic, social, and cultural rights. "Western human-rights groups, which have traditionally focused only on civil and political violations, are looking again at economic rights, and hope eventually to persuade governments to place the right to a house or a meal on an equal footing with the right to vote."[9] Critics of traditional approaches to protection are calling for a new approach to human security, which highlights rights in the areas of health, education, and employment.[10]

Some organizations have taken specific steps to strike a better balance between economic, social, and cultural rights and civil and political rights. In August 2001, Amnesty International implemented a policy decision with wide-ranging implications for itself and for the humanitarian enterprise more broadly. That organization adopted as its mission "to undertake research and action, focused on preventing and ending grave abuses of the rights to physical and mental integrity, freedom of conscience and expression, and freedom from discrimination, within the context of its work to promote all human rights."[11] This statement does not distinguish between advocacy for civil and political rights, on which it has concentrated in the past, and efforts to ensure economic, social, and cultural rights.

"At its heart, Amnesty International is and remains a movement fighting for individuals whose rights are violated," explained the organization's Secretary General Irene Khan in announcing the change in policy. "The difference is that from now on, we will work, not only against torture or for prisoners of conscience, but against all forms of discrimination, whether they affect political and civil or economic, social and cultural rights."[12] The organization envisions expanding its expertise over time so as to lay to rest the doubts expressed by the *Economist:* that having "successfully chastised torturers and despots," Amnesty International will fail to become "equally effective in the greyer worlds of health, housing, and labor policy."[13]

Such shifts in paradigm and policy have major ramifications for the programming and profile of rights agencies. In working to outlaw child labor in India, for example, Human Rights Watch has moved beyond an earlier boycott of imports made by children to embrace the need for a program of alternative economic and educational opportunities for those involved. Human rights groups now also devote more attention to efforts to strengthen the capacity of indigenous human rights counterparts in order to prevent violations and to monitor those that occur. Recognizing that nonengagement has its own costs, rights groups have diversified their tool kit, relying less on publicly "shaming" governments and instead collaborating with them to end violations. These changed understandings and strategies have in turn increased the possibility of collaboration with relief and development agencies in the field.[14]

From each side, the perceived convergence of relief and rights represents a major conceptual breakthrough. "Many humanitarian organizations serve as providers both of material assistance and protection," notes Michael McClintock of Human Rights Watch, "while human rights organizations now increasingly address questions of basic needs in their research, reporting, and advocacy, particularly in armed conflicts and in addressing related refugee and international displacement issues."[15] Aid groups themselves increasingly frame their activities in human rights terms. The possibility of rapprochement has improved as aid practitioners have taken a closer and more politically savvy look at the causes of the need for assistance and as their rights colleagues have begun to give greater attention to bread-and-butter rights and a longer time horizon.

Both relief and rights groups are aware of the risks of continuing to go their own separate ways. If potential synergies present win-win possibilities for both sets of actors, functioning in isolation may produce lose-lose outcomes. The absence of protection for civilian populations, to cite a dramatic example, has arguably extended the prevailing conflicts and increased the need for emergency assistance. In the Caucasus, "inadequate protection and the ensuing vulnerability of civilians often has led to increased militancy among segments of the population." The Gali region of Georgia/Abkhazia in 1995–98 and the city of Samashki in Chechnya in 1996 provide cases in point. "Exposed civilians repeatedly have taken up arms, mined the perimeters of their villages, and formed loose-knit, self-defense cadres to protect themselves or to secure and safeguard the resources they need for the survival of their families."[16]

Despite such growing mutuality between relief and rights groups, considerable asymmetry remains between the two. Relief activities are much more amply funded than rights work. The panoply of aid actors has no counterpart on the rights side, where institutions are less numerous and personnel fewer. (While a plethora of actors creates dilemmas, a dearth of them has its own difficulties.) Indigenous rights groups are more exposed than their assistance counterparts. Moreover, assistance needs are being more adequately met while many exposed populations continue to lack the most rudimentary physical security, to say nothing of other facets of human rights protection. Indeed, "supposed sovereign prerogatives, intentional targeting of civilians, insecurity of aid operations and personnel, and the high degree of politicization endemic to all of the conflicts have collectively stacked the odds against effective protective responses."[17]

Asymmetries notwithstanding, humanitarian action is now understood in more inclusive terms to encompass *both* the delivery of relief and other life-saving and life-supporting assistance *and* the protection of basic human rights. The assistance component of the humanitarian enterprise involves activities such as providing emergency food, medicine, and shelter, helping societies rebound from current emergencies, and strengthening indigenous coping mechanisms to avoid future crises. The rights component, too, covers a host of activities such as interposing one's self as a physical barrier to deter human rights violations, providing physical presence to a vulnerable community, monitoring the actions of governments and insurgents, arranging evacuation of at-risk people, advocacy with political actors, and diplomatic intercession.[18]

But the nomenclature debate remains largely unresolved. Although activities to provide emergency aid and protect human rights more clearly affirm a common commitment to human security and dignity, differences remain regarding how such activity at its most inclusive should be labeled. For a number of years, the Humanitarianism and War Project has used the term "humanitarian action" to encompass both assistance and protection. Some others prefer "human rights" as the chapeau for both sets of activities. Still others use "protection" as the overarching concept, since protection is a basic prerequisite for realizing the full spectrum of rights and accessing relief assistance.

Perhaps the most illuminating and future-oriented framing of the relief and rights connection is offered by analyst Hugo Slim in an article entitled "Dissolving the Difference between Humanitarianism and Development: The Mixing of a Rights-Based Solution." Slim recalls the little-known fact that at the time of their adoption in 1949, the Geneva Conventions were shorn of a draft preamble — viewed at the time as too political — that would have situated humanitarian law squarely in a human rights context. For its part, "development," too, had been approached as a process without a firm footing in fundamental rights — economic, social, and cultural as well as civil and political. "The (re)discovery in the 1990s that both humanitarianism and development are 'rights-based,'" Slim concludes, "ended, once and for all, the distracting dichotomy set up between the two." Indeed, the way forward lies, as Slim suggests, in affirming at the conceptual level a common rights foundation to all assistance activities, whether short-term emergency aid or longer-term development assistance.[19]

We have participated in, and learned from, this evolution in understanding the interface between relief and rights. Our early work was criticized for lack of attention to rights issues. Gilbert Loescher found *Mercy under Fire: War and the Global Humanitarian Community* "closer to most relief and development agencies than to human rights organizations." He expressed disappointment at the absence of "bold proposals to develop mechanisms and models to counter the trend towards prioritizing assistance over protection and to provide UN and NGO integration of assistance and protection in situations of internal conflict."[20] William Demars faulted what he perceived as our assumption that "all humanitarian action falls under a single set of shared norms, muffling the often boisterous contestation between advocates of delivering physical relief assistance, protecting human rights, aiding refugees and displaced persons, and the Red Cross vision of responding to victims of war."[21]

Our more recent studies have examined the interplay between relief and rights in greater detail. *Protecting Human Rights: The Challenge to Humanitarian Organizations*, designed as a practical guide for aid officials, encourages efforts to frame and conduct relief activities in ways that would deter human rights abuses. One of the examples provided involves social service programs that include a regular home-visit component, carried out where possible by international personnel. The design reflects the reality that "The presence of medical personnel, social workers, mental health professionals, clergy, and others in social service or health-related fields is often accepted by authorities or combatants" who would turn back card-carrying human rights monitors.[22]

War's Offensive on Women: The Humanitarian Challenge in Bosnia, Kosovo, and Afghanistan also approaches protection and assistance in holistic fashion. Often targeted by war and suffering disproportionately from it, women require not only access to the basic essentials of everyday life, including health care and other services, but also protection against violence and other forms of abuse and exploitation. Our study urges that humanitarian organizations use a gender perspective in tailoring activities to the particular situation. Such a perspective, undergirded by a human rights framework, takes into account how the different roles, opportunities, and constraints of men and women influence their needs and their ability to respond in times of crisis.[23]

Practical Applications

Clarification of the conceptual relationships between the delivery of relief and the protection of human rights is beginning to have operational implications for both sets of agencies. In fact, the focus of attention has shifted from understanding the connections at the level of policy to adapting agency programs to reflect the new awareness. In operational terms, some promising stirrings are taking place, but agencies still have a significant distance to go.

The two organizations with the most explicit international legal obligations for protection are the ICRC and UNHCR. The ICRC's mandate is framed by the Geneva Conventions and Protocols, which seek to limit the means and methods of warfare and to protect those who do not (or who no longer) participate in hostilities. The ICRC views its assistance activities as complementary to its protection work: as, in its own words, reverse sides of the same coin. While its aid activities have increased in scale, they are generally an integral part of a protection strategy. The ICRC has spurred its colleagues to examine the connections between relief and rights and to tone up their performance.[24]

Also embracing a protection mandate, UNHCR has a division of international protection and a cadre of staff with specific protection portfolios deployed in the field. UNHCR views all its employees in a given country as protection officers, whether their specific tasks involve providing shelter, liaising with governments, or monitoring population movements and human rights abuses. Yet UNHCR's protection work has experienced tensions with its aid activities, with the latter often upstaging or undercutting the former.

The difficulties were evident in the Republic of Georgia in 1994–95 and the former Yugoslavia in 1992–93. In the case of Georgia, UNHCR developed a program to encourage the return of people who had fled the Gali region of Georgia/Abkhazia. We concluded that "the UN [had] displayed questionable judgment in promoting the rapid return of refugees" into circumstances in which their security would prove precarious.[25] In the former Yugoslavia, the issue early in the 1990s concerned not the return but rather the evacuation of minorities. The painful dilemma, in the words of one UNHCR official, was that "it's hard to find a balance between saying that people have a right to stay in their homes, and saving lives. If you step in too quickly, they run; if you wait, they can die."[26]

In reality, the toughest choices in the former Yugoslavia were not between assistance and protection but rather between protecting human rights *in situ* or through evacuation. "In the context of a conflict which has as its very objective displacement of people we find ourselves confronted with a major dilemma," observed then-UN High Commissioner for Refugees Sadako Ogata in November 1992. "To what extent do we persuade people to remain where they are, when that could well jeopardize their lives and liberties? On the other hand, if we help them to move, do we not become an accomplice to 'ethnic cleansing'?"[27]

Reflecting on the situation almost a decade later, the former high commissioner still struggles with the ethical dilemmas involved. "All the refugees I met over the past 10 years have been victims of governments and authorities. But if we tried to protect the human rights of these victims by fighting against the authorities, we might not be able to preserve their lives. What should we provide for these people who have fled their homelands? We must consider not just their abstract human rights but their concrete needs, such as food, medical treatment, and educational opportunities. What refugees really want is to be able to live normal lives in safety with their families. As a practical matter we must approach the authorities for these things and try to get them to cooperate on the basis of humanitarian considerations."[28]

The view from the field in the former Yugoslavia was, if anything, even more excruciating. "A major human rights dilemma for UNHCR in the former Yugoslavia," recalls a young Ugandan UN volunteer seconded to the refugee agency, "was whether to carry out large-scale evacuations of vulnerable people, which would literally mean that UNHCR — the refugee protector — could be seen as helping to create refugees. The alternative," as he saw it, "was to attempt to provide protection and security to threatened minorities where they lived, a totally unrealistic option in a situation of ethnic cleansing."[29] Our own study concluded that UNHCR's protection policy in the region "should have been weighted from the start more clearly toward facilitating people's departure from life-threatening circumstances."[30] As with other dilemmas, the challenge is not to find a solution without untoward consequences but to identify the least objectionable among unsatisfactory alternatives.

Will protection against human rights abuses receive higher priority from UNHCR in the coming years? In a meeting with NGOs early in his tenure, Ogata's successor, High Ruud Lubbers, expressed his view that UNHCR "had no other raison d'être than protection."[31] More recent statements have raised doubts about whether he will be able to increase the relative priority of protection. The notion of preventive protection — that protection efforts should be stepped up in order to make it unnecessary for vulnerable minorities to flee their homes — is a positive one. Yet unless activities are energetically pursued to reduce exposure, preventive protection risks thwarting the exercise of the right to seek asylum. Early in the new decade, serious funding cutbacks also threatened UNHCR's *bona fides* in protection work.

In recent years the UN system as a whole has given higher priority to integrating, or "mainstreaming," human rights into its various activities and programs. Following the World Conference on Human Rights in Vienna and the creation of the Office of the UN High Commissioner for Human Rights (OHCHR) in 1993, the integration of human rights across the system received direct impetus from Secretary-General Kofi Annan's reform program of July 1997. The status of the "mainstreaming" of human rights that he mandated was the subject of an ECOSOC review in 1998 and thereafter of our own study, *When Needs Are Rights*.[32] The mainstreaming of gender issues in the UN system also received impetus from the 1993 World Conference.

Our 1998–99 study on the integration of human rights found wide disparity among the UN's four major operational humanitarian organizations (UNHCR, UNICEF, WFP, and UNDP). UNICEF was showing signs of major institutional transformation, reflected in and spurred by its promotion of the Convention on the Rights of the Child. Several other agencies were content to add a human rights position to the organization chart and to repackage current activities in human rights terms. Of the four secretariat entities examined, the Departments of Peacekeeping and Political Affairs were downplaying their own human rights–related mandates while OHCHR and OCHA were asserting little leadership.

Revisiting the issues two years later, we found several encouraging developments. Accelerating its efforts, UNICEF had embarked on an ambitious program of workshops and staff training on human rights and humanitarian law, seeking to ensure that all UNICEF country programs incorporate human rights principles. The traditional view of children as victims in need of assistance is giving way to approaching them as rights-holders whose rights must be actively protected. UNICEF had challenged states that violate children's rights, for example, the Russian Federation for the impact on children in Chechnya of its prosecution of the war. OHCHR itself and OCHA, however, as well as the UN Divisions of Peacekeeping Operations and Political Affairs, continued to lag behind other agencies.

Since our study, UNDP has launched a new Human Rights Strengthening (HURIST) program, undertaken jointly with OHCHR. UNDP country program officers are being trained and human rights activities integrated into UNDP country programming. In Yemen, UNDP worked with the government to integrate, with World Bank backing, the rights to food, education, and health into a poverty-reduction strategy within the country's national development plan. The Universal Declaration of Human Rights served as the basis for Nepal's development plan which, reflecting discussions at the local, regional, and national levels, infused human rights principles into Nepal's development assistance framework. Mauritania's poverty-reduction plan, also approved and supported by the World Bank, makes specific reference to eliminating slavery, a major human rights issue there. Many in UNDP's field offices have found that including human rights in a country's normal economic and social planning cycle is the most effective way to mainstream human rights and obtain the necessary budgetary support for rights-related activities.

In peacekeeping operations, the human rights division of the UN Observer Mission in Sierra Leone (UNOMSIL) and the human rights component of the UN mission in Angola (MONUA) have forged closer working relationships with aid agencies. Those human rights units organized and led joint training sessions and workshops on international human rights and humanitarian law with major UN agencies, the ICRC, and NGOs, including Save the Children, Oxfam, CARE, MSF, and World Vision. A joint working group of relief and rights agencies drafted a common humanitarian code of conduct for Sierra Leone that was based on and reflected human rights principles. In Angola, the human rights unit conducted joint visits with aid agencies outside their usual working areas and forged other productive and cooperative initiatives.

The peacekeeping operation in Sierra Leone also successfully enlisted humanitarian actors in the effort to gather credible information and ensure more comprehensive coverage and more effective advocacy. The Sierra Leone Human Rights Committee included a broad array of local and international aid actors, along with human rights NGOs and human rights personnel from the peacekeeping operation. By working with the much larger number of relief workers present in Sierra Leone, the committee was able to draw greater attention to the human rights situation and effectively advocate for accountability mechanisms such as a truth commission and special court.

Such country-level activities represent a "bottom-up" approach that is often neglected or omitted from reports available from agency headquarters. In some instances, more dynamism and creativity seem to exist at the field level; in others, headquarters statements of policy have yet to find operational resonance. One initiative that seeks to close the gap between headquarters and the field is a study by the Inter-Agency Standing Committee, "Growing the Sheltering Tree," which seeks to document successful and potentially replicable examples of protecting human rights through humanitarian action. The experience of field officers is pooled, with the working group at UN agency headquarters analyzing and disseminating the lessons identified.

Beyond the UN system but also reacting to it, NGOs have demonstrated a new level of interest in these interface issues. The process of rethinking relationships between relief and rights was evident at, and spurred by, a UNHCR-convened conference in March 1999 promoting its collaboration with both sets of NGOs.[33] The meeting showcased recent developments and spurred future collaboration. While most relief NGOs have come to acknowledge the relevance of human rights issues to their work, they have taken different stances regarding how as assistance agencies to make the connections.

Some agencies see human rights concerns as legitimate in their own terms but highly politicizing and diversionary, recalling the view within the mainstream aid community evident in the response to the Ethiopian famine in the mid-1980s. Others affirm human rights as an alternative optic for presenting what they are already doing, resulting in a modest repackaging of current activities. Still others see rights-based programming as requiring more fundamental changes. They have reformulated their mission statements away from the language of moral obligation and beneficiaries, of victims and voluntarism, to the language of legal obligations and entitlements, of rights-holders and claimants.

As within the UN system, new conceptual understandings of the interface are beginning to influence day-to-day activities in the field. Following the March 1999 protection workshop, northern NGOs have taken the lead in convening twenty-seven training workshops for staff and nine for training trainers on the subject. Individual NGOs have made significant structural changes. The New York–based International Rescue Committee has formed a protection division, integrating rights-related activities into ongoing programs and undertaking new rights-oriented initiatives. Maintaining access for aid activities, however, with its implied limitations on public criticism of human rights abuses, remains a top agency priority.

Significant institutional change is also under way within CARE U.S. In the late 1990s, the agency carried out a detailed review of its activities in four countries, seeking to determine the extent to which relief activities were — or might have been — sensitive to human rights issues and sharing its results with other CARE affiliates. More recently, CARE U.S. has created a Rights-Based Approach Reference Group to promote attention to such issues throughout the agency. Training in rights-based programming has been provided to between six hundred and eight hundred staff in field, regional, and headquarters offices.

In earlier years, CARE had "shied away from examining root causes and considering how we might address them." Now, reflecting a remarkable change of orientation, structural issues are no longer off limits.[34] "Relief, rehabilitation and development assistance," observes a CARE staff person in Rwanda, "is more than a favor that we provide to people. CARE's work is a public declaration of belief in human rights."[35] Even though putting flesh on those rights is an operational challenge that is still in the process of being met, the perspective on assistance activities has fundamentally changed. "Whereas calls for generosity can only pluck weakly at the sleeves of rich governments," notes the *Economist*, "perhaps unsubtle claims of legal obligation will twist their arms."[36]

Discussions within and among NGOs highlight broad differences between European and U.S. aid groups. Our research on the relief/rights interface received quite different responses among the aid groups in Geneva and New York in 1999, reflecting differences in institutional culture and programmatic emphasis. Members of the Steering Committee for Humanitarian Response, the Geneva-based consortium of major multinational NGO families, treated the proposition that relief groups were also human rights actors as self-evident. Most European agencies were comfortable with the political dimensions of humanitarian action, including rights issues. Their U.S. counterparts, by contrast, remained more nervous about the association.[37] In broad compass, however, the institutional and cultural gap between U.S. and other NGOs has begun to narrow.[38]

Dilemmas and Discoveries

During the past decade, significant progress has taken place in understanding the relationship between relief and rights and in the interactions of both sets of organizations. No longer arrayed in warring camps, the two see themselves increasingly as cohorts in a common struggle, though tensions remain. A number of dilemmas have arisen. Recent experience also offers some discoveries about how to manage these dilemmas more effectively.

First is the evident tension between the neutral and impartial delivery of assistance and the more politically charged protection of human rights. Aid agencies have traditionally prided themselves on their neutrality, even though their unwillingness to acknowledge the political implications of their activities has sometimes confused neutrality with naiveté. Their commitment to neutrality has served both as a core principle and as a strategic device to keep them out of political thickets. Collaboration with political authorities, they have felt, requires tempering criticism in the interest of continued humanitarian access. They have thus kept their distance from rights groups, whose work they have construed as monitoring and challenging, "naming and shaming," and riveting media and public attention on violators and violations.

In recent years, however, discoveries in both relief and rights communities have helped ease the tensions between the two. A more probing analysis by each has narrowed the gaps and nurtured appreciation of the contribution of the other. Most aid agencies functioning in highly politicized settings, while they seek to avoid political agendas, are now more prepared to acknowledge the political context and ramifications of their work. Like their rights counterparts, aid groups also engage with the political authorities and sometimes contest limitations on access to persons in need of assistance.[39]

As it has become more comprehensive in approach, conversely, rights work has developed a new appreciation for the contributions and constraints of aid agencies. UN human rights field operations in recent years "have begun to do much more than monitor, investigate, and report on human rights violations. They also seek to engage the authorities in long-term, sustainable projects addressing the root causes of rights violations."[40]

Experiencing difficulties in finding local counterparts, rights groups have developed greater respect for the working relationships that aid agencies have established with indigenous institutions. Here, too, a fuller understanding of the challenge has highlighted the wisdom of a both/and rather than an either/or approach.

As aid groups take a more probing look at the issues, some are questioning whether trade-offs indeed exist between the more adversarial stance traditionally associated with rights advocates and the more collaborative posture of assistance providers. "Have we ever been denied or lost access to our target population because of an agency statement or advocacy position?" a UN official asked his colleagues during one of our interviews in early 2001. The fact that his team could cite no single case in point suggested that the dilemma may be less vexing than is often assumed. In fact, in the same interview, the situation in Burundi was highlighted, where rights-based aid programming was being carried out without compromising agency access or safety.

Yet in some instances efforts to protect basic human rights have increased the difficulties of aid providers. On a trip to Afghanistan in September 1997, Emma Bonino, then director of ECHO, visited a women's hospital in Kabul. The Taliban authorities had granted permission for her visit but not for filming at the hospital by the large accompanying CNN camera crew. Her arrest spurred a human rights campaign, A Flower for the Women of Kabul, mounted the following March on the International Day of Women. Whatever the value in Europe of the mobilization, the Taliban authorities in the days following the hospital visit registered their displeasure by arresting six women employees of international aid agencies.[41]

Despite ongoing tensions, aid agencies — as they have become more active in advocacy on humanitarian issues — have discovered more common ground with rights groups. In their effort to achieve a ban on antipersonnel land mines, for example, rights groups such as Human Rights Watch and Physicians for Human Rights were joined by aid agencies such as Handicap International, World Vision, and Oxfam. Firsthand testimony regarding the impact of mines on civilians effectively countered statements by government officials who were intent on minimizing such effects.[42]

In short, what has been traditionally viewed as the "assistance-protection dichotomy" is no longer understood as such. Another example from Afghanistan illustrates the point. Aid agencies found that in areas where livestock flourished, the Taliban had difficulty recruiting fighters. Elders told Taliban recruiters that young men were needed to guard village cattle and thus could not be spared for fighting. The Taliban accepted the explanation because of their desire that the local population, including fighters, be fed. Assistance programs that benefited livestock thus translated into greater protection for all.

Increasingly, well-planned assistance is seen to constitute a type of protection — and strategically mounted protection a form of succor. Conversely, inattention to abuses of rights is implicated in heightened need for emergency assistance. "If refugees do not receive sufficient assistance," one analyst has pointed out, "many will turn to prostitution, be recruited into armed forces, or turn to illegal activities — all of which are protection issues." Rights-based assistance programming offers a means of bridging the divide.[43]

Translating a concern for human rights into operational assistance activities, however, remains a major challenge, as does respecting the comparative advantages of relief and rights groups. Yet the momentum within the humanitarian enterprise for doing so is now increasingly well established. Aid groups are taking care not to become, pure and simple, human rights groups, and rights groups not to position themselves essentially as aid delivery mechanisms. Each type of group is respecting the "specificities" of the other.

A related problem concerns the need for independence and yet the difficulty of achieving it. Aid agencies have frequently come under criticism for doing the bidding of donor governments, which sometimes lace humanitarian activities with heavy short-term political agendas and pressures. Conversely, human rights monitoring, during the Cold War and since, has also been viewed in recipient countries as expressing a Western or Northern political agenda. Rights and relief groups thus share a common dilemma: how to maintain their integrity when activities are often underwritten by, and undertaken from bases in, donor countries.

Here the discovery has been that independence is more indispensable for both sets of institutions than had been understood, again both as a core humanitarian principle and as a key operational strategy. "If agencies delivering services in wars become increasingly dependent on the funding, logistical assistance, and authority of parties to the conflicts in which they operate — be they governments or intergovernmental bodies — their humanitarian integrity may appear to be compromised and their capacity to perform their humanitarian mission reduced."[44] The integrity of human rights initiatives mounted by UN human rights bodies or by government-funded NGOs or research groups is equally precious — but also equally vulnerable.

Accordingly, relief and rights agencies are giving increasing thought to accepting only those resources that do not compromise their independence, either in objectives or scale. A more circumspect approach, however, itself involves tough choices. The grants and contracts that provide essential wherewithal to extend an agency's reach may also call into question its *bona fides*. An organization may find it necessary to reject resources from a donor government within the conditionality specified just as it may refuse to accept humanitarian access under the strictures imposed by the host political authorities.[45]

Relief and rights groups also experience dilemmas related to tensions between short- and longer-term needs and solutions. Succumbing to the "tyranny of the emergency," aid agencies have typically engaged in fast-paced responses to suffering, showing little patience for addressing — sometimes even for comprehending — the underlying causes of distress. Rights organizations too often focus on immediate violations or incidents, paying less heed to the systemic causes of abuse. Faced with the need to identify structural remedies, their recommendations have often seemed superficial, perfunctory, and unrealistic. More probing analysis of how to design and implement projects that address root causes of the human rights violations, which is badly needed, is beginning to emerge.

The discovery here, too, is that the dilemma should be acknowledged and the inherent tensions creatively managed. Both relief and rights groups, the emerging consensus holds, need to pursue a "tortuous ethical calculus that should draw upon interdisciplinary data and analysis on the full spectrum of human rights, from assessments of basic needs to the requirements for protection from looters, sexual violence, and marauding armies." Such a calculus "should integrate concerns for meeting a population's needs for food and fresh water today, for example, with reflections about the ultimate prospects for survival and self-sufficiency or for debilitation, oppression, famine, and war."[46]

Warmhearted concern about suffering needs to be paired with hard-headed analysis of root causes. Nevertheless, the result may still relieve but not resolve the tensions. Aid groups need to acknowledge that their relief efforts may indeed prolong conflicts and thereby make their beneficiaries subject to continuing human rights abuses — but that their efforts remain imperative nonetheless. Seeing the picture whole makes it more possible to fit together relief and rights interventions, however uneasily, as essential components in the larger humanitarian enterprise. Perhaps the more compassionate ethos of relief can learn from the more tough-minded approach of rights groups, and vice versa.

Another dilemma involves how the wider humanitarian task is framed and how collaboration between relief and rights agencies is pursued. The humanitarian enterprise involves a wide array of such agencies, with diverse and distinctive mandates. Organizations such as the ICRC and UNHCR with mandates for both assistance and protection face the challenge of balancing protection and assistance activities and finding synergies. Agencies with either relief or rights mandates, but not both, are faced with the challenge of forming effective collaborative arrangements with other organizations within the larger common effort.

Here the discovery is rather self-evident: No agency can meet the full array of assistance and protection needs single-handedly. Moreover, when needs are themselves rights, each agency has a stake in the performance of the overall enterprise: assistance agencies in the protection of rights, and rights agencies in the satisfaction of needs. Accordingly, as the connections between needs and rights have become more clear, specific relief and rights agencies have forged partnerships. Operational collaboration forces practitioners to address difficult issues such as agreeing on a common strategy vis-à-vis the host political authorities and the media, and protecting and sharing confidential information. Progress has been slow because trust requires time to develop.

A final dilemma involves the continuing tensions among specific human rights or categories of rights. In international law, human rights are universal and indivisible, although their universality has been contested, both by voices from the global South and by social scientists. In recent years, however, the transcultural nature of humanitarian impulses and of respect for human rights has become more evident. "Sterile debates about universality and indivisibility are now increasingly giving way to vigorous discussions led by local NGOs on how best to incorporate international human rights standards into their respective societies."[47] Asian values, for example, may be distinctive, but they do not countenance genocide.

The two "baskets" of social/economic/cultural and civil/political rights are also finding a better balance. Our conference on the relief/rights interface witnessed a sharp clash of viewpoints on how the two baskets should be understood. One human rights expert held that "No human rights should be pursued at the expense of other human rights." Another countered that, "Indivisibility of human rights is a counsel of perfection to be rejected."[48] Common ground is being discovered which affirms the indivisibility and mutually reinforcing nature of rights, yet acknowledges the need to establish priorities and make choices for the short and longer term. Again, dichotomies may be accommodated within a negotiated strategy.

The discovery that rights are complex and interconnected illuminates the tough choices that operational agencies face, whether on matters of assistance or protection. International law is important, but often not dispositive. "During the first decade of the post–Cold War era, the previously discrete fields of human rights, humanitarian, and refugee law have begun to coalesce.... Yet growing congruence in the legal realm has generated a certain tension in the field. Human rights monitors, aid personnel, and refugee officials now literally stumble into each other visiting prisons, government officials, refugee camps, and hospitals. At one point or another they also seek out local NGOs. Mandates overlap and competition for resources and visibility is great."[49]

Our *Humanitarian Practitioner's Guide to International Human Rights Law* provides a resource to aid personnel in identifying the human rights dimensions of their work and exploring the use of law and a rights-based approach to their activities.[50] However, the study itself cautions that the application of international law to everyday practice is not self-evident and the best efforts of humanitarian practitioners to bring to bear its resources on their day-to-day work are no guarantee of success.

In sum, the emerging approach is to harness the respective strengths of relief and rights agencies. The waning of ideology, at least before September 11, facilitates efforts to capitalize on the comparative advantages of each. Human rights "fundamentalism" — the notion that the full spectrum of internationally recognized human rights should be demanded of and respected by all governments forthwith — is now viewed as unrealistic and unconstructive. So, too, however, is aid "fundamentalism" — the idea that the right to humanitarian assistance should trump all concerns about any violations of rights that such aid may entail. Reflecting a decade of experience, both fundamentalisms are being tempered with pragmatism.[51] The emerging wisdom holds that all rights should be recognized, even though ensuring respect for them at the operational level requires strategic choices.

Thus tensions remain, reflecting dilemmas inherent in the nature of conflicts themselves as well as in the humanitarian response. As with the dilemmas of coordination, the challenge is not to select one of the horns of each of the dilemmas but rather to manage skillfully the tensions inherent in each. While "one size fits all" approaches may be tempting, the heterogeneity of circumstances guarantees that one size will not fit all. Indeed, painstakingly analyzed, dilemmas may become *more* rather than *less* complex, *more* rather than *less* of a management problem.

The new awareness of the interaction between relief and rights, as well as the new level of dialogue and collegiality among relief and rights agencies, is encouraging. As the awareness crystallizes and spreads, the humanitarian challenge becomes appreciated in its widest possible frame, its elements addressed comprehensively and jointly. The need to rebalance resource commitments so that protection activities receive more equitable treatment vis-à-vis relief delivery is also now acknowledged.

The effectiveness of the humanitarian enterprise will surely benefit from a continuation of these trends, although pressures to return to the status quo ante abound. Scrap the emphasis on child rights, U.S. officials recently told UNICEF executives, and concentrate on vaccinations. Such pressures to backsliding notwithstanding, the trend is worth sustaining, even though for the time being, the data regarding the improved results of "rights-based programming" vis-à-vis more traditional approaches remains fragmentary.[52]

4

Strengthening Local Capacity

When the Humanitarianism and War Project research team arrived in the Middle East in June 1992, we received an unexpected barrage of criticism regarding the world's response to the Gulf crisis. My colleagues encountered it in Turkey and Syria; I heard it myself in Jordan, Iran, and Iraq. By the time of our arrival, most of the million-plus Third Country nationals who had fled Iraq through Jordan had returned to their countries of origin. Yet that largely successful resettlement was overshadowed by a residue of bad memories around the region. Our interviews were laced with recurrent criticism of the international effort.

The initial aid response had come from civil society organizations and government ministries in Jordan and Iran, not from the lumbering international humanitarian apparatus. Yet months after the crisis, donor governments were still refusing to reimburse the Jordanian authorities for funds they had advanced. Iran, an international pariah at the time, had failed to receive resources proportionate to its refugee caseload. "We got the refugees," said the Iranians, "but Turkey got the funds."[1] Throughout the region, national Red Cross and Red Crescent Societies were unhappy with the heavily Western and Christian thrust of international relief efforts and the lack of coordination with their own work. Some found the entire relief effort arrogant and off-putting.

The international humanitarian enterprise has a strong rhetorical commitment to strengthening local institutions in countries affected by crises. To fail to enhance their capacity, aid officials persuasively argue, would leave conflict-affected societies vulnerable to recurring emergencies. Many individual relief and rights organizations have policy affirming their intention to work in partnership with indigenous actors. The expressed goal is to enable their hosts to respond better to future crises and to play a more active role in their own civil societies.

Yet the humanitarian enterprise has proven itself better at delivering life-saving assistance than at strengthening local capacity. In the heat of each new crisis, the scramble to save lives often eclipses the sought-after partnership

with local institutions, which in comparison seem diversionary and dila-
tory. Moreover, relationships established during long-lived emergencies are
difficult to change as collaborative possibilities emerge for reconstruction
and development. The heavy externality of international relief interventions works against the expressed preference for greater mutuality and local
participation.

This chapter reviews the dilemmas that humanitarian organizations confront in strengthening local institutions. In examining the rich experience
of the past decade, the chapter highlights a number of discoveries about
the challenge of managing the dilemmas. The discussion takes as a point of
departure the experience of the Gulf crisis in 1990–92, which illuminated
problems that have characterized subsequent emergency responses as well.
The fact that only modest improvement has occurred during these years
casts doubt upon the sincerity of the humanitarian enterprise in strengthening local capacity and calls into question the lesson-learning process.
The absence of significant improvement also points to the deeply rooted
and dysfunctional power relationships that underpin the humanitarian
apparatus.

Conceptual Issues

Accurate framing of the categories of actors is an important first step in analyzing their interaction. The customary parlance of "international" agencies
and "national" agencies seems self-evident. "Internationals" have activities
in multiple countries: UN organizations such as the World Food Program,
bilateral aid donors such as the United States Agency for International Development and the U.K.'s Department for International Development, and
NGOs such as Oxfam and Save the Children based in developed countries.
The "nationals" are institutions in crisis areas: the Guatemalan ministry of
health, the Liberian council of churches, or CARE West Bank–Gaza.

Yet such terminology is misleading. Why is a ministry of health in a
crisis country that receives funds from a score of such international agencies
any less international than individual bilateral donors themselves? Why is
a national or local NGO in an emergency-affected country that manages
funds from ten different donors any less international than an NGO based
in Europe that works in ten countries? The assumption that international
agencies have superior expertise, greater resources, and a larger role to play
than those closer to the scene — themselves ostensibly parochial and limited
in their capacity and contribution — has come under overdue scrutiny in
recent years.

The term "national" as applied to institutions in crisis countries is itself
somewhat misleading. Government ministries are indeed national, although
in situations of armed conflict their reach extends only as far as the areas

under central government control. Institutions of civil society — religious organizations, civic groups, professional associations, NGOs — are often national in name only. Some, created by or for international actors in search of counterpart organizations, lack authentic roots. Often the distinguishing feature of a "national" organization is an office in the capital city rather than nationwide clientele or credibility.

Even the term "local" has limitations. Local institutions include a wide range of actors, each with strengths and limitations: traditional tribal leaders, religious authorities, women's groups, secular NGOs, and local officials associated with national government ministries. In the case of Mozambique, the traditional leaders enjoy widespread community respect but are highly patriarchal, religious authorities are recognized as established providers of social services, women represent the majority clientele for humanitarian services but an oppressed one, and some secular NGOs have close connections to government officials and to local economic or even criminal elites. Faced with an array of claimants of the "local" mantle, international actors face difficult dilemmas in selecting those institutions whose capacities they will seek to strengthen. Yet choose they must, inasmuch as (to adapt the American aphorism that "all politics is local") effective humanitarian action requires local authenticity and traction.

In some respects, the categories of "foreign" and "indigenous" or "external" and "internal" are preferable to "international" and "national"/ "local." The former categories are more descriptive and less value-laden, as long as the word "foreign" does not conjure up images of extraterrestrials and the word "indigenous," notions of primitive and hapless societies. The terms "indigenous" and "internal," however, share some of the limitations inherent in "national" and "local." Faced with these difficulties, this chapter and the research on which it is based continue to speak for the most part of "international" and "local" actors. The challenge, of course, is to establish a division of labor that respects the comparative advantages of both sets of actors. The critical question involves how the international humanitarian apparatus in all of its foreignness may better strengthen and reinforce local capacities in all of their unevenness.

A related conceptual step involves clarifying the purpose of relationships between international and local institutions. In *Patronage or Partnership: Local Capacity Building in Humanitarian Crises,* we examined the dynamics of the interaction between the two sets of agencies in six country settings. The data, much of it assembled explicitly by or in collaboration with nationals from the countries involved, confirmed that many international agencies approach strengthening local capacity as a means to an end — that is, as an instrumental exercise geared toward equipping local organizations to deliver emergency assistance or to protect fundamental human rights.

Only a few organizations see capacity building as an end in itself, an investment in the ability of indigenous entities to function over the long haul independently of outsiders. While development groups often describe their function as working themselves out of a job, relief agencies emphasize that the shorter-term nature of their task sets serious limitations on how collaborative they can be and still succeed in their life-saving ministrations. In fact, many emergency aid staff, interviewed in the throes of emergencies, express the view that capacity-building is at root a development rather than a relief function.

The need for quick action thus upstages longer-term perspectives. "Attempts to strengthen local capacity," our case study of Sri Lanka found, "may appear to obstruct the efficient delivery of emergency relief supplies." As a result, expatriate agencies "often see only the short-term disadvantages in capacity building."[2] Indeed, one of the downsides of the pervasive post–Cold War debate on "humanitarian intervention" is that it focuses on the criteria for intervention, including the perceived disarray of national and local institutions, rather than on the impacts of the intervenors, humanitarian as well as political-military, on those institutions.

An instrumental approach to humanitarian action can be the enemy of serious capacity building, as has been the experience in Sri Lanka. Our review of the international response to the crisis there, entitled "Means without End," concluded that "the strengthening of local capacities does not appear to be a key focus in the United Nations system within war areas."[3] Data that the project collected and analyzed from other conflicts bears out this observation, although the criticism may apply less to the approach that some NGOs take. By and large, however, patronage routinely upstages partnership across the humanitarian enterprise.

On a more positive note, many humanitarian organizations are beginning to sense that, from a longer-term perspective, process is as crucial as product. From an extended vantage point, helping local agencies to play an enhanced role in their own societies should become at least as important as delivering services. Implementing such an approach requires proceeding more collaboratively in responding to crises — utilizing, for example, expertise and resources from the affected country and region and placing a higher priority on consultation and joint action. Assisting in the empowerment of local agencies also requires a change in the current emphasis among donors and agencies on "deliverables," which attaches higher priority to the material aspects of relief programs than to less quantifiable tasks such as nurturing leadership and strengthening capacity.

While some agencies have yet to embrace a less instrumental approach, many agree at least in principle that relationships need to be managed in ways that do not set back the abilities of indigenous organizations to function over the long haul independently of outsiders. Otherwise, what begins as a marriage of convenience may soon become a source of marital discord.

The key question is not just "What works?" but also "What lasts?"[4] For agencies committed to saving lives and preventing rights abuses, however, "process" issues are unsettling.

Indispensability of Local Actors

The humanitarian impulse is, in its broadest terms, human — that is, universal. Indeed, most cultures have their own traditions of succor and protection of the vulnerable. Yet despite the universality of humanitarian values, the humanitarian enterprise as an organized undertaking has a predominantly Western approach, ownership, and organized constituency. Association with indigenous traditions and institutions offers a needed point of entry into countries requiring external assistance. Forging a connection with that context reflects the importance of local institutions and provides a check on inappropriate interventions.

In crisis after crisis, the first response to human need comes from local individuals and institutions who share their own resources without benefit of outside assistance or reinforcement. Even in high-profile emergencies receiving massive foreign inputs, the scale of locally contributed resources may in the end be more substantial still, and certainly altogether indispensable to the process. Moreover, in the absence of making such connections early on, external initiatives are often frustrated and short-lived.

On the first day of the exodus of Third Country nationals from Iraq triggered by Iraq's August 2, 1990, invasion of Kuwait, Jordanian families in Amman took food from their pantries to the border to share with the new arrivals. They were joined by the Jordanian Red Cross and Red Crescent Society and other local civic organizations. The actions were, from all accounts, not a political statement about the conflict but an expression of human solidarity with people who had just made a grueling six-hundred-mile trip with only the resources they could carry with them.

Likewise in the Caucasus, some of the worst effects of sudden mass displacement were averted in 1995 and 1996 by the willingness of Ingush and Daghestani citizens to house the Chechens who had been forced to flee their homes because of the conflict with the Russian Federation. Some Ingush families hosted as many as thirty displaced Chechens, in spite of the generalized economic hardships facing people in the region from the collapse of the Soviet system. International humanitarian agencies in camps and communal shelters cared for only a minority of the displaced. "Strong kinship support networks and traditions of self-sufficiency... diminished the need for outside material inputs."[5]

African traditions of hospitality also run deep. Many communities espouse an ethic that embraces sharing food, clothing, and shelter with people in need and reaching out to strangers. Local traditions of hospitality are

frequently rooted in deeply held religious beliefs. Indeed, evidence suggests, in the words of one African scholar of Ethiopian nationality, that
"humanitarian actions and impulses are part of the common heritage of
humankind."[6]

Yet Africa in recent years has received so much foreign aid, the same analyst notes, that its own humanitarian traditions have become obscured.[7] One
bellwether of the destructiveness of the Sudan's civil war has been the erosion
of the country's vaunted traditions of hospitality across the dividing lines of
tribe, race, and religion. In various other countries, too, massive population
displacement and its longer-term social, economic, and ethnic impacts have
eroded deeply rooted traditions. Daghestani hospitality toward the tens of
thousands of displaced Chechens waned considerably when small numbers
of Chechen fighters began to use their country of refuge as a launching pad
for attacks on Russian federal forces.

In Haiti during the period of military rule following the 1994 coup,
Haitians themselves were "usually on the front lines in dealing with the
underlying crisis that engendered food shortages, working with local populations to deal with the impact and define coping strategies, and working
with other social actors to address the underlying issues that aid and abet
crisis." International actors, however, had great difficulty connecting with
the "myriad collection" of voices that were expressing, even during the military rule, a strong and vibrant commitment to democratic social change.[8]
The sparse and fragile links forged between international actors and internal change agents during the coup period arguably delayed the necessary
momentum for social reconstruction once Aristide was reinstated.

In crisis after crisis, traditional coping mechanisms for dealing with major
emergencies exist at the family, community, and national level. In fact, the
Ethiopian famine of the mid-1980s surfaced on the international screen only
after local coping mechanisms had largely been exhausted. By the time families arriving at feeding centers caught the international eye, they had sold
off most of their possessions and had vacated their lands. The experience
underscored the need for early warning systems and assistance earlier on in
the process to reinforce local coping capacities, people's first line of defense.

Some nations in crisis, of course, have greater private and governmental
resources to draw on than others. *Patronage or Partnership* deliberately
selected countries whose civil society institutions were at different stages
of development, ranging from largely nonexistent or embryonic to vibrant.
Drawing on data from one country each in Asia, Europe, Latin America
and the Caribbean and from two in Africa, our case studies examined the
impacts of differential stages of civil society development on crisis responses.

We also reviewed contributions that local actors made at various stages
of emergencies, whether in the run-up to crises, during the heat of conflicts,
or in postconflict reconstruction. While some civil societies are more robust

and well organized than others and some governments more action-oriented than others, the civil societies and governmental infrastructures of countries undergoing crises form the first line of defense in emergencies.

Our research tested the hypothesis that the world's humanitarian apparatus would play a more direct role in countries with less well developed institutions of civil society and a more behind-the-scenes role in countries with more mature institutions. To our dismay, we found that the particular shape of an international response to a given emergency is determined more by factors inherent in the external humanitarian apparatus than by the developmental stage of local institutions or even the particular stage of the conflict. Analysis of the six cases concluded that whether humanitarian action nurtured or undermined local capacity had more to do with the attitudes of the major foreign — and, for that matter, indigenous — actors, whether combatants, politicians, diplomats, or aid officials, than with the size and maturity of the indigenous institutions themselves.

In Sri Lanka, belligerents brushed aside the well-rooted institutions of a mature civil society. In Mozambique, foreign aid agencies created "national" NGOs that, years later, lacked the firm local roots enjoyed by preexisting groupings such as traditional birth attendants. In Haiti, a Canadian NGO did better at connecting with local civil society and meeting its objectives after its expatriate staff had fled and had turned over operations to its existing Haitian employees than it had with Canadians on the ground.

In short, the existence of civil society institutions does not guarantee that they will form the cornerstone of an externally driven humanitarian response. Conversely, the apparent absence of such institutions need not stymie outside efforts to strengthen local capacity. The fact that a society has few private, nonstate structures should not deter humanitarian organizations seriously committed to strengthening local capacity.

Whatever their stage of development, however, for most countries civil strife is not a situation in which institutions continue to function as in normal circumstances. The existence of conflict places such structures under duress, making public and private institutions and leadership vulnerable to insecurity and politicization. As observed in our case study of capacity building among Guatemalan refugees and in Guatemala, "[E]mergencies, by definition, mark a break with a population's history, often accompanied by shifts in environment, production, community ties, and relations with outside actors. The exceptional nature of these shifts creates severe limitations on efforts at long-lasting changes."[9]

The point is a fundamental one, if somewhat obvious. Strengthening local capacity during times of civil strife is far more difficult than during periods of relative stability. Even where outside actors are committed to partnership with, and to respecting and nurturing the self-reliance of, indigenous structures and leadership, the impacts of their involvement may carry in the opposite direction. Activities among Guatemalan refugees geared toward equipping the women for return to their homes following the war thus promoted skills that did not suit the situation awaiting the women on their return. "They learned to further their interests as a matter of 'right,'" our study concluded, ill-preparing them for a Guatemala "where there is no institutional or cultural means of establishing rights" or of satisfying them.[10]

Local actors are key, but equipping them for the challenges they face is not an easy process, even when foreign actors are thoroughly committed to partnership.

Externality of the Humanitarian Enterprise

The international response to the crisis in the Persian Gulf also highlighted the essentially foreign character of the international humanitarian enterprise. "Crises, particularly those of the magnitude of the Gulf," we wrote in 1992, "exacerbate the tendency to import foreign experts, field workers, and relief items irrespective of the human and material resources available locally and of the potential contributions of indigenous institutions. This tendency leads to increased costs and prevents the country concerned from benefiting from commercial opportunities. It also narrows the potential for cooperation, coordination, and institution-building with national authorities and local populations."[11]

Why is outside assistance so little attuned to capacity building? First, external perceptions often define emergencies. One crisis that caught the world's attention during the 1990s involved the expulsion of some 250,000 ethnic Georgians from Abkhazia in 1993. In responding to the needs of those who resettled in the Zugdidi area of Georgia and in the capital of Tbilisi, international agencies soon realized that the Abkhaz conflict was only one of three crises causing hardship for civilians in Georgia. Tensions between Georgians and Ossets and between supporters and opponents of Georgia's former president Gamsakhurdia were also creating serious displacement. Moreover, while one in twenty Georgians suffered directly from the conflicts, most Georgians had been seriously affected by the collapse of the former Soviet Union. Aid organizations that framed the humanitarian challenge in terms of responding to conflict-affected populations risked fanning tensions with others requiring aid and bypassing fledgling post-Soviet governmental structures that needed support and encouragement.[12]

Second, in major crises foreign actors often frame the problem in terms of what they have to offer rather than what may be most needed in the circumstances. In the case of Georgia, while relief for the displaced was indeed urgent, assistance to build indigenous capacity to protect human rights and to move the former command economy to its post–Cold War market orientation was also imperative. Dealing with people displaced by conflict without addressing broader macroeconomic policy issues was a recipe for frustration and confusion. Yet the alternative of tackling the broader issues would have stretched humanitarian agencies beyond their mandates and resources.

In the case of Ethiopia, where aid-bearing outsiders approached the famine in the mid-1980s as a function of climate rather than of repressive and counterproductive government policies, the international response in terms of megatons of food aid left the underlying problems unaddressed. In the case of gender, the needs of women have often been overlooked by an international apparatus unattuned to their circumstances.

Third, outside assistance favors external actors at the expense of local ones. In the case of Haiti during the 1990s, the view from afar rightly accentuated problems of poverty, a stagnating economy, authoritarianism, and inefficiency. Yet that view also obscured the vitality that existed at the community level. "The myriad civil society organizations, traditional social organizations such as *soldes* and *eskwad,* youth groups, women's organizations, neighborhood organizations, peasant organizations, and cooperatives have developed strategies and gained experience in dealing with their problems."[13] In fact, the engagement of precisely such organizations brought innovation and success to the use of international food aid.

Fourth, the global humanitarian edifice is, by nature and design, an external construct. Each of the major components of the artifice — donor governments, bilateral and multilateral aid agencies, NGOs, and the International Red Cross and Red Crescent movement — has its own respective lines of communication with organizations in conflict areas. The increasing familiarity of these external actors with each other can be an asset, as noted in our Kosovo study, where many of the officials, as well as their institutions, had collaborated with each other before arriving in Skopje, Tirana, or Pristina. Yet the established inner circle of foreign actors is often difficult for national and local actors to penetrate. Indigenous NGOs experience difficulty gaining access to the conference rooms, including the international NGO forums, where discussions of humanitarian strategy take place, succeeding sometimes only after the emergency is past.

Fifth, competing agendas between external and indigenous actors drive wedges between the two sets of institutions. The Bosnia crises surfaced a fundamental element of competitiveness between foreign and indigenous actors for available international funding. "It is widely believed by Bosnian NGOs that as long as there is money for international NGOs in Bosnia, they will not leave. Further, international NGOs will rarely advise donors to work through Bosnian organizations as long as there are financial possibilities for themselves."[14] The crisis response also positioned foreign donor agencies and their in-country agents in direct competition with the host government and its own network of governmental and nongovernmental implementing partners.

Our study concluded that, without the benefit of a tradition of private-sector entrepreneurial and voluntary action, the Bosnian public had little understanding of NGOs, while local authorities viewed private agencies as foes of the government and competitors for international funds. "Despite much talk of participation and consultation, donors essentially ignore Bosnian NGOs when preparing their projects and programs, focusing on their own priorities and agendas."[15] In one instance as embarrassing as it was incriminating, a donor received an application from an international NGO that had neglected to substitute "Bosnia" for "Bulgaria," where the form had last been used.

Competing agendas may also involve clashing political objectives. International funders necessarily make choices between governmental and non-governmental recipients. In Mozambique at mid-decade evidence existed of "a deliberate attempt of the donor community to weaken the government rather than to promote a healthy balance between state and civil society activities."[16] Revisiting the issues in Mozambique several years later, we found that donors' innovative attempts to channel funds for the health sector through government structures at the national, provincial, and local levels represented a notable exception to broader patterns.

Indeed, the generally positive experience in the health sector in Mozambique was limited in impact by donor preference for funding NGOs rather than other government entities, including the ministry of planning and administration. The approach taken ignored the paradoxical reality that "state legitimacy must be reinforced first in order [for external funders] to cultivate a viable independent grassroots force that can engage it."[17] The recent experience in Afghanistan, described in the epilogue, offers something of a variation on the same theme. The interim government agreed to at the Bonn meeting in December 2001 lacked popular legitimacy and national scope, with donors doubtless soon to be tempted to fund international NGOs in a vain effort to detour the flagrant problems of government authority and accountability.

Local institutions, too, often have political agendas of their own. For years the International Federation of Red Cross and Red Crescent Societies has labored to encourage its national affiliates in crisis countries, often headed by government officials or political appointees, to function in keeping with the movement's core principles of neutrality, impartiality, and independence. During and after the conflict in Bosnia, the president of the Republik Srpska Red Cross was the wife of political leader Radovan Karadzic. In the Federal Republic of Yugoslavia, the secretary of the Serbian Red Cross was a member of Slobodan Milosevic's party and a candidate for local elections. Following Milosevic's departure, senior personnel in the Serbian Red Cross were replaced, but political affiliations figured in some appointments at the branch level. The need for insulating humanitarian agencies from political agendas is not limited to crisis countries. National Red Cross societies in the United States and some other Western countries have charters stipulating membership of government officials on their respective boards.[18]

Finally, the preponderant externality of the humanitarian enterprise is reinforced by the media, which routinely ignores the forward line of response in the form of the resources of host governments and civil societies. "During the Gulf crisis, western media concentrated on the international activities of donor governments and the Allied Coalition, the UN, and NGOs. As a result, the critical humanitarian role played by the governments and peoples of the region was obscured."[19]

The media generally seeks out the foreign elements in a relief operation, interviewing persons who speak its language and are of interest to its viewers and readers back home. Expatriate aid workers, largely white, and international military forces, preferably in battle fatigues, make better copy than locals performing the same tasks. Who is doing the job often receives more attention than does the nature of the job being done. The international public is often unaware that its resources are being channeled through local institutions and leadership as well.

Media attention, of course, has positive benefits, such as giving the wider world a sense of participation in a crisis and generating added financial resources and political momentum. Yet its preoccupation with two sets of stereotypes — international Good Samaritans and abject local victims — contributes to delusions of humanitarian grandeur among foreign aid agencies and distorted public perceptions of the relative scale and importance of international largesse. Local actors are understandably distressed at bearing the lion's share of the humanitarian burden yet being marginalized in the public eye. Had UN information officers cultivated African media with the same zeal they displayed toward the BBC, Reuters, and the *New York Times,* Operation Lifeline Sudan would arguably have been perceived in Africa itself as less foreign and might have generated more regionwide interest and support.[20]

Getting the Balance Right

Strengthening local capacity, approached as an integral part of the more immediate process of responding to humanitarian emergencies, requires getting the balance right between foreign and indigenous actors. Given the importance of engaging local resources in the face of the overwhelming externality of the international humanitarian apparatus, the challenge is to nurture the former while constraining the latter. The reality that indigenous institutions require outside assistance and that outside agents need viable connecting points in crisis areas lends urgency to the balancing act. Neither the interdependence of need nor the logic of the partnership, however, has yet made an effective division of labor noticeably easier to achieve.

One of the best-case examples of realizing the potential synergies between the foreign and the indigenous involves an NGO food security project in Haiti.[21] This initiative used food assistance purchased locally in Haiti from small producer groups with funds provided by the Canadian government to a Canadian NGO, the Centre canadien d'etude et de la cooperation internationale (CECI), to sustain local cereal-processing and trucking operations and to distribute assistance to some sixty thousand needy beneficiaries. CECI's staff of Haitian nationals reconfigured and continued these activities throughout the period of the coup and of international economic sanctions following the recall of Canadian NGO personnel by the Canadian government for security reasons.

A number of factors contributed to the redesigned project's success. The NGO staff of "trained and competent professionals" from Haiti reconceptualized a traditional food aid program that had existed before the coup so as to "build on local capacities and stimulate national production, while at the same time complying with criteria for [international] humanitarian assistance programs."[22] Their knowledge of the local scene allowed them to forge partnerships with existing grassroots producer organizations. Locally produced and milled cereals came to constitute 80 percent of the volume of the food aid and (due to the cost of edible oil that continued to be imported from Canada) 50 percent of the cost of the program.

Foreign actors also played key roles. The Canadian government approved a new grant to the NGO, waiving the required presence of Canadian personnel on the ground. The Canada-based NGO continued to support the operations of its local staff in Haiti. Indeed, based on the experience, CECI has given its indigenous staff in other countries a larger role in decision making and operations. A CIDA evaluation gave the program high marks for its economic, social, and institutional impacts. FAO recognized its accomplishments with a special food security award.

A somewhat less successful example that highlights the need for a strategic balancing of external and indigenous elements concerns "assistance by remote" in the Caucasus. This approach involves using either indigenous personnel employed by foreign agencies or indigenous agencies themselves to sustain humanitarian work in situations of extreme insecurity. The strengths and weaknesses of the various options available were discussed in a series of workshops held in the Caucasus in 1997 that helped inform *Humanitarian Action in the Caucasus: A Guide for Practitioners*.[23]

Confirming the Haitian experience, local employees of international agencies in the Caucasus represented an indispensable resource when expatriates were unwelcome or unwilling to take the risks of continued direct involvement. The emphasis in the Caucasus discussions was on finding ways to sustain humanitarian activities through facilitating and supporting the continued efforts of local actors, whether locals employed by international agencies or local organizations themselves. Yet workshop participants were clear that on occasion humanitarian activities might need to be withdrawn or suspended.

Discussions sought to identify a series of "disengagement indicators" to help reach such a critical decision.[24] Anticipating the likely fallout of withdrawal, one of the concerns expressed was that the disengagement of internationals would expose or punish local NGOs associated with foreign relief operations. "Militant elements would enjoy greater impunity due to weaker local NGOs and the absence of the deterrent effect of international aid agencies."[25] The extreme insecurity in the Caucasus underscored the reality that a commitment to local institution-building limits the freedom of expatriate organizations abruptly or without consultation to disengage from insecure theaters of operation. If capacity building is to have any meaning, international humanitarian actors are not simply free to go — or perhaps even to come — entirely on their own terms.

Experience elsewhere confirms the extent to which engagement with foreign agencies can be hazardous to the health of indigenous employees and institutions. A dramatic example took place in Rwanda in 1994, where militant elements entered buses that were evacuating expatriate personnel during the genocide, removing and taking to their death the agencies' Tutsi employees. Debriefed in Nairobi after the incidents, UN personnel were in a palpable state of shock as they tried to come to terms with the fate of their colleagues — as contrasted with their own stays of execution.

In more recent years, international organizations, including the UN system itself, have made stronger policy commitments and more specific arrangements to protect indigenous as well as expatriate staff. The differential treatment received by the two categories of personnel, however, remains clear confirmation of the externality of the organized humanitarian enterprise. International media in the latter months of 2001 gave extended coverage to the arrest and trial of eight expatriate aid workers for proselytization in Afghanistan, to their release from the Taliban authorities fleeing the U.S. bombing, and to their removal from the country with the help of U.S. Special Forces. Negligible coverage has been devoted to the even greater vulnerability of the sixteen Afghan nationals also arrested and doubtless more likely to suffer harassment and torture.[26] Only the rare news account noted that the national staff were eventually freed along with the expatriates.[27]

Such experiences in Haiti and the Caucasus, Rwanda and Afghanistan suggest the need for a basic strategy geared to getting the indigenous/foreign balance right. Such a strategy should accentuate the indigenous, at the same time injecting safeguards to lessen the chances that the wrong institutions and questionable leaders benefit from external collaboration. The strategy should also keep foreign involvement at a generally low profile, at the same time realizing the powerful positive influence that outside resources and involvement can exercise on the behavior of the warring parties and on the dynamics of conflicts. Such a strategy should also differentiate between NGOs and other civil society institutions that reflect popular aspirations and those that are little more than extensions of political, religious, personalistic, or other extraneous agendas.

A strategy of rebalancing foreign and indigenous elements would also need to distinguish among various kinds of activities and programs so as to maintain the comparative advantages of the respective actors in each. Efforts to protect human rights may prove more vulnerable for indigenous staff and therefore preferable for expatriate personnel to undertake. Conversely, relief work may be less sensitive as an area for local staff to be engaged in and not require expatriate presence.

Even this generalization needs qualification. In Rwanda in February 1997, four members of the UN Human Rights Field Operation were killed near Cyangugu. Ambushed in a UN vehicle while en route to a meeting were two internationals, whose bodies were mutilated, and two local staff. Being expatriates — in this instance, from Great Britain and Cambodia — provided no special protection. In Haiti during the final months of the coup, conversely, assistance efforts had to be suspended because they jeopardized the safety of local staff and civilians.

Foreign human rights organizations have done even less in the way of local institution building than have aid groups, although that situation, too, is changing.[28] Within the past several years, for example, Human Rights Watch has worked with partner agencies in crisis countries, both to encourage their own monitoring of abuses and to provide opportunities for advocacy in Northern countries and at the UN Security Council. The new policy directions that Amnesty International embraced in late 2001 have implications for the texture of its relationships with indigenous organizations.

Recurrent institutional obstacles still remain to getting the balance right between the foreign and the indigenous. Many donors do not actively support strengthening local capacity, focusing instead on activities with more measurable and visible results and with quicker fund disbursement rates. Many donors, too, do not provide funding to underwrite essential administrative support costs, including training, of indigenous NGOs. Short time frames for grants, funding tied to procurement of aid materiel in donor countries themselves, and rigid conceptual understandings of relief and development all work against the necessarily slower and more holistic approach to capacity building. Many humanitarian agencies themselves still respond to emergencies first and think about capacity building later.

A number of correctives and safeguards now seek to strike a better balance between the two sets of actors. Among these approaches are the following:

- Moving beyond the "one size fits all emergencies" approach to design programs tailored to specific local settings
- Incorporating local expertise and contextual knowledge into international needs assessment missions
- Framing the humanitarian task in its broader terms, no longer making the immediate relief of suffering the overriding objective
- Enlisting development agencies, perspectives, and resources from the outset rather than sequentially
- Working to avoid the normal "bidding war" among foreign organizations that inflates local salaries and drains leadership from indigenous institutions
- Including indigenous organizations as full participants in coordination meetings and other discussions of program strategy
- Devising informal ways as well to reach out to indigenous institutions and leadership

Some agencies — U.S.-based NGO Lutheran World Relief is one — no longer operate their own programs of emergency assistance, instead channeling resources received from Northern governments and private contributors to partner organizations. In some crises — Bosnia is an example — NGO coalitions and roundtables include indigenous as well as foreign groups. A number of NGOs have paired reduction in their hands-on relief roles with a stepping up of advocacy efforts. The creation of national NGO chapters in crisis areas (e.g., World Vision/Zimbabwe or Save the Children/Liberia) has helped put indigenous and foreign agencies on a more equal footing. Yet extensions of Western agency consortia are no guarantee of local ownership or traction. Moreover, decentralized decision making may reduce the coherence of an international agency's global programs or on its own sense of ownership and accountability.

One creative example of a recalibration of the balance between international and indigenous actors involves response to the Gujarat earthquake of January 2001. Early on, a number of international NGOs, some of them without previous experience in India, sent needs assessment missions to the scene with an eye to exploring ways to become operational. Coordinating meetings chaired by Indian NGOs, however, confirmed that the situation was demonstrably well in hand. "The best thing we could do was to provide financial support," reported a Mercy Corps official, "and get out of the way."[29] Acting on his recommendation, the agency made a grant to an

Indian NGO, Chetna, for its work in strengthening local NGOs, along with limited amounts of material aid.

Despite significant strides toward greater mutuality, however, a preponderant externality continues to characterize the humanitarian enterprise.

Dilemmas and Discoveries

A better balanced international humanitarian apparatus offers a tool to assist in managing the dilemmas inherent in strengthening local capacity. Indigenous institutions represent the front lines of humanitarian response to crises, but when difficulties become overwhelming, outside assistance may be indispensable. External involvement will need to take into account longer-term impacts on indigenous structures, however. Can a relief operation be considered a success if, although the patient survives, the local emergency medical team that will treat the patient's next emergency remains marginalized or incapacitated?

The process of selecting local interlocutors involves dilemmas as well. In Mozambique, each set of local institutions has its limitations. "[M]any voices that might help the modern health sector are found in traditional forms of associational life rather than in the nascent national NGOs." Embracing traditional civil society structures to the exclusion of local government structures that deliver services, however, may delay the validation that the state requires for its role in postconflict reconstruction to become a reality. That said, state structures themselves have limitations. "Working with the provincial administration and central government bureaucracy militates against enhancing local capacities."[30] In such circumstances, finely tuned "both/and" strategies are preferable to "either/or" choices.

NGOs in donor countries, too, have their own strengths and weaknesses. Many NGOs represent expressions of the humanitarian concerns of their citizens, confirmed in voluntary contributions to their work. Yet many U.S.-based groups are anything but nongovernmental in their revenue sources and retain their credentials as private institutions. Applicable U.S. legislation allows "private voluntary organizations," the American equivalent of NGOs, to receive as much as 80 percent of their resources from nonprivate sources. On the European Continent, NGOs receive significant amounts of funds from their own governments, some functioning as extensions of various labor and other social and political movements.

The humanitarian enterprise also faces a dilemma in the area of product and process. The current emphasis on relief delivery uses quantifiable indicators within stated time frames to measure success. One recent study uses the "output culture" as a term to describe post–Cold War humanitarian assistance.[31] Strengthening local capacity, however, also requires more intangible benchmarks and longer-term horizons. Practitioners find themselves caught between the effectiveness criteria of donors and their own commitment to assisting local partners. Managing this dilemma necessitates clarifying expectations on both sides and developing indicators that put strengthening capacity on a more level playing field with traditional objectives in health, nutrition, and other sectors.

Managing the dilemmas associated with strengthening local capacity requires scrutiny of the agendas and policies of the external institutions that purport to build indigenous institutions. While the existing literature tends to focus on what is meant by "capacity" in crisis areas themselves, the credentials and agendas of international actors also require review. Research needs to enlist and reflect indigenous actors and analysts as well, as our own has sought to do. The time has come to break the invidious but accepted circle: *outside* actors do studies for *outside* use paid for by *outside* resources *using* external criteria to judge *internal* capacity building. The nature and success of capacity building look different depending on vantage point.

Capacity building, like coordination, is ultimately about power: the sharing of power and resources, of limelight and accountability. Efforts to strengthen local institutions sooner or later bump up against the political economy of the humanitarian enterprise, in which donors have more power than implementing agencies, Northern NGOs than Southern NGOs, military actors in the aid sphere than civilian ones, providers than beneficiaries. My colleague Sue Lautze's caution is thus well placed: An emphasis on local capacity building should not be allowed to serve as a ruse for relieving the international humanitarian apparatus of the onus of adapting itself more fully to local needs. The project is launching new research that picks up where *Patronage or Partnership* leaves off to examine the political economy of the humanitarian enterprise, seeking to identify and address the imbalances in power that undermine its effectiveness.[32]

Dilemmas also attend choices about sustaining humanitarian activities in situations of insecurity. The perils that expatriate personnel face may point to the use of indigenous surrogates, but the stepped-up involvement of local staff and partners contains perils for them and their sponsors. Indeed, extreme situations may arise in which no viable solutions are available for sustaining humanitarian activities, with or without local intermediaries. Again, the experience in Sri Lanka is illuminating, where "Neither the state military nor the separatist guerillas will allow an independent network of local communities to flourish in areas under their control.... State and guerilla interference in every aspect of the relief activity is debilitating to the nurture of local leadership."[33]

Perhaps the situation is not quite so bleak. Even in deeply militarized areas in Sri Lanka where authorities attempt, often brutally, to assert total control over humanitarian action and local communities, some local leaders and organizations have been able to carve out a modicum of humanitarian space. Thanks to the strong support such groups have nurtured from the communities in which they work, the authorities would have to answer to local citizens for unpopular decisions. Moreover, the availability of outside funding, combined with strong leaders who have developed influential connections, provides a degree of protection against manipulation. Thus, within limits that local partners and communities themselves carefully define, capacity-building efforts in places such as Sri Lanka quite appropriately aim to reinforce stronger leadership and a greater sense of community ownership of externally supported activities.[34]

Dilemmas such as these cannot be solved on the basis of global generalizations for policymakers or prescriptive nostrums for humanitarian program managers. Such dilemmas, though, may be skillfully managed, drawing upon available experience and competent analysis. International actors may work with and through local organizations, being careful to take into account their weaknesses. Conversely, indigenous actors may draw on international support, taking care to make their own informed judgments about what is in their own best long-term interests.

The experiences of the past decade demonstrate that getting the relationship right is possible, and that clear payoffs are available for doing so. In Haiti, knowledgeable and professional indigenous staff were able to adapt and sustain activities that would otherwise have been forced to close, leaving local people bereft of their benefits. In Chechnya, indigenous institutions managed programs when the presence of foreign personnel could no longer be sustained.

The conclusion of an earlier study of drought and warfare in the Sudan written by Francis Deng and myself in 1992 suggests a desirable division of labor. The thrust of the study has since been validated by other crises.

> [E]mergency operations should maintain a more discreet international profile. On the one hand, expatriate presence facilitates international cooperation and helps to interject innovation, efficiency, and experience gained in other crises. On the other hand, nationals and expatriates must be able to work together in all phases of emergency operations and development cooperation. A more sensitive approach would be to reinforce the resourcefulness of indigenous populations and to capitalize on proven survival techniques. Particular attention should be given to selecting expatriate staff in terms not only of the technical expertise required but also of the ability to manage human relationships in cross-cultural situations.[35]

Replacing patronage with partnership — or, more realistically, increasing the partnership roles of local institutions in global humanitarian action — requires fundamental changes in the international enterprise. Although traditions of patronage die hard, reform requires a rebalancing of the established division of labor between foreign and indigenous actors. Reform requires working between crises to position the system to respond better in the next emergency and broadening the understanding, the mandates, and the time horizons of humanitarian organizations.

In the humanitarian regime of the future, the mobilization of local institutions and their strengthening needs to be seen as essential rather than diversionary. Solutions lie not in approaching one set of actors or the other as the panacea to humanitarian response, nor in stigmatizing either set for its demonstrated limitations. The way forward lies in finding creative ways to manage the necessary tensions between the two. The implications of this approach are explored in the discussion of humanitarian architecture in chapter 7.

5

Humanitarian Politics

In 1972, I participated in an initiative by the Sudan Council of Churches to assist people returning to the southern Sudan from exile in neighboring countries. The moment was a propitious one, thanks to the Addis Accords, a peace agreement facilitated by the World Council of Churches that brought down the curtain, for a time, on a conflict that had rent the nation asunder since 1955.

Our encampment of aid workers from a variety of World Council– related groups pitched its tents in Juba, site of the regional government established under the Accords. Occasionally Joseph Lagu, commander of the southern forces during the civil war, would stop by to see his longtime friend, my colleague and Norwegian Church Aid representative, Oystein Stabrun.

I remember being nervous about his visits. Should aid workers be fraternizing with soldiers, especially ranking ones? Would that draw the relief effort into a political crossfire at a time when the country was finally positioned to move on? Why not simply deliver food, blankets, clothing, agricultural tools, and shelter materials to returning refugees and stay out of the political arena?

The limitations of sticking to my humanitarian knitting and the value of my colleague's reaching out to southern Sudanese leaders are now clear. Humanitarian agencies nowadays realize the need to familiarize themselves with the political-military landscape, even while seeking to preserve their neutrality — or, more precisely, as an investment in preserving their neutrality. Differences still play themselves out, reflecting not only individual and agency variations but also divergent comfort levels between European and U.S. agencies on engaging with the political realm.

The post–Cold War era has witnessed major changes in the interaction between the humanitarian enterprise and political, diplomatic, and military actors. This chapter focuses on the interface between the enterprise and the political sphere, examining conflicting understandings of politics and neutrality, the recent evolution of international norms and the role of advocacy in promoting such changes, and the erosion of the traditional understanding of sovereignty through humanitarian activities. The following chapter on coercive humanitarianism reviews interactions between the humanitarian enterprise and the use of military and economic force.

Politics and Neutrality: Conflicting Paradigms

The ongoing debate within our research group on the nature of politics and humanitarian neutrality provides a window into the wider dispute that engages politicians and diplomats, policy makers and practitioners. The interface between humanitarian action and politics has been a leitmotiv of our research since its inception. From our precursor work on Operation Lifeline Sudan in 1990 through our most recent publications on politics and conflict, our emphasis has been not on the delivery of humanitarian assistance and protection in its own right but rather on the dynamic interrelationships between humanitarian action and the political sphere.

Much of our early work viewed politics as a threat to effective humanitarian work. In settings such as Central America and the Caucasus, we observed the intrusive impacts of the political-military strategies of the belligerents on evenhanded humanitarian efforts. We commented on the "infiltration" of donors' political agendas into the allocations and activities of aid groups. The "damages" confirmed the wisdom of scrupulous adherence to the principle of neutrality: that humanitarian action be based solely on need, eschewing extraneous agendas, whether political or ideological, religious or cultural. The challenge faced by the enterprise, as we saw it, was to function in highly politicized environments without embracing a political agenda or making major concessions to political pressures. "Politicization" was a pejorative term describing the infiltration of politics; humanitarian advocacy was a means for resisting such inroads and expanding the space for principled humanitarian action.

Stepping back from case studies of individual conflicts, our latest work has proposed a more elaborate framework for understanding the relationship between the humanitarian and the political. In *Politics and Humanitarian Action,* S. Neil MacFarlane, a political scientist and international organizations specialist, describes politics as a value-neutral arena in which interests are identified, priorities established, and resources allocated. In that arena, humanitarian organizations press politicians and diplomats for greater sensitivity to humanitarian values and greater space for relief and rights work. MacFarlane's *Humanitarian Action: The Conflict Connection* takes further the theme that humanitarian action cannot be isolated from politics. The humanitarian enterprise, as he sees it, should work to avoid exacerbating — and where possible to ameliorate — the conflicts to which it responds.

In MacFarlane's view, "politics is about process, not ends. It is a form of behavior and a set of institutional mechanisms whereby individuals and groups seek to accumulate and use power to pursue their objectives. Politics is neither good nor bad, although the ends that people pursue may be good or bad, and the consequences — whether advertent or inadvertent, good or bad." Politicization can thus be positive rather than pejorative, depending on its outcomes. "Politicization means rendering political," in his view. Advocacy is a political act, and a positive one at that. In fact, he says, advocacy represents an instance of "the infiltration of political agendas into the conduct of humanitarian action."[1] In a journal article with Thomas G. Weiss, who shares his views, MacFarlane comments that "[T]he humanitarian imperative can not be pursued effectively by seeking to maintain artificial barriers between the humanitarian and the political. Instead, aid agencies should consciously engage in political processes in order to realize their objectives."[2]

In my foreword to MacFarlane's *Politics and Humanitarian Action,* I note that "While his 'take' occasionally differs from [my] own, he analyzes the data dispassionately, draws conclusions carefully, and makes recommendations persuasively. Certainly his thesis that 'the humanitarian imperative is best served not by avoiding the political process but by consciously engaging it' deserves consideration."[3] Indeed, the dialogue within our research group has sharpened up the issues, though we lack unanimity on a template for understanding the interplay between humanitarian action and politics.

I, for one, have difficulty approaching politics as "value neutral" when the political institutions in countries beset by major crises are so often tilted against those in need of assistance and protection. While I embrace the notion of advocacy with political authorities by humanitarian organizations on behalf of their values and clientele, the proposition that relief and rights groups should embrace political agendas seems dangerous and diversionary.

I also find it helpful to distinguish short-term political or foreign policy interests from longer-term ones, the former being generally invidious to humanitarian action, the latter more supportive of it. Again, MacFarlane differs. "The distinction between short- and long-term policy or political objectives and long-term ones is problematic," he observes. "Often short-term ones are supposed to contribute to long-term ones but in practice they are identical. From the perspective of donors, at least the liberal ones and the UN, one could argue that their long-term policy goal is the construction of societies in which the treatment of populations is based on human dignity. In the short term, that policy goal translates into relief, protection, and conflict prevention, management, and resolution. Are these 'bad' because they are short-term political objectives?"[4]

This difference of viewpoints provides a point of entry into the interplay between humanitarian action and politics that our research illuminates. The divergence reflects not only a difference among ourselves as analysts but also a division within the enterprise itself regarding how humanitarian action should be situated in relation to politics. Broadly speaking, three major positions exist.

The ICRC views the humanitarian and the political spheres as separate and distinct, with authentic humanitarian organizations required to remain neutral on political issues. Neutrality, the principle that "the Red Cross may not take sides in hostilities or engage at any time in controversies of a political, racial, religious or ideological nature," is a central tenet. "Red Cross institutions must beware of politics as they would of poison, for it threatens their very lives," wrote Jean Pictet twenty years ago. "Indeed, like a swimmer, [the ICRC] is in politics up to its neck. Also like the swimmer, who advances in the water but who drowns if he swallows it, the ICRC must reckon with politics without becoming a part of it."[5]

The ICRC's insistence on insulating from politics its own humanitarian activities, which it describes as matters of "charity" rather than of justice, leaves no doubt about its view. Charitable activities are undertaken without reference to the underlying injustices implicated in people's suffering. While the ICRC eschews politics, its day-to-day conduct demonstrates that the sought-after separation is maintained not through sealing off its work off from the political sphere but rather through intensive engagement of the political authorities at every level. "Only if you're politically savvy can you be politically neutral," says one veteran manager of several ICRC relief operations, Urs Boegli.

He points out that in embracing the principle of neutrality, ICRC staff are anything but neutral regarding the victims of armed conflicts. "We don't give a damn about Greater Serbia," he notes, "but we do get exercised about ethnic cleansing and rape when it is used there as a tactic of war."[6] Noting that it has "a bad odor" if construed as passive, "Neutrality frees us from the politics of the situation and allows us to use our energies for the humanitarian aspects of the same problem."[7] While his organization prefers quiet conversations with the authorities, the ICRC may go public on behalf of the victims when private remonstrances prove ineffective.[8]

Other humanitarian groups have sought to redefine the concept of neutrality to allow for greater engagement with the root causes of crises. Some groups have embraced the concept of nonpartisanship as more in keeping with their commitments to justice, which requires addressing political issues such as powerlessness and power that underlie vulnerability. In proposing the Providence Principles of humanitarian action in our 1993 *Handbook for Practitioners,* we suggested that the principle of neutrality, while fully valid for the ICRC, did not reflect the approaches of other humanitarian agencies, particularly those with roots in religious and social justice movements.

Confronted by the same ethnic cleansing and violence with which the ICRC deals, other groups are committed to "speaking truth to power," even if this requires that they address broader political issues. Nonpartisanship reflects the core concept that "Humanitarian action responds to human suffering because people are in need, not to advance political, sectarian, or other extraneous agendas. It should not take sides in conflicts."[9] The concept allows humanitarian organizations, acknowledging the political implications of their activities, greater flexibility to speak to political issues, while still stopping short of embracing a political agenda of their own.

The U.S. NGO Catholic Relief Services (CRS) thus recognizes that "conflict situations and the provision of humanitarian assistance are inherently political, but...the CRS response will be strictly non-partisan."[10] While I myself have great respect for the clarity and consistency of the ICRC's approach, my own views resonate with the nonpartisanship paradigm, which allows for greater activism on humanitarian issues in the political arena.

A third category of humanitarian organizations, finding neither neutrality nor nonpartisanship possible, affirm the importance of taking sides with the poor and oppressed. This approach is reflected in the work of the Mennonites, a religious group known for its quiet and persistent activities in peace building, often at a distinctly local level. Fully committed to work across political and other fault lines, Mennonite agencies encounter situations in which they view solidarity as more important than neutrality. "If one side in a conflict has the preponderance of military power and is inclined to use violence to support its side, maintaining neutrality becomes hard."[11] While the agencies committed to neutrality and nonpartisanship also in one way or another affirm their solidarity with the victims of armed conflict, groups that align themselves with the vulnerable place an even higher premium on such solidarity. For some, solidarity involves simply affirming the humanity of those who suffer; for others, that identification has a definite political component as well.

Tensions between neutrality and solidarity are evident in the comments of an official of the U.S. NGO World Vision, Thomas Getman, posted in the Middle East and writing in anguish in January 2001 at a time of runaway violence between Jews and Palestinians. "Our primary role as a humanitarian agency," he observes, "must be the delivery over the siege blockades of the annual Christmas Epiphany/Muslim Ramadan gift clothing and food packages for the children of poor families. This is in parallel to the support for the near-catatonic mothers who with their traumatized children participate in psycho-social drama groups to manage the terror to which they are subjected." World Vision is also committed, he observes, to "continue sustainable water, health and education development projects which will survive and hopefully thrive no matter how the oppression deepens."

The violence that lends urgency to such activities reminds Getman:

we in the NGO community cannot become partisan, allowing ourselves to be recruited for either side in the Israeli election or for one
side in the ongoing Palestinian/Israeli negotiations. But even as I try
to be faithful to that principle, it is hard in the extreme — impossible,
in fact — not to speak out about the monstrous arrogance of power
being imposed in a racist way. Palestinians are not guiltless and, if we
can believe reports, they have participated in excessive responses too
because of their despair and desire to be free. So what we must stand
for is justice for the oppressed poor on either side of the Green Line.
In reality, however, there are many more people suffering injustice on
one side than the other.[12]

Within the humanitarian community, different paradigms for conceptu-
alizing the humanitarian and the political and for guiding day-to-day work
thus are present. The difference in viewpoints does not concern the need for
humanitarian actors to become more knowledgeable about political forces
and agendas in individual conflicts. The political naiveté that characterized
humanitarian action during the Cold War is no longer a viable option, although some agencies continue to frame relief activities in narrow terms that
downplay their engagement with the political. Instead, the telltale difference
involves how agencies approach the political. The figure of "three degrees
of separation" may be a helpful one.

Separating itself most studiously from the political, the ICRC is committed to neutrality, which it seeks to preserve through refraining from taking
positions on political issues unrelated to the conduct of its humanitarian
activities. Other humanitarian actors, espousing a lesser degree of separation, view themselves as nonpartisan — stopping short of becoming actors
with their own political agenda but still engaging the authorities on essentially political issues. Still others, espousing virtually no separation at all,
find neutrality undesirable and adopt a more avowedly political posture.
Continuing differences in approach notwithstanding, a new and welcome
sensitivity across the humanitarian enterprise acknowledges the importance
of such paradigms and of the political.[13]

Other analysts have offered other typologies. My colleague Thomas G.
Weiss uses the categories of classicists, minimalists, maximalists, and soli-
darists.[14] Hugo Slim speaks of humanitarian prophets, such as the ICRC,
and humanitarian priests, other operational aid agencies.[15] Mark Duffield
distinguishes between neutral humanitarianism and what he terms the "new
or political humanitarianism" in which humanitarian action is part and parcel of a complex of relief, development, and social reconstruction activities
responding to "the new wars."[16] While not necessarily more satisfactory
than these other constructs, the approach that emerges from the project's

research does seek to reflect the rich and varied day-to-day experience of humanitarian practitioners in actual conflict settings.

Real-Life Interactions

Practitioners and analysts concur in the view that during the past decade, political authorities at every level have become much more active interlocutors in humanitarian matters. Interactions between political institutions and with the humanitarian enterprise take place at three levels. At the *local* level, governments and insurgents manipulate humanitarian access to advance their political-military objectives while seeking the presence of international assistance and personnel to legitimize their causes. At the *regional* level, governments affected by instability have important political interests in the outcomes of nearby conflicts. They frequently host large refugee populations, a potentially destabilizing element, and serve as staging areas for humanitarian initiatives.

At the *international* level, governments address perceived political interests unilaterally as well as through the UN Security Council, the world's preeminent political body, and in other intergovernmental arenas. The Security Council has found itself at the convergence of twin trends that have characterized the post–Cold War era: "the higher humanitarian component in political decision-making and the greater assertiveness of humanitarian interests in the political arena."[17] The former is the subject of this section, the latter of the next.

The council's engagement with humanitarian issues has grown steadily over time. As analyst Ted van Baarda has observed, "For nearly twenty-two years, between its establishment and the Six Day War of 1967, the Council passed no resolution on the humanitarian aspects of any given armed conflict." Since that time, the council's involvement has been reluctant (until 1979), moderate (until mid-1990), and intensive (in the 1990s). By decade's end, the humanitarian dimension of international peace and security had come to provide a central justification for many of the actions taken by the council in major emergencies.[18] The council is now routinely engaged with humanitarian matters, viewing abuses of human rights and large-scale unmet human need as threats to international peace and security. Other political authorities and forums, whether international, regional, or national, are also more seized with humanitarian issues.

From a humanitarian standpoint, the council's involvement has been something of a mixed blessing. On the positive side, as Ambassador Eliasson notes earlier, placing the human being in the center of political discussions is "an increasingly accepted formulation and norm." Confirming that reality, an independent study conducted for the IASC notes that "Humanitarian assistance is no longer seen as an activity which can take place outside the normal boundaries of international relations. . . . [I]t is part and parcel of a more complex and political response to crisis."[19] But drawbacks come along with the higher profile status. The council, observes one international law professor, offers "humanity à la carte," proceeding selectively in a pick-and-choose fashion that "cannot help but be discriminatory."[20] Humanitarian space, newly expanded at various levels, is at the same time more subject to political intrusion.

Influential member states, particularly the Permanent Five with veto power, have used the council to advance their specific national interests. In April 1994, the United States, responding to Presidential Decision Directive 25 — formulated partially in reaction to the deaths of U.S. military personnel in Somalia the previous year — prevailed upon the council to reduce the number of UN peacekeeping personnel in Rwanda during the genocide, rejecting the desperate request of the UN general on the ground for more troops.[21] Acting on its own national security agenda, China shortened the extension of the UN peacekeeping mission in Haiti and blocked authorization of UN military observers to oversee the Guatemalan peace agreement to protest those two countries' relations with Taiwan. China later blocked extension of the mandate of peacekeeping troops to Macedonia on similar grounds.

Perceived national interests can also exert a more positive international influence. Political considerations led the French government to prevail upon the council to authorize Opèration Turquoise, blessing the deployment of French troops to Rwanda in June 1994 at a time when multilateral troops were not to be augmented.[22] The presence of politically active Haitian diaspora groups in the United States and Canada promoted the dispatch of U.S. troops to restore President Aristide in 1994 and, following their departure, the commitment of Canadian leadership to reconstruction efforts.[23]

Studies carried out by the project early in the decade highlighted the mixed nature of the new political context for humanitarian initiatives. The experience in the Caucasus provided cases in point. For humanitarian organizations assisting people affected by the conflicts in Chechnya (a republic still within the Russian Federation), in the enclave Nagorno-Karabakh in Azerbaijan (also involving Armenia), and in Georgia (where three conflicts existed side by side), politics was a major factor to be addressed.[24]

The collapse of the Soviet Union ended the USSR's superpower status and, in effect, the Cold War itself.[25] In a broad sense, the passing of the Cold War opened up access to large areas of the former "Second World" that had been closed to Western humanitarian initiatives. The need to secure cooperation from the Russian Federation on other international agenda items, however, has constrained the extent to which governments and aid agencies have been willing to challenge the traditional notion that political authorities should exercise exclusive and unchallengeable control over relief and rights matters. The suffering of Chechens during the 1994–96 war provides a case in point.

While some governments have raised human rights concerns with the authorities, Russia's continuing political importance has discouraged insistence on the proposition that the claim of sovereignty carries unavoidable humanitarian obligations. Russian authorities excluded UN organizations from assisting in Chechnya proper, although they responded positively to a December 1994 Russian request to set up operations in the neighboring republics of Dagestan, Ingushetia, and North Ossetia. The UN appeal in 1996 for "persons displaced as a result of the emergency situation in Chechnya" was somewhat misleading, as the appeal excluded those still within the republic.[26] While some UN officials were anxious to help in Chechnya proper, no evidence exists "that UN organizations pressed Moscow for permission to work inside Chechnya at any time during the war."[27] UN acquiescence in Russia's exclusive management of the crisis also meant that few political modalities of protection were exercised in New York or Geneva.

No ranking UN official set foot in Chechnya during the critical years beginning with the deployment of Russian troops in late 1994. The first to do so was UN High Commissioner for Human Rights Mary Robinson, who, visiting Grozny in March 2000, criticized Russian troops for rights abuses.[28] A report to the Human Rights Commission by human rights groups, published in March 2001, was also sharply critical of the Russian authorities for violations such as summary executions, rape, and torture.[29]

Russia's resistance to such criticisms and its reiteration of the traditional understanding of sovereignty presented the international community with the worst of all worlds: the government's assertion of its legal rights within its territorial jurisdiction, yet its failure to meet its humanitarian obligations to the Chechen population or to allow others to do so. More recently, the Council of Europe and the OSCE have obtained agreement from the Russian authorities to station personnel in Chechnya. On a more negative note, however, Russia's membership in the antiterrorist coalition following the September 11 attacks has had the effect of "aligning the United States with Russia's frequent attempts to ascribe the insurgency to Islamic extremists from abroad."[30]

During the decade, the impacts of politics on humanitarian work in the Caucasus, both at the international level and within the Russian Federation, have been significant. On the negative side of the ledger, diplomatic initiatives in peace processes have often "made humanitarian activity more difficult or dangerous. Risks have become especially acute when diplomatic arms of the UN in Abkhazia or the OSCE in Chechnya have become properly exercised on humanitarian issues but without first consulting with the humanitarian community." Ill-advised diplomatic moves have placed relief and rights operations and personnel in jeopardy. They have also compromised the independence, impartiality, and neutrality of humanitarian actors and appropriated humanitarian action in the pursuit of political agendas.[31]

On the positive side are instances in the Caucasus and elsewhere in which well-conceived diplomatic intercession has expanded access to vulnerable populations and augmented the protection of civilians. Diplomatic initiatives have also improved the security of aid operations and personnel, undermined impunity and enhanced accountability, and moderated the behavior of combatants and of diaspora populations in their support of conflict. The result of such successes has been a net plus for humanitarian interests, often bringing diplomatic and political benefits as well.

What options are available for structuring the interface between humanitarian action and politics at various levels? In a 1995 study called *Humanitarian Politics,* we identified three approaches used in one theater or another to manage the inevitable tensions between humanitarianism and politics.[32] The first involves the subordination of humanitarianism to political goals. Exemplified by Cold War policies, political ideology becomes the main driver behind humanitarian response. In a second approach, "cure-all humanitarianism," emergency responses become a high profile but ultimately unsatisfactory substitute for measures to address the root causes of violence, as exemplified by the international response to the crises in Somalia, Rwanda, and the former Yugoslavia.

The third approach — in our view the most effective one — places humanitarianism in a limited partnership with politics. "[H]umanitarian and political action need to be conceived and implemented on parallel tracks, each reinforcing but not preempting the other," we concluded. "Neither humanitarian nor political action is sufficient in itself; both are necessary. Absorbed as part of a political strategy, humanitarian action may suffer. Devoid of humane values, political action can precipitate a humanitarian disaster. Political action benefits from making space for humanitarian action; humane values require supportive politics to sustain them."[33] That interaction was indeed one of the lessons of UN peacekeeping under the UN Transitional Authority in Cambodia (UNTAC) and the UN Observer Group in El Salvador (ONUSAL).

Chapter 7 returns to the issue of structuring future humanitarian action in relation to the political sphere.

Advocacy and International Norms

The mixed nature of involvement by political actors such as the Security Council, regional organizations, individual states, and belligerents in humanitarian action has both reinforced and reflected the second post–Cold War trend: that of stepped-up engagement by the humanitarian enterprise in the political arena. Whether or not advocacy is a violation of neutrality or an investment in its preservation, humanitarian efforts during the first post–Cold War decade have widened appreciably the space available for relief and rights work.

A consultation on humanitarian access held at Brown University in early 1991 provides a benchmark for gauging the evolution in international norms during the decade. The gathering reviewed the utility and feasibility of a new humanitarian convention that would clarify, reinforce, and extend the provisions of existing law. The group affirmed the viewpoint expressed by the UN secretary-general in 1985 that in the prevailing political climate, "an attempt to 're-negotiate' existing principles could lead to weakening them."[34] Rather than advocating the development of new law, the consultation encouraged governments that had not yet done so to ratify existing conventions and pressured all governments to demonstrate greater fidelity to existing law.[35]

If the 1991 consultation were to be reconvened a decade later, members would be pleasantly surprised at what has transpired in the interim. Significant changes in international law and international relations during the first post–Cold War decade (some are listed in the time line in appendix 1) now place stricter limitations on how wars may be conducted and how authorities may treat civilian populations. Among the legal landmarks are the creation of war crimes tribunals to deal with violations of international humanitarian law in the former Yugoslavia (1993) and Rwanda (1995) and the agreement in principle to create an international criminal court with universal jurisdiction over crimes against humanity (1998), a war crimes tribunal for Sierra Leone (2001), and movement toward the creation of a genocide tribunal for Cambodia (2002).

The fiftieth anniversaries in 1999 of both the Geneva Conventions and the Universal Declaration of Human Rights have provided occasions for reviewing and reaffirming the importance of those earlier achievements. The use of the occasion by the secretary-general to announce that UN peacekeeping activities would henceforth be bound by international law was a step forward.[36] The decade has also seen significant incremental progress in clarifying and codifying international norms in humanitarian, human rights, and refugee law.

The growing vulnerability of civilians and humanitarian personnel in situations of armed conflict has led to a number of steps designed to strengthen and extend existing legal norms. Following up on two resolutions by the Security Council and some fifty-four recommendations, the secretary-general has made three reports on the protection of civilians in armed conflict designed to promote a more effective normative framework on protection issues.[37] His most recent report in 2001 includes a section on criminal prosecution for violations of international humanitarian and human rights law.[38] In 1994, the General Assembly approved the Convention on the Safety of United Nations and Associated Personnel, which entered into force on January 15, 1999.

Illustrative of the incremental gains in the sphere of international law is the negotiation of the accord to ban antipersonnel land mines, a process that culminated in the signing by 122 governments of the mine ban treaty in Ottawa in December 1997 and its taking effect on March 1, 1999. The success of the initiative reflected the fruits of well-coordinated efforts by four sets of actors, which are analyzed in our study.[39]

NGOs formed the International Campaign to Ban Landmines, provided firsthand documentation of their destruction of human life and limb, and organized broadly based national campaigns in many countries. Operational relief agencies such as Medico International, Handicap International, and World Vision — as well as rights groups such as Human Rights Watch and Physicians for Human Rights — played key roles. *The ICRC* provided its own documentation from the field, organizing conferences that reached out to weapons manufacturers and military combat engineers while also engaging international humanitarian law experts. The *United Nations* registered its own concerns through the secretary-general, OCHA, and UNICEF. *States* such as Canada and Norway provided major leadership. The engagement of governments, who would need to ratify and implement a convention that required major alterations in their own practice, was indispensable. Out of the dynamic interaction among these four groupings was forged the broad-based and ultimately successful campaign to ban land mines.[40]

Coming into force in 1999 after having been dismissed a few years earlier as a virtual impossibility, the mine ban treaty represents an accomplishment of major humanitarian, political, and legal proportions. The Cold War residue of more than 100 million mines had proved a major obstacle to economic reconstruction and social progress in more than sixty countries. The treaty, of course, did not defuse this legacy of ordnance with the stroke of the signatories' pens. Its fuller implementation needs to be energetically encouraged and carefully monitored.

Yet "as of August 2000, the number of mine victims in high-risk places such as Afghanistan, Cambodia, and Mozambique had decreased significantly; more than twenty-two million stockpiled antipersonnel mines were destroyed; more than 168 million square meters of land were de-mined; and production dropped dramatically from fifty-four to sixteen known producers."[41] In political perspective, "The treaty was a striking achievement not least because it was resisted by the most powerful state in the international system."[42] In a singular display of cosmetic humanitarianism, the Clinton administration paired its decision not to sign the treaty with an announcement of a "global demining initiative" geared to "end the plague of landmines by 2010."[43] Given U.S. opposition, the treaty itself would not have materialized at all had not a number of concerned governments played a leadership role.

The success of the initiative has been heralded as the result of the "new" phenomenon called advocacy promoted by a "new" breed of nonstate actor, the NGO. Placed in the context of earlier events, however, the advocacy exemplified in the land mines campaign is not a post–Cold War invention, nor did NGOs suddenly spring full-blown onto the scene. A hundred years earlier, when governments at the Hague Peace Conference in 1899 agreed to ban the dumdum bullet, they did so in response to a worldwide initiative by civil society organizations which, as in the land mines action, relied on field-level information on inhumane effects documented by medical professionals.[44]

A close look at the historical record also tempers florid generalizations about the ban as "harbinger of a new diplomacy" in which NGOs overcame for the first time the resistance of states to placing humanitarian concerns over perceived security interests. We concluded instead that the convention is evidence of "revitalizing a pre–World War II style of disarmament negotiations rather than establishing an entirely new approach to international diplomacy."[45]

The campaign also lends itself to instructive comparisons with initiatives to create an international criminal court, to halt the use of child soldiers, and to ban small arms transfers. In the first two instances, the formulation of the problem in clear-cut humanitarian terms helped generate the political momentum that produced successful efforts to create international law constraining state sovereignty. The absence of a humanitarian focus in the more disparate effort to ban small arms has contributed, we found, to its lack of success.[46]

A second example of progress in the evolution of international norms involves provision for internally displaced persons (IDPs). More numerous during the post–Cold War era than refugees, IDPs are persons who, although forced to leave their homes, have not crossed an international border. Legally speaking, they therefore fall outside the protections of the 1951 Convention relating to the Status of Refugees and outside the formal mandate of UNHCR.[47]

In 1992 at the request of the UN Commission on Human Rights, the secretary-general created the position of representative on IDPs and appointed Francis Deng to fill it. Reflecting extensive fact-finding and troubleshooting in a variety of crises as well as discussions in a variety of forums, including the General Assembly, a set of thirty Guiding Principles for Internal Displacement was presented to the commission only six years later. These principles are consistent with the provisions of existing humanitarian, human rights, and refugee law which, taken separately, however, are "too diffused and unfocused to be effective in providing adequate protection and assistance for the internally displaced."[48] In 2000, the IASC established an Inter-Agency Network on Internal Displacement to address IDP issues at the more operational level.

Governments have thus far stopped short of embracing the IDP principles as formal elements of international law. However, "The response by advocates of the principles, including UN agencies, the ICRC, NGOs, and a number of supportive states, has been to act on the basis of the principles irrespective of their official legal status. The principles have now been widely disseminated and are being promoted and applied by the broader humanitarian community. Thus far, the approach appears to be effective, and there is now growing support for a formal mechanism to monitor compliance."[49]

Not having achieved formal legal status, the IDP principles are an illustration of what the International Commission on Intervention and State Sovereignty, in material quoted in the following section, calls "developments in international relations" rather than of explicit changes in the law itself. Yet the principles do offer a platform for challenging inhumane practices. In November 2001 during the peak of the fighting in Afghanistan, the representative of the secretary-general on IDPs and the special coordinator on internal displacement made an urgent appeal to "all parties to the conflict to undertake immediate and sustained efforts to provide greater protection to the displaced and civilian population and to respect their rights as guaranteed by international humanitarian and human rights law."[50]

The examples of the land mines ban and of protection for IDPs suggest a gradual but significant evolution in the international norms that provide the broad political framework for humanitarian action. The changes reflect stepped-up levels of advocacy by the various actors comprising the humanitarian enterprise. For years, the UN Security Council has received regular input on humanitarian matters from the ICRC. In recent years, UN organizations and NGOs have played an increased role. In February 1997, the Security Council held its first-ever meeting with NGOs, who briefed the council on complex emergencies in Africa. Numerous meetings on other topics have subsequently been held.[51]

Engagement by humanitarian organizations with the political sphere has influenced decision-making bodies and political actors at other levels as well. At the regional level, emergency aid to people in countries hosting refugee populations has defused tensions, representing a concrete form of burden-sharing and expanding humanitarian space. Field-level programming of assistance has successfully reduced the inroads of politics into humanitarian activities by addressing the political fears of the host authorities. Political interests have thus proved neither immutable nor necessarily negative vis-à-vis the humanitarian enterprise. In the case of donor states, humanitarian actors have found ways to broaden the states' frequently parochial involvement in political and humanitarian action and to relax the often tight time frame and strict conditionality of the assistance provided.

Yet major problems at the political/humanitarian interface remain, some of them Cold War residues. These problems include the selectivity with which interventions are mounted and the double standards evident in the world's highly variable responses from one crisis to the next.[52] The existing problems are complicated not only by the preponderance of internal (as contrasted with international) armed conflicts but also by the phenomenon of "failed states," which often make it difficult for humanitarian actors to find reliable interlocutors. In sum, recent experience confirms that changes in law, however important, require ongoing vigilance over state practice.

Humanitarian Action and the Erosion of Sovereignty

The conduct of relief and rights work during the past decade has played a significant role in influencing the evolving international understanding of state sovereignty. Both the assertion and the delegation of the prerogatives of sovereign political authorities at various levels shape the context within which humanitarian initiatives are mounted.

"State sovereignty denotes the competence, independence, and equality of states," notes the International Commission on Intervention and State Sovereignty (ICISS), an expert panel whose creation in 2000 at the initiative of the government of Canada demonstrated the significance of changes in the once largely inviolable preserve of sovereignty. "The concept is normally used to encompass all matters in which each state is permitted by international law to decide and act without intrusions from other sovereign states. These matters include the choice of political, economic, social, and cultural systems, and the formulation of foreign policy. The scope of the freedom of choice of states in these matters is not unlimited; it depends on developments in international law (including agreements made voluntarily to limit sovereignty) and international relations."[53] Four specific areas of interaction between humanitarian activities and state sovereignty are examined here.

First, recent experience underscores now-higher expectations of sovereign political authorities. They are obliged either to discharge their humanitarian obligations or to request outside help. The Sudan offers a dramatic case in point. In 1988, a major humanitarian initiative by the ICRC and several NGOs was stillborn when the Khartoum authorities and the SPLA refused to agree to the presence of international humanitarian personnel. During that year alone, some 250,000 Sudanese died of war and famine. The following year, the more assertive UN approach of Operation Lifeline Sudan (OLS) won agreement from both parties, with the UN mounting programs through pre-agreed corridors of tranquility north and south. Noting the contrast already in 1992, we observed that "Rising moral expectations that now influence international response to such tragedies and the increasing globalization of humanitarian action mean that suffering which might have been ignored in the past can no longer be tolerated today."[54]

The Sudan initiative was followed in 1990 by the use of military force to protect civilians in northern Iraq from abuses by their own government. The commitment of the United States in Somalia in late 1992 carried the new brand of assertive humanitarianism forward. However, following the retrenchment in American and U.N. policy after the loss of soldiers' lives in Somalia in 1993–95, the latter half of the decade witnessed fewer dramatic sovereignty overrides. "The flawed intervention in Somalia left an international community increasingly reluctant to engage in other complex emergencies, particularly where it means military involvement," noted an independent review. "Having been shocked by the obstacles to and consequences of intervention, the international community was to be faced only two years later with the accusation that its reluctance to intervene in Rwanda contributed to the decision to withdraw UNAMIR, and the subsequent genocide."[55]

Despite such retrenchment, assertive international action staged a comeback late in the decade in Kosovo and East Timor. In the former, NATO in 1999 launched "the first major bombing campaign intended to bring a halt to crimes against humanity being committed by a state within its own borders."[56] In the latter, following election-related violence in August 1999 and the deployment of the International Force for East Timor (INTERFET), the UN temporarily assumed sovereign powers. The experience of the decade as a whole suggests that while political authorities are now expected to behave more humanely, the willingness of the community of states to insist on such behavior remains uneven and the institutional enforcement mechanisms still highly improvisational.

Second, the exercise of sovereignty by political authorities was shown to be capable of either facilitating or frustrating humanitarian action. Examples from the Sudan and Tanzania illustrate both aspects.

The Sudan government took pains to frame its consent to OLS as a voluntary exercise of sovereignty. "We have, in effect, conceded sovereignty over a large part of our territory to the United Nations," noted Dr. Ohag Mohamed Musa, minister of welfare, zaakat [charity], and relief. The authorities exercised sovereignty in delegating specified prerogatives. The insurgents, who at the time were committed to "one Sudan" and did not claim sovereignty themselves, nonetheless exercised their own authority in agreeing to provide international agencies with access to areas they controlled. The UN, represented in the negotiations by UNICEF Executive Director James P. Grant, considered agreement by both parties a precondition for launching its initiative.

In the early months of OLS, a UN official observed that "We're always testing the concept of sovereignty and being tested. If the government has loaned us its sovereignty, it may always reclaim it."[57] Indeed, reclaim it the authorities did. In reasserting control in November 1989, President Bashir complained that Sudan's sovereignty had been violated by NGOs, which, in association with OLS, were allegedly supporting the rebel cause and introducing military supplies into the south. Bashir's initial decision to allow OLS to function had been sharply criticized by the National Islamic Front and in the local media, which pictured the undertaking as an assault on Sudanese sovereignty.

The Sudan experience demonstrated a contribution by humanitarian actors in promoting legal norms. OLS imposed a certain discipline on both sets of belligerents. The initiative served as a means, at least in 1989, for bringing the practice of the Sudan government, a signatory to the Geneva Conventions and Protocols, more nearly into conformity with international humanitarian law. While not a party to those agreements, the SPLA expressed its willingness to respect them, although the insurgents, too, fell short of agreed international standards.[58]

The government of Tanzania delegated to UNHCR extensive authority for managing the humanitarian response to the refugee crisis in Ngara district, where on April 28, 1994, some 250,000 Rwandans crossed into Tanzanian territory. Granted the power to select the NGOs that would work in the district, UNHCR chose twelve and rejected forty, with the government expediting visas accordingly. While, as noted earlier, UNHCR's exercise of this function created some unhappiness among NGOs, most conceded that this choice made for more effective relief operations. The government also granted access directly into the area for the relief flights that UNHCR approved. The delegation of such authority represented a departure from the normal procedure of having government officials in charge of accreditation, visa, import, and transport functions.

The near-term results were overwhelmingly positive. "The government's approach to sovereignty played an important role in the emergence of an effective coordination scheme in Ngara."[59] Yet in late 1996, the Tanzanian authorities reasserted their prerogatives, pushing Rwandan refugees back across the border without much consultation with, or involvement of, the agencies.

In cases such as these where sovereign powers have explicitly delegated their authority to humanitarian actors, international programs to provide assistance and protection have been the direct, albeit temporary, beneficiary. In the absence of such delegation of authority, humanitarian actors have a less clear mandate. Aid agencies may also be viewed as having interposed themselves between the authorities and their citizens, usurping political functions in settings where the host government is unable or unwilling to provide the necessary services.

That relationship, indeed, represented a third aspect of the experience of the decade, one that cautions humanitarian actors against preempting, or being perceived as preempting, sovereignty. The relief effort in Mozambique provides an example of calculated international efforts to undermine the sovereignty of the national authorities. During the long-lived civil war throughout the 1980s and into the early 1990s, relief agencies provided assistance to civilians in areas controlled by the government or by the insurgents. The number of NGOs involved, many of them heavily funded by donor governments, increased from 7 in 1970 to 70 in 1985 and 180 in 1990.

In what soon came to be known pejoratively as the Donors' Republic of Mozambique, there "seemed to be a deliberate attempt of the donor community to weaken the government rather than to promote a healthy balance between state and civil society activities." To be more specific, "the government was obliged to surrender temporarily elements of sovereignty as a condition for the peace process to come to fruition. . . . The policies, with a particular emphasis on privatization and the market, were set by the donor consortium, and implementation was deliberately placed in the hands of the myriad NGOs."[60]

Since assistance and protection are, in the first instance, the responsibility of sovereign political authorities, inability to meet those responsibilities often constitutes a political embarrassment. Yet aid agencies sometimes appear quite oblivious to the sensitivity of the functions they assume. While UN organizations are not beyond high-handed behavior, NGOs in particular have been criticized for the naiveté of their approach. On the one hand, the critique goes, they pride themselves on their purported neutrality and denigrate what they view as the politicized efforts of other actors. On the other hand, they are themselves engaged on highly political terrain, interacting with belligerents, governments in conflict regions, and international donors.

Drawing on experience in government, military, and NGO posts, Andrew Natsios conveys the view held by some that humanitarian actors need to roll up their sleeves and enter the political fray. "As long as NGOs see their work as separate and distinct from the politics of foreign policy, or in its most condescending form as superior to politics and foreign policy, they will not be considered serious players and will be unable to influence the policy debate except at the margin."[61] Without doubt, humanitarian actors who press governments to enable relief and rights activities by overriding national sovereignty and who themselves function as surrogate sovereigns are themselves involved in high-stakes politics.

Fourth, relief and rights work has made modest but significant inroads into the requirement that humanitarian action receive the advance consent of the political authorities. While not difficult to arrange in situations of natural disaster, consent — "the expression of sovereignty"[62] — may be much harder to extract in settings of civil strife and failed states. Not only are the political circumstances more highly charged; sovereignty-asserting insurgents who command access to civilian populations in areas not controlled by central governments need to be drawn into the negotiations as well.

To deal with cases in which the political authorities fail to request demonstrably needed assistance or protection, UN member states have put into place more assertive ground rules than existed during the Cold War. Following debate in the General Assembly in 1991 sparked by dissatisfaction with the disjointed UN response to the crisis in Iraq, governments approved a painstakingly negotiated formulation for the terms of international access to distressed populations. "The sovereignty, territorial integrity and national unity of states must be fully respected in accordance with the Charter of the United Nations," reads the resolution. "In this context, humanitarian assistance should be provided with the consent of the affected country and in principle on the basis of an appeal by the affected country."[63]

A perfunctory reading of the text, negotiated under the leadership of Swedish Ambassador Jan Eliasson, would hardly suggest a new approach to sovereignty. Nothing is said about a generic international "right" or "duty" to intervene in situations of humanitarian extremity. However, the formulation places governments on record agreeing that "consent" rather than a formal request may trigger humanitarian assistance. That consent may come from "the affected country" rather than from the host government itself. Moreover, "in principle" — but, by implication, not necessarily in every instance — the government will need to request such assistance. The fact that aid "should be provided" in response to such a request implies that in some instances international aid may be nonconsensual.[64]

In these four respects, the interaction between the humanitarian enterprise and sovereign political authorities has contributed to an evolution in the understanding of sovereignty itself. In the words of the Sovereignty Commission mentioned earlier, "sovereignty has been eroded by contemporary economic, cultural, and environmental factors. Interference in what would previously have been regarded as internal affairs — by other states, the private sector, non-state actors — has become routine."[65] Contributing to this more general erosion, humanitarian action has injected substantive obligations into the traditional understanding of sovereignty, benefiting in turn from the duties now perceived as more incumbent upon would-be sovereign authorities.

Dilemmas and Discoveries

Recent interactions between the humanitarian enterprise and political institutions have highlighted a number of dilemmas; the attempt to manage them has produced a number of discoveries. Three dilemmas and five discoveries are noted here.

The first dilemma concerns the content and exercise of sovereignty. Assistance and protection are in the first instance the responsibility of sovereign states rather than transnational or nonstate actors. The sooner the authorities meet those responsibilities and the more fully, the better. Most analysts would probably agree with the former prime minister of the Sudan, Dr. Gazuli D'Faallah who, as OLS began operations, observed that "The solution to the tension between sovereignty and humanitarian concern lies in redefining the sovereignty issue. Within the sovereignty of states, all these humanitarian concerns can be addressed."[66] When governments meet their obligations, overriding their sovereignty is moot. Infusing sovereignty with humanitarian content is better than having to challenge the inaction of reluctant or recalcitrant authorities.

Being invited to assume sovereign functions on a temporary basis, as in the Sudan and Tanzania, is also preferable to seizing those functions, as in Kosovo. The sensitivity of needs and rights is such that outsiders inject a tricky dynamic into the scene, even when authorities request their involvement and even when it is only for a short time. Delegations of sovereignty should therefore be treated with care. Its temporary stewards need to be alert to the perception that humanitarian action makes international institutions and foreign personnel "pseudo-sovereigns" in their areas of involvement. Eventually, responsibility and accountability revert to resident political authorities or to newly created institutions.

Sovereign authorities are today under more clear, if still uneven, international pressure to meet their humanitarian responsibilities. Doing so can garner international political points. Those responsibilities themselves have been increasingly clarified in law (for example, as regards antipersonnel mines) and custom (as regards IDPs). Sovereign authorities are, in effect, on notice: international humanitarian action no longer requires their request or consent in each and every instance.

The "use or lose" status of sovereignty, however, is not without its difficulties. When political authorities use their sovereignty to accomplish humanitarian objectives, the profile of humanitarian activities may be reduced and the pace slowed. By contrast, wresting sovereignty from the authorities may provide more scope for international humanitarian action but create its own problems, both immediate and longer term.

The second set of dilemmas is a function of the higher political profile of humanitarian concerns. Increasing involvement by political institutions such as the UN Security Council has given higher visibility to humanitarian values. However, the council's new level of engagement, selective and uneven in nature, has at the same time undermined the universality of humanitarian action. Suffering in Liberia and Tajikistan does not exercise as dramatic a claim on international resources, diplomatic or humanitarian, as did malnutrition in 1992 in Somalia and human rights abuses in 1999 in East Timor.

Greater attention to humanitarian crises is of course welcome. Lest the perfect become the enemy of the good, many agencies do not defer action in one crisis because a more critical emergency somewhere is not receiving due attention. Yet the need exists to capitalize more fully and creatively on available political interest and humanitarian resources to ensure greater proportionality in the overall response to global demands. The characteristics of many politically driven responses such as massive financial and material aid, short time frames, early exit strategies, and scant attention to local capacity also complicate the longer-term success of humanitarian undertakings.[67]

The third set of dilemmas involves the pervasiveness of politics in the humanitarian sphere. Responding to crises in which sovereignty is contested and issues are highly politicized confronts humanitarian actors with difficult choices. If they seek to insulate themselves from the political, they are viewed as naïve. If they immerse themselves in the politics of conflicts, they risk undercutting their humanitarian mission. If they concentrate on operational aid activities, they may give inadequate attention to managing the essential relationships with local, regional, and international political authorities. Managing those relationships, however, can be a time-consuming and delicate task. In interposing or imposing assistance and protection, they may fuel or perpetuate conflicts.[68] Withholding humanitarian activities, however, provides no assurance that widespread suffering will be ended any sooner.

Politics may represent either a boon or a bane to humanitarian interests, or, more likely, some combination of both. The actions of political authorities at the local, regional, or international level may be beneficial or harmful, or both. The assertion of sovereignty by host political authorities can open up access for international agencies and personnel, or bar them from the scene. The devolution of sovereignty to humanitarian actors can simplify their work or create longer-term difficulties.

Humanitarian organizations respond variously to the challenge of managing the interface with the political landscape, reflecting their self-understandings, mandates, and cultures. Some make neutrality their cardinal tenet, which they interpret as delimiting their ability to address the underlying causes of conflicts and human need. Others affirm nonpartisanship or solidarity, or both, which afford greater space for addressing broader social, economic, and political issues. Each of the three basic approaches has its respective strengths and weaknesses. Taken together they reflect the strength and vitality of the humanitarian community. In the heat of emergencies, however, they are often a source of disharmony and stress among agencies already working under duress.

The newfound realization of the politics of humanitarian action does not necessarily translate into a greater ability to resist or manage the inroads of politics. Agencies are only beginning to realize that "the capacity to control the impact of humanitarian action on conflict requires a substantial knowledge base regarding the conflict and the socioeconomic and political context."[69] Managing the dilemmas of politics and conflict requires a set of skills, detailed in chapter 8, that agencies are only now beginning to cultivate. One such skill is the capacity to analyze the political-military circumstances in which humanitarian action is mounted and to frame and weigh options and likely impacts. Another skill needed is the commitment and capacity to engage political authorities and belligerents on humanitarian issues.

Advocacy, while not exclusively a post–Cold War invention, can be an investment in more effective humanitarian action and a creative way of managing the dilemma between humanitarian neutrality and political action. Agencies that labor to remain neutral vis-à-vis the warring parties in their daily conduct of conflicts can be advocates in the political arena on issues related to the humanitarian imperative, values, and space. Those reluctant to be publicly identified with political activism may join or support coalitions that speak on behalf of the wider community, thus indirectly contributing to the broader effort while preserving a semblance of anonymity.

Out of the struggle to understand and manage such dilemmas have come several discoveries. First, the necessarily political nature of humanitarian action, a dimension largely ignored or sidestepped during the Cold War, is now unmistakably clear. Assistance and protection activities, now as then, take place on highly political terrain and have decidedly political repercussions. Politicization is the case whether or not humanitarian organizations themselves have a political agenda, as some host political authorities allege, some donors and analysts encourage, and some humanitarian organizations acknowledge.

Second, a fundamental, unresolved, and in some quarters still unconceded tension exists involving the different roles of the United Nations as regards politics and humanitarian action. Recent experience illuminates the extent to which the UN system is at one and the same time the focal point for efforts to develop a more effective humanitarian apparatus and the very arena in which state sovereignty is most zealously defended. This paradox has major implications for the humanitarian architecture examined in chapter 7.

Third, given the pervasive reality of politics, an overriding need exists to go beyond lamenting its ravages and to protect the integrity of humanitarian action. Our studies demonstrate not only the variegated interplay in conflict after conflict between humanitarian actors and the political process but also the rewards to the enterprise from understanding the interplay more fully and managing it more adroitly. The challenge is not to deny or finesse the dilemmas but rather to manage the tensions associated with them. The benefits of creative management accrue to political and diplomatic as well as humanitarian actors.

As it matures, the enterprise counts among its ranks fewer "humanitarian fundamentalists" who believe that humanitarian considerations should override all other concerns. Many people now realize that humanitarian imperatives are "only one — and not necessarily the most significant — among a complex set of factors that impinge on the definition of interest and the formation of policy."[70] At the same time, the humanitarian enterprise is increasingly committed to broaden that definition and to elevate the relative importance of humanitarian values within the political process. The extent to which the new antiterrorism campaign in Afghanistan and beyond represents a setback to efforts to move the human being closer to the center of the political firmament is examined in the epilogue.

Finally, recent experience suggests that for all of the dichotomies and tensions between humanitarian action and the political and diplomatic activities of sovereign authorities and institutions, certain underlying common interests provide the basis for positive synergies. In the political sphere, for example, "the actual interests of humanitarian and political institutions are far more complex and far less adversarial than generally perceived."[71] In the diplomatic sphere, win-win combinations are also possible. As data from the Caucasus and elsewhere shows, independent humanitarian activities can benefit from broad diplomatic support while themselves contributing to the amelioration of conflict and to postconflict reconstruction.

Thus, a decade-plus into the post–Cold War era, politics has become infused with greater humanitarian content, while humanitarian action has attained greater political impact. The age-old tension between sovereignty and solidarity continues to shift gradually and unevenly in favor of a new sense of the common obligations of humankind. Those obligations have implications for political and diplomatic as well as humanitarian actors. The humanitarian enterprise has emerged both as significant factor in bringing about that shift and as a major beneficiary of it.

6

Coercive Humanitarianism

In April 1995, the U.S. Marine Corps convened one in its series of Emerald Express exercises at the First Marine Expeditionary Force's headquarters at sprawling Camp Pendleton in southern California. Gathering together humanitarian personnel from the UN, donor governments, and NGOs, high-level diplomats, and military brass, the conference featured intensive presentations and discussions on collaboration between military and humanitarian organizations.

"We see humanitarian tasks as a full-fledged military mission," said Lt. Gen. Anthony Zinni in opening the meeting. "They are not futuristic." The exercise also involved simulations under the hot sun of real-life challenges faced by humanitarian and military personnel: roadblocks thrown up by insurgents, field hospitals under attack, and helicopter gunships ferrying supplies and personnel. The expeditionary force was clearly taking its new responsibilities seriously.[1]

The previous chapter examined the interactions between the humanitarian enterprise and political actors, assessing their changing dynamics during the first post–Cold War decade. This chapter reviews interactions between the enterprise and coercive military and economic instruments. Three such instruments are highlighted: the use of military force in support of international peace and security, a concept that now includes action to address unmet human needs and human rights abuses; the utilization of military forces to carry out humanitarian functions such as assistance and protection; and the application of economic sanctions to achieve humanitarian purposes.

International responses to the crises of the 1990s have established a trend toward a more coercive approach to humanitarian action. The use of nonconsensual instruments is now more routine, even though the fuller engagement of military and economic force in the service of humanitarian objectives is proceeding unevenly from conflict to conflict. The fact that the military forces involved are anything but monolithic makes generalizations difficult, as does the fact that economic sanctions and their policy objectives vary also from situation to situation. Differences exist, too, in the attitudes among humanitarian organizations toward coercive humanitarianism.

Broadly speaking, however, acceptance is growing of the legitimacy and appropriateness of using military force in support of humanitarian values and of having military assets play a contributing role in broader relief and rights activities. This acceptance may, in fact, be one of the more significant aspects of the otherwise elusive post–Cold War "peace dividend." The expanded use of military force and forces, however, is not without complications. Economic sanctions, too, have been a mixed humanitarian blessing. Indeed, after a sharp increase in their utilization, sanctions are now being used with greater attention to recurrent negative humanitarian impacts.

The Use of Military Force
for International Peace and Security

The first purpose of the United Nations, reads Article 1 of its Charter, is "to maintain international peace and security." While the General Assembly may discuss issues of international peace and security and act when the Security Council fails to do so, "primary responsibility" is lodged with the council.[2] In the face of threats to or breaches of international peace and security, the council may take preventive or enforcement action, including the use of economic or military force, to maintain or restore international peace and security.[3]

The current state of the art is captured in remarks by Secretary-General Kofi Annan to the General Assembly in September 1999. "State sovereignty, in its most basic sense," he said, picking up on a theme of our previous chapter, "is being redefined by the forces of globalization and international cooperation." After "a century of unparalleled suffering and violence," he observes, greater consensus now exists on the need to intervene to thwart serious abuses of basic human rights. "Just as we have learned that the world cannot stand aside when gross and systematic violations of human rights are taking place, so we have also learned that intervention must be based on legitimate and universal principles if it is to enjoy the sustained support of the world's peoples."

The secretary-general then identifies one of the dilemmas of intervention arising from recent experience. He contrasts the situation in Rwanda, where the community of nations responded with "inaction in the face of mass murder," with that in Kosovo, where NATO responded but without a UN mandate. He invites those people who feel that "the greatest threat to the future of international order is the use of force in the absence of a Security Council mandate" to ponder whether they would have objected to NATO intervention to stop the genocide in Rwanda. Conversely, he asks those people who believe that the Kosovo action "heralded a new era when States and groups of States can take military action outside the established mechanisms of enforcing international law" to ponder the dangerous implications of states making such judgments. He challenges the Security Council and the UN as a whole to "forge unity behind the principle that massive and systematic violations of human rights — wherever they take place — shall not be allowed to stand."[4]

Within the broad framework that is evolving within the UN with respect to the use of force for humanitarian purposes, relief and rights organizations are divided among themselves regarding such use. As a result of the experiences of the 1990s, many people believe in the importance of military force, or at least the threat of its use, in support of humanitarian values and objectives such as gaining access to victims of starvation, halting genocide, or addressing other situations of humanitarian extremity. Some agencies have encouraged the UN or individual governments to intervene, with military force if necessary, to address humanitarian needs. Others view such matters as political issues beyond their own areas of competence.[5] Complicating the situation further, individual relief and rights officials often have their own personal views about the appropriateness of military force, views that may or may not correspond to the policies of their organizations, if indeed such policy exists.

The debate about the use of military force involves issues of principle and practice. Issues of principle are reflected in discussions during the past decade of "humanitarian intervention," to which the secretary-general alluded. Debate has focused on the existence of a right of intervention (*droit d'ingérence*) or, beyond that, a duty to intervene (*devoir d'ingérence*). The French government and leading French academics and others have endorsed both, arguing that military and economic force is a legitimate means of protecting human rights and human dignity from abuse.[6] Indeed, they say, unwillingness to intervene on behalf of abused populations suffering under obstinate governments would mock the humanitarian imperative and strengthen the hand of belligerents who flout international norms. Humanitarian intervention is the clear and compelling right and even duty of the community of states.

The ICRC counters that since civilians have what is, in effect, a right to assistance and protection under international humanitarian law, and since sovereign states have a duty to provide neutral and impartial humanitarian organizations with access, authentic humanitarian action may be incompatible with military coercion. While force may be legitimate and necessary in maintaining international peace and security, humanitarian law does not envision imposing assistance through force. Since humanitarian assistance as framed by the Geneva Conventions and Protocols is a matter of consent, "humanitarian intervention" is an oxymoron. Accordingly, the ICRC as an agency "cannot... be associated with armed action for humanitarian purposes."[7] In order to protect its neutrality, the ICRC mounts humanitarian action independently of the belligerents to a conflict.

While the ICRC position protects its own interests and underscores its own institutional distinctiveness, its validity is reinforced by some other international legal experts. International humanitarian law, observes Ted van Baarda, "is a neutral body of law which does not seek to affect the status of the parties to the conflict nor of the conflicting claims. Acting as neutrals, humanitarian organisations can achieve the necessary degree of trust in order to have access to all victims of armed conflict." Unlike the UN Security Council, which can judge the merits of the conflicting claims of warring parties, "in order to operate on both sides of the frontline, humanitarian organisations have to stay out of the merits of the conflict as such."[8]

Issues of principle are thus linked to matters of humanitarian practice. "The threat of force, and the will to use it," remarked UN High Commissioner for Refugees Sadako Ogata in 1997, reflecting the bruising experience of the decade, "becomes essential where consensual arrangements have no chance of success. Enforcement . . . may undermine neutrality and engender risks for impartial humanitarian action, but are strict neutrality and effective protection not often incompatible? Humanitarian responses should serve first of all the protection of people."[9] For governments to provide humanitarian assistance unreinforced by the necessary military assurances of its delivery and of the safety of its agents, proponents argue, would be imprudent and ineffectual, a counsel of despair.

The ICRC seeks to delink issues related to the use of military force from the humanitarian activities that the organization carries out. In its view, while force is a legitimate tool of international diplomacy and while peace-keeping operations can "provide greater security and avoid more deaths," the delivery of humanitarian assistance cannot be sustained at the point of a gun.[10] "Ninety-five percent or more of humanitarian needs," an ICRC official has noted, "can be met only with the consent of [the political-military] authorities," reinforcing the need to win agreement from belligerents to its involvement.[11]

Association with coercive action, however justified such action is in its own terms, may undermine humanitarian access to victims on all sides of conflicts. In fact, the use of military protection for aid operations may prove provocative. "Any attempt to use force has a whiplash effect throughout the entire operation," noted Madame Ogata's chief of UNHCR operations for Bosnia and Herzegovina in June 1993, expressing a different view from her own. "The minute you use force, you make the entire [humanitarian] operation untenable."[12]

An example of the divided opinion within the humanitarian community on the use of force is provided by the reaction of NGOs to the deteriorating security situation in Mogadishu in late 1992. CARE and the International

Rescue Committee wanted to see additional UN troops committed to Somalia in an effort to reduce the violence. Oxfam and MSF feared that a larger contingent would lead to an escalation of the strife and make aid operations even more vulnerable. On December 19, the professional association InterAction sent a letter on behalf of a number of NGO signatories to the U.S. national security advisor, General Brent Scowcroft. Observing that "humanitarian agencies cannot work effectively in Somalia without greater security," the group urged deployment of "appropriately armed UN security forces tasked with protecting emergency supplies and staff." In December, a U.S. military contingent landed in Mogadishu.[13]

Rights groups are also divided on the appropriateness of the use of force and of advocacy for or against its exercise. Amnesty International "has refused to advocate or oppose military action under any circumstances," even when the stated objective of such action is the prevention of human rights abuses. "It argues that this position is necessary in order to distance the organisation from selective actions of governments and to maintain Amnesty's strict impartiality, which protects the group from government manipulation." Human Rights Watch, by contrast, makes determinations on a case-by-case basis, using criteria including "the scale of the abuses, whether non-military means have been exhausted or would prove effective, and whether the intervention is likely to do more harm than good." Human Rights Watch favored military intervention in northern Iraq, Somalia, Bosnia, and Rwanda but did not take a position on Kosovo.[14]

If opinion among relief and rights groups and among politicians is divided, unanimity is also elusive on the politico-military side of the UN and in the foreign offices and defense ministries in national capitals of troop-sending countries. Some countries are willing to have their military assets used in support of international peace and security. They train specialized contingents for duties, including humanitarian work, involved in consensual peacekeeping and coercive peace enforcement duties. Others are more cautious. "We field an army, not a Salvation Army," U.S. Secretary of Defense William I. Perry noted in 1994. "Generally the military is not the right tool to meet humanitarian concerns."[15] Notwithstanding the opening vignette and other signs of more openness to humanitarian involvement, official U.S. policy still remains tightly circumscribed.

However the debates about the principle of using force to protect international peace and security have proceeded and whatever the impacts of using force on humanitarian activities, the general trend during the decade has been toward the more assertive — if still selective and uneven — application of military coercion in support of expressed humanitarian objectives. The ICRC is now more isolated in its views and generates less sympathy for the distinctions it seeks to make than a decade ago. That trend is confirmed in the following review of the expanded roles played by the military in recent humanitarian crises and in the most recent crisis in response to Afghanistan, described in the epilogue.

The Use of Military Forces ▾
for Humanitarian Tasks

The application of military force in support of international peace and security, including humanitarian operations, is one element in the larger construct called "military humanitarianism."[16] The use of that term demonstrates differences of views within our research group, mirroring a similar divergence within the wider humanitarian and policy community as well. As with the concept of politicization discussed in the previous chapter, some see military humanitarianism as pejorative, others as positive, still others as value-neutral. Some applaud the present trend that involves harnessing the military to tackle humanitarian tasks; others decry it; still others accept it as more or less inevitable.

Thomas G. Weiss, cofounder of the Humanitarianism and War Project, sees the advent of military humanitarianism, which he defines as "the application of deadly force without the consent of a sovereign state to sustain human values," as reflecting the coming of age of post–Cold War humanitarian action.[17] He welcomes it, along with what he calls "militarized humanitarian intervention,"[18] as an indication that the community of states is finally getting serious about assisting and protecting vulnerable civilian populations.

My view is quite the opposite. I see military humanitarianism, like humanitarian intervention itself, as a contradiction in terms. In my view, both represent negative developments that cast a serious cloud over the effectiveness of the humanitarian enterprise itself. In fact, much of the data accumulated by the project and reflected in many of its publications caution against an embrace by humanitarian organizations of the military as a partner.

Our study *NATO and Humanitarian Action in the Kosovo Crisis* joined the issue by using the term "humanitarian" to apply only to activities carried out by civilian organizations. We did so to distinguish relief and rights agencies, whose sole reason for being was humanitarian, from military forces that from time to time assume tasks in the humanitarian sphere.[19]

At the workshop convened by the Netherlands Foreign Ministry in November 1999 to review our recommendations, a participant from the Dutch armed forces challenged our approach as reflecting a clear bias against the military. He was correct in the sense that international humanitarian law does not exclude military forces from humanitarian activities. The military often carries out medical work among victims of armed conflicts.[20] Our research team believed, however, that as a matter of principle and practice, humanitarian action is — and should remain — first and foremost civilian in character.

Our review of the contribution of NATO forces to the humanitarian challenges of the Kosovo crisis examined the tensions created by their status of those forces as cobelligerents. Their hands-on contributions to the aid effort were appreciable, particular in the early going in Macedonia and Albania. Their dual roles as warriors and healers confused the situation badly, however, and ended by seriously undermining the work of legitimate relief and rights organizations. We concluded that "military assets used during the Kosovo crisis played an important surge protector function at a time when humanitarian organizations were overwhelmed by the scale of the refugee crisis." However, we saw "the future role of the military in the humanitarian arena as exceptional rather than routine."[21]

What is the most appropriate role for the military in the humanitarian sphere? Our first study examining that issue, *Soldiers to the Rescue: Humanitarian Lessons from Rwanda*, identified three major humanitarian functions that national military forces have assumed within the larger international response to major humanitarian crises. Such forces have fostered a secure environment for civilian populations and humanitarian organizations, supported the activities of humanitarian agencies, and provided direct assistance to civilians in need. This tripartite typology of functions, evident in the response to the Rwanda emergency, has been borne out in other post–Cold War crises as well.[22]

The first function, *fostering a secure environment* for civilian populations and humanitarian activities, is an area of clear comparative advantage for the military. Humanitarian agencies on their own can do little to maintain basic law and order, nor do they wish to. Ironically, however, international military forces in Rwanda did least well at this, their most indispensable function. They turned out to be *least* available when *most* needed: during the genocide in 1994 and again in 1995–96 when insecurity in Rwandan refugee and IDP camps was most problematic. Moreover, the troops that were on hand labored under rules of engagement (for example, with respect to the protection of their own forces) that inhibited their ability to provide security for civilians and humanitarian operations.

To be sure, the UN peacekeeping force UNAMIR mounted courageous efforts to shelter Tutsis and moderate Hutus in the first days of the violence in and around Kigali. Yet what UNAMIR was authorized to do and the numbers of troops available to Major General Roméo Dallaire fell far short of the mark. Operating within a more robust framework, French troops in Opération Turquoise succeeded in providing security in southwest Rwanda for two months beginning in late June 1994. As noted earlier, however, their efforts, highly political in nature, had the dubious outcome of buying time and protection for Hutus involved in the genocide.

By contrast, "The prohibition against most US forces from leaving the Kigali airport [and] the reluctance of the Japanese [troops] to work in refugee camps circumscribed what the troops themselves were able to achieve."[23] The rules of engagement of each contingent reflected the relative willingness of the respective political authorities — for example, in Washington and Tokyo — to have their forces assume risks.

International military forces deployed in the Rwanda crisis were more successful in a second task: that of *supporting the work of humanitarian agencies*. In the Rwanda emergency, they assisted in the transport of civilian aid personnel and supplies, using the logistical and organizational, engineering and other technical capacities for which militaries are well known. U.S. and other forces assisted UN and other aid organizations with the heavy lifting of relief supplies into the Rwanda theater. Yet again, their support services were available largely following the mass exodus from Rwanda, not during the genocide.

Moreover, accessing those services was also often difficult for aid agencies. In one instance, Oxfam–UK and Ireland sought to arrange transport on ideally suited large-payload U.S. military jumbo jets for bulky piping needed to bring potable water to refugee camps in Goma, Zaire. A combination of bureaucratic delays and aircraft diversions and repairs caused the critical shipment to arrive more than two weeks later than would have been the case had the NGO chartered commercial space. "The whole thing was a disaster," commented Oxfam's emergencies director, who accepted some of the blame himself for not pursuing the commercial option. As a result, he said, his NGO would be less willing to cooperate with the military in the future.[24] While some such difficulties can be ironed out through cooperative memoranda of agreement, structural and cultural differences between humanitarian and military institutions constitute a recurring problem.

The UN World Food Program (WFP), the premier multilateral logistician, confirmed the limited utility of the military's logistics capacity for humanitarian groups. WFP has extensive experience moving large quantities of food and vehicle fleets into fast-onset disasters, some of them remotely located. "In most cases we can probably arrange airlifts far quicker than the military can into places they wouldn't be prepared to go at a fraction of the cost," observed one WFP manager. Yet he took care not to rule out the use of military logistics in certain circumstances: for example, in areas served by secure and accessible airports in the early stages of crises when the scale of resources needed may require transport beyond what aid agencies can quickly provide or charter.[25] The numerous provisos, however, confirm our view that the utilization of military logistics capacity should be the exception rather than the rule.

In the third area, *hands-on relief delivery,* various national military contingents became involved in the Rwanda emergency to an unprecedented extent. In Goma, the work of French and U.S. troops in burying bodies, digging latrines, purifying water, and providing emergency medical services made a major difference to the overall humanitarian effort. Throughout the region, national contingents from countries such as Canada, Israel, Japan, and the Netherlands — some in concert with UNHCR, others on their own — provided direct services to people uprooted by the conflict. Media coverage of the troops as aid providers helped generate resources for the broader aid effort. What attracts the media? asked CNN's Charles Bierbauer. "Plight and might. No matter how desperate the indigenous situation, the story gets better when the troops arrive."[26]

In retrospect, however, the troops' direct assistance was less pivotal than it appeared at the time. Epidemiological data showed death rates in Goma already beginning to decrease by the time U.S. troops arrived.[27] The military also proved expensive, although differences in accounting practices and a lack of transparency in military accounting make the comparative cost-effectiveness of military and civilian options impossible to establish. In some instances, the aid agencies of donor governments reimbursed their militaries for services provided; in others, the services were contributed by defense ministries at no cost to the aid effort. Some individual initiatives proved to be very expensive. The cost of health services provided by Israeli Defense Forces to a mere five thousand Rwandan refugees for a single month totaled $7 million.[28]

Progress has been made since the Rwanda crisis in each of three military/humanitarian functions. Even during that crisis, relationships became less ad hoc and more structured. Military and humanitarian organizations separately and together have reviewed their experiences and clarified their division of labor.[29] The Camp Pendleton exercises are one such occasion; another was the establishment in 2001 of a liaison unit at the U.S. Central Command in Tampa to facilitate direct communication between UN and NGO aid agencies and military officials monitoring the evolving situation in Afghanistan. Many humanitarian organizations are now involved in ongoing dialogue with the military in one forum or another.[30] The thrust of many of the current exchanges is less to expand the areas of collaboration than to "improve the effectiveness of humanitarian response while preserving [humanitarian] independence."[31] The idea established by the Rwanda response — that the commitment of troops by sovereign states represented an exercise of global responsibility — has also become more widely accepted.[32]

Discussions within NATO in particular are reprioritizing the roles of the military, reflecting experience in Rwanda and other recent crises. In a policy document that its nineteen members have newly agreed to, NATO affirms that the primary function of its troops is to perform "security re-lated tasks."[33] Hands-on activities by the military are envisioned only in exceptional circumstances: for example, when lives may be saved, and then only in collaboration with humanitarian agencies and civil authorities. Bi-lateral civic action activities by individual national contingents are also discouraged.

This revision of priorities corresponds to what many aid agencies are themselves encouraging. "Fostering security is a complex, political issue given the relation to state sovereignty, the questions of mandate and use of force, and the security factor," notes Ed Schenkenberg, coordinator of the International Council of Voluntary Agencies. "However, if the mili-tary wants to have a meaningful role in future civil-military cooperation, it should fill the gap that it, and not humanitarian organizations, can fill."[34] While NATO officials see the more circumspect delineation of military roles as helpful, they and others caution that "political pressure to become in-volved [in civic action work] can be overwhelming." The newly formulated NATO policy, delimiting the civic action roles of its forces, is expected to be the subject of more detailed operational guidance by mid-2002.[35]

In retrospect, the hands-on role of the military in the early phase of the Kosovo crisis illustrates the need for greater clarity in the division of la-bor. In April 1999 at the request of UNHCR, NATO troops responded to the massive influx of Kosovar Albanians into Macedonia and Alba-nia by speedily erecting tents and providing other emergency services.[36] Other humanitarian organizations, however, expressed the view that such aid activities should have been mounted by card-carrying civilian aid groups instead. Even though they conceded that the aid agencies were badly over-matched initially, the resort of donors to the military reflected the results of a pattern of underfunding UNHCR and other civilian organizations, not any inherent comparative advantage of the military. While an element of turf protection may have figured in their assessment, serious policy issues were also involved. A serviceable humanitarian apparatus requires year-in, year-out care and feeding by donors so that quick-onset emergencies do not overmatch its capacity.

The performance of civic action work by INTERFET troops in East Timor, undertaken by the military at its own initiative, also became "a source of irritation" to aid groups.[37] Once again an element of turf pro-tection may have been involved in the desire of humanitarian organizations to be the preferred vehicle for hands-on aid work. Yet serious issues of com-parative advantage were also involved. It is noteworthy that humanitarian officials from both the United Nation and the U.S. government discouraged U.S. military forces from engaging in civic action work in Afghanistan in 2001–2.

An example from Kosovo demonstrates both the indispensability of the military in guaranteeing physical security and the limits to what international troops may accomplish. As part of the UN Mission in Kosovo (UNMIK), UNHCR and the Organization for Security and Cooperation in Europe (OSCE) cochaired a joint minorities task force, based in Pristina, that closely monitored incidents directed against minority groups and then identified areas in which the Kosovo Force (KFOR) would deploy troops to enhance civilian security. In one instance in the Prizren region, the erection of a checkpoint, manned by Turkish troops, reduced attacks by Kosovo Albanians on several villages populated by Serbs and Slavic Muslims and also discouraged harassment of aid workers. KFOR also sought to contain violence between ethnic groups in the city of Mitrovica and elsewhere.

Illustrating the complexity of the policy choices in the area of protection, however, an NGO coalition, the Minorities Alliance Working Group, questioned the approach taken by KFOR. "While eminently justifiable on the grounds of ensuring short-term security, some KFOR activity nonetheless merits scrutiny on the grounds that it is effecting long-term ghettoization of minorities, or is interfering with the natural tendencies of people in post-conflict environments to begin, at some point, to interact constructively. While in no way diminishing the importance to peacekeeping of keeping hostile populations apart when circumstances are explosive, keeping them apart unnecessarily is counterproductive and unsustainable."[38] The criticism involves not the need to have the military foster a secure environment but rather the strategies according to which the necessary security is provided.

In the absence of effective protection for their operations, humanitarian organizations have tried a variety of innovations. In April 1991, when the Allied Coalition was intent on withdrawing from northern Iraq, the prospect of arranging access for a UN peacekeeping force or observer mission to provide security for ongoing UN aid operations and resident personnel seemed dim. Negotiations with the Iraqi authorities produced agreement on what became known as the UN Guards Contingent in Iraq (UNGCI), a unit of armed and uniformed UN personnel drawn from staff that provide security at UN installations around the world. While the experiment was initially successful, thanks in part to the presence of Allied Coalition troops on the ground, the contingent was withdrawn when the security situation became more precarious after the ground troops had departed. Visiting Iraq in June 1992, our team concluded — rightly, as it has turned out — that the UNGCI would have limited replicability in other settings.[39]

The need for security in the camps for Rwandan refugees in eastern Zaire in 1994 produced a different approach. As early as September 1994, UNHCR requested UN assistance in maintaining order in the camps. Reviewing the situation, an assessment team of UN and Zairian officials suggested deploying UN peacekeepers. However, the secretary-general's request to troop-supplying countries received no takers. In desperation, UNHCR arranged in early 1995 to deploy and train a Zairian Camp Security Contingent (ZCSC). Drawn from the nation's Presidential Guard and trained by the UN, the contingent is credited with helping, belatedly, to maintain security in the Goma camps. Yet the ZCSC did not succeed in wresting control of the camps away from Hutu leaders or in controlling the flow of arms and paramilitary forces back into Rwanda.[40] As with the UNGCI, the outcome has not been replicated elsewhere.[41]

A third variation involves hiring security guards from the local population. In Somalia, aid agencies — and, for that matter, even the UN peacekeeping force itself — contracted with "technicals," armed personnel deployed to protect staff and to guard compounds and supplies. The experience failed to provide the security needed, since the technicals brought to their duties the clan rivalries implicated in the country's civil strife. Their contract fees undoubtedly fueled the war, and some technicals were implicated in the theft of the very humanitarian assets they were paid to protect.

More recently, humanitarian organizations have contracted with international security firms to provide protection for operations and personnel in places such as Sierra Leone, Angola, and the Congo. The number of such firms and staff has mushroomed as security specialists from the Cold War have sought new employment. At the local level, private security firms have also enlisted ex-combatants from local conflicts to guard humanitarian assets. The use of such firms and personnel raises major policy and operational issues for the humanitarian enterprise, including the compatibility with international humanitarian law of using armed security personnel.

Facing the likelihood that the private security option will become more widely available, humanitarian organizations are now seeking to identify ground rules to guide the use of such personnel, both international and local. They are concerned that firms such as Executive Outcomes and Sandline, already providing protection for multinational corporations, will associate humanitarian activities with controversial commercial operations in conflict areas. A recent conference at Tufts University explored some of the critical issues.[42] "The security sector is becoming better organised and is emerging as a 'player' in the aid response, able to advise where and how aid should be offered," noted a conference paper. "The potential exists for security companies to offer advice that reflects interests other than purely humanitarian ones and to coopt humanitarian aid to external commercial and political interests."[43]

Many aid agencies have sought to develop greater in-house expertise on security matters, whether by secundment of trained personnel or by direct hiring. More intergovernmental organizations, both at headquarters and in the field, are now retaining staff advisors with defense and security backgrounds, including retired intelligence or military personnel and still-active employees on loan from ministries of defense of UN member states. A group of aid workers visiting the headquarters of one UN humanitarian organization in the spring of 2001 received a briefing on the agency's work from a former British intelligence operative. They did not doubt his competence in the security realm or the need for his expertise, but they questioned his credentials for presenting the humanitarian objectives and activities of his new employer. In late 2001, a former Defense Department official was nominated to be head of AID's Office of Foreign Disaster Assistance, the U.S. government's focal point for humanitarian response.[44]

The failure of the community of states to respond effectively to recent threats to international peace and security, much less to provide security for humanitarian operations, has spurred efforts to find new ways of harnessing national military assets for multilateral purposes. One new creation, initially proposed by the Danish government, is a UN Stand-by Forces High Readiness Brigade (SHIRBRIG), which is now providing troops for peace-keeping activities in Ethiopia and Eritrea. Other proposals include one from the Canadian government to develop UN rapid-reaction capability and one from the European Union for a rapid-reaction force. Each would interface with humanitarian needs and organizations in situations into which they were deployed.

What is the status of the current trend toward military humanitarianism? Dialogue is proceeding between humanitarian and military organizations on the issue of harnessing national and international military forces for tasks in the humanitarian sphere, sharpening up the distinctive contributions of each set of organizations, civilian and military. The responsible use of military assets as a feature of global stewardship among sovereign states is increasingly accepted, by both political and humanitarian actors. Many humanitarian organizations increasingly support the use of force to counteract violations of international humanitarian norms, but some organizations are also anxious to maintain a certain distance between their activities and those of the military. New multilateral configurations are emerging, but serious problems including issues of mandates, cost, and accountability have yet to be addressed.

Economic Sanctions

Also available to coerce policy change are economic sanctions, which have emerged during the 1990s as an instrument of choice. "Whereas the Council had only imposed sanctions twice in the first forty-five years of its existence, against Rhodesia in 1966 and South Africa in 1977, during the 1990s, the Security Council imposed comprehensive or partial sanctions against Iraq (1990), the former Yugoslavia (1991, 1992, and 1998), Libya (1992), Liberia (1992), Somalia (1992), parts of Cambodia (1992), Haiti (1993), parts of Angola (1993, 1997, and 1998), Rwanda (1994), Sudan (1996), Sierra Leone (1997), and Afghanistan (1999). In addition, member states imposed unilateral, bilateral, or regional economic sanctions more than three dozen times during the 1990s."[45]

The objectives of sanctions during this period included "to reverse territorial aggression, restore democratically elected leaders, promote human rights, deter and punish terrorism, and promote disarmament."[46] Sanctions enjoy a privileged place in the UN Charter and in the tool kit of international diplomacy. They are situated, along with military force, among the coercive instruments available for deployment in an effort to maintain or restore international peace and security.[47] They offer a means for asserting and protecting humane and democratic values short of resorting to military force and its often lethal and inhumane consequences.

The experience of the decade suggests that sanctions have more often than not had a negative impact on the welfare of civilians, at the same time failing to achieve their stated political objectives. A study undertaken by the Humanitarianism and War Project and two colleague institutions[48] examined the relationship between humanitarian pain and political gain from sanctions imposed by the UN against South Africa, Iraq, the former Yugoslavia, and Haiti.[49] The project also carried out its own reviews of international sanctions against Iraq and the former Yugoslavia and of regional sanctions against Haiti and Burundi.[50] In each of these countries except for South Africa, the degree of civilian pain exceeded to one degree or another the resulting political gain. Only in South Africa did sanctions, encouraged and supported by many of the country's black population, play a significant (although not altogether decisive) role in ending apartheid.[51]

Economic sanctions have been regularly linked to three sets of negative humanitarian impacts.[52] First, by their very design, sanctions increase the scale and depth of human suffering. They seek policy change through the exertion of pressure on the authorities that civilian suffering is expected to generate. Second, they complicate the ability of international organizations to provide assistance and protection. Aid agencies need to import humanitarian essentials and personnel at a time when most imports and travel are restricted. In this sense, observed a WHO official in Belgrade in 1993, sanctions make humanitarian work "almost impossible."[53] They pose issues for humanitarian actors similar to those associated with the use of military force. While agencies may welcome the international effort to change the policies of regimes, the actual impacts of sanctions take their own toll and complicate humanitarian work.

Third, sanctions politicize the work of aid agencies by associating them with the suffering that the sanctioning authority is imposing. "The United Nations kills, and then hurries to walk in the funeral," said one observer in Jordan in 1992 as he surveyed the devastation wrought early on by UN sanctions against Iraq.[54] The unpopularity of the UN among the warring parties in the former Yugoslavia led a UN aid worker based in Croatia to have business cards printed up for use in Bosnia that omitted his Zagreb address.[55]

In Haiti, we concluded that sanctions proved "a liability to the poor, a boon to the de facto authorities and their supporters, and a hardship to humanitarian organizations," who were divided among themselves about their utility and appropriateness. In fact, "sanctions were more damaging to humanitarian organizations than to the regime against which they were invoked."[56] Indeed, in crisis after crisis, sanctions, seeking simultaneously to mete out pain and to cushion its effects, produced schizophrenia within the humanitarian enterprise and beyond.

At the UN's request, we brought our research to bear on a specific set of operational issues: the extent to which sanctions might be made more humane. We reviewed the functioning of the existing arrangements whereby certain humanitarian items are often exempted when sanctions are imposed. Such exemptions, in our judgment, represented "the hinge between the use of sanctions to achieve stated political objectives and the protection of the rights of civilian populations in targeted countries to receive humanitarian assistance."[57] The exemptions varied widely from situation to situation, with political considerations playing a major role in determining exempt and nonexempt items. The process of reviewing requests from individual agencies for exemptions was characterized by delays, both intentional and unintended, and by a lack of transparency in decision making.

We recommended a series of steps that the UN might take to move from an ad hoc approach to "a more regime-like system characterized by agreed principles, rules, and procedures."[58] To help defuse the politicization surrounding sanctions discussions, we proposed a methodology for pre-assessing and monitoring their impacts, using quantitative and qualitative indicators in the five areas of public health, economics, population displacement, governance and civil society, and humanitarian activities. We analyzed the advantages and disadvantages of each of the three major options for exemptions — institution-specific, item-specific, and country-specific.

In recent years, misgivings by many humanitarian organizations and by some states have helped generate reforms in international sanctions policy and practice. The thrust of the changes has been to target sanctions more specifically against political elites, to take into account likely humanitarian impacts before sanctions are imposed, to monitor the impacts once sanctions are in place, and to fashion a more effective system to exempt humanitarian essentials, thereby shielding vulnerable civilians from the brunt of enforcement measures.

In essence, the pain-gain calculus is being rethought and acceptable levels of civilian suffering reconsidered. Negative humanitarian impacts are being viewed as not only undesirable from a humanitarian standpoint but counterproductive from a political one. The assumption that civilian hardship will produce policy or regime changes in undemocratic countries is being questioned as autocratic leaders often turn sanctions to their own advantage, manipulating public opinion through the "rally 'round the flag" effect. Moreover, the concept of following the traditional progression in Chapter VII of the UN Charter from economic to military coercion is being revisited. In Iraq, economic sanctions were not given a chance to accomplish their objectives, while in Haiti the application early on of military instead of economic force would arguably have been more humane.

The response of the UN Security Council to an assassination attempt in Ethiopia in 1995 on the life of Egypt's President Hosni Mubarak provides an encouraging harbinger of new directions. When the Sudan failed to comply with the Security Council's request to extradite three suspects to Ethiopia, the council found its lack of compliance a threat to international peace and security and imposed diplomatic sanctions.[59] However, a more wide-ranging set of sanctions on travel and air transport, provisionally approved, was never implemented. Imposition of the ban was initially delayed until the UN Department of Humanitarian Affairs could assess its likely impacts on civilians and the extensive aid operations under way.[60] While the impacts were estimated to be minimal, the council ended by not imposing the proposed sanctions, reflecting in part concerns flagged in the UN's preassessment report.

In recent years, the Informal Working Group of the Security Council has sought to develop recommendations on improving the effectiveness of UN sanctions. Although agreement has yet to be reached, a working paper makes a number of proposals that would add momentum to the trend toward politically smarter and more focused sanctions with fewer unanticipated or untoward humanitarian impacts. At the same time, a subcommittee of the IASC on sanctions has made some progress in agreement on a methodology for monitoring the humanitarian impacts of sanctions. These recommendations are described in chapter 7.

Dilemmas and Discoveries

The experience of the decade highlights a number of recurring dilemmas related to the association of the humanitarian enterprise with military and economic coercion. Attempts to manage these dilemmas have produced a number of discoveries.

The first dilemma is a function of the now-higher profile of humanitarian action. The more frequent invocation of international peace and security as a rationale for coercive measures in the early post–Cold War era has both pluses and minuses from a humanitarian vantage point. On the plus side, the broader importance of meeting emergency human needs and protecting fundamental human rights is now affirmed. On the negative side, the Security Council's exercise of its coercive authority may call into question the neutrality and consensual nature of humanitarian action in such settings. With that danger in mind, the secretary-general has challenged the council to act with greater consistency and urgency.

The humanitarian enterprise is divided in its appraisal of the new visibility of humanitarian action. Some relief and rights organizations welcome the expressed intentions of applying military and economic coercion to improve the humanitarian situation of the civilian populations with which they work. They encourage the use of military force in particular, stressing only that force be more consistently applied from crisis to crisis. Other organizations look askance at the human fallout from those policies and keep their distance from association with them. Still others consider such matters beyond their areas of mission or competence.

The second dilemma involves the pros and cons of using military force and forces. Two lessons have emerged from the decade: that military force may be needed to protect vulnerable civilian populations and humanitarian personnel, and that its application may have deleterious effects on civilians and humanitarian operations. The tension between humanitarian objectives and negative consequences, however, creates difficult choices for the humanitarian enterprise.

"If the humanitarian community does not accept any protection, it might, on occasion, find itself in a situation where it can deliver no assistance at all," notes Ted van Baarda. "If, on the other hand, the humanitarian community accepts military protection whole-heartedly and unreservedly, the warring parties will distrust humanitarian organizations and not allow them to pass. Somewhere along this line a modus vivendi may have to be found and a decision has to be made about the price, in political currency, humanitarian organizations are willing to pay."[61]

The process of establishing a clearer role for military force and forces in relation to humanitarian objectives is now proceeding apace. Humanitarian organizations find themselves situated along a broad spectrum. The ICRC is most insistent on operational autonomy; the UN's organizations are more willing to collaborate with military forces. NGOs find themselves at various points in between. European agencies are generally more circumspect about cooperation with military forces, and U.S. organizations are more willing to "pay the price." We return to the issue of structuring civilian/military relationships in the following chapter on humanitarian architecture.

The third dilemma is that while military forces have their liabilities when pressed into the service of humanitarian objectives, the alternatives have their drawbacks as well. In recent years, reflecting the general lack of availability of military forces, private security firms are increasingly employed.

As with the use of military forces, however, the utilization of such firms has raised serious questions about the integrity of the humanitarian effort. Whether working relationships are cultivated with private security firms or military forces, such collaboration involves not only the purchase of services but also association with their respective institutional cultures. Relief and rights groups are only now beginning to review the options and issues.

A fourth area of tension involves the need for a clearer division of labor between civilian and military actors in the humanitarian sphere. The experience of the decade suggests that military forces have an uncontested comparative advantage over humanitarian organizations in providing security. Their second-most critical function includes providing support for humanitarian organizations. Least essential and most overlapping with the work of aid groups is the hands-on provision of emergency assistance. NATO policy and doctrine is moving to confirm the essential division of labor that most humanitarian organizations favor, even though such provisions may give way to political pressure in times of crisis.

Within humanitarian operations themselves, tensions arise between what such activities require in the way of security and the effects that sometimes result from attempts by the military to provide the requisite security. Many humanitarian actors now acknowledge the need to make discerning judgments regarding how to position their activities in relation to military and peacekeeping forces and, in the case of the more broad-gauge agencies, on larger issues of international peace and security as well.

Fifth, as with military coercion, economic sanctions have pluses and minuses. Properly framed, managed, and monitored, sanctions can accomplish both political and humanitarian objectives. Sanctions that cause hardship among civilians in ill-conceived attempts to put pressure on intransigent regimes may achieve neither their political nor their humanitarian goals.[62] Politicians and diplomats tend to minimize the hardships that sanctions cause both to civilian populations and to aid operations while, conversely, humanitarian organizations may overemphasize their negative impacts. It is high time to introduce reforms into the discussion, imposition, and monitoring of sanctions that promote a more systematic and less improvisational approach.

Efforts to manage these dilemmas have produced a number of discoveries. The first involves the importance of conceptual clarity. Concepts such as "humanitarian intervention" and "military humanitarianism" have become a kind of shorthand for a pragmatic approach to the challenges of the post–Cold War era. These concepts have placed on the defensive people who have sought to preserve the consensual and civilian character of humanitarian action and to take a more principled approach to charting their operational courses of action. Used loosely, the terms have confused rather than clarified the debate about the essentials of humanitarian action and the role of the military in it. Greater circumspection in terminology would contribute to more productive discussions and, ultimately, more effective action.[63]

The importance of effective multilateral mechanisms, both humanitarian and military, represents a second discovery. In settings of internal armed conflict, the need is heightened for humanitarian activities that avoid the bilateral political agendas of individual governments or groups of governments. The involvement of outside military forces in both Rwanda and Kosovo had a heavy bilateral element, with individual national contingents playing high-profile roles. Even in UN peacekeeping undertakings, national troops have their own distinctive features. Productive humanitarian action, particularly in settings of internal and international armed conflicts, arguably requires effective multilateral mechanisms in which both humanitarian organizations and UN-related military forces play complementary roles. "[B]ilateralism is particularly ill-suited to humanitarian action in a setting where the main donors to the humanitarian effort are also belligerents in the conflict."[64]

Third, a considerable potential payoff is to be had by clarifying the ground rules that will guide humanitarian organizations in encounters with coercive political instruments, and, conversely, the factors that will trigger the application of military and economic force. Relief and rights groups have made headway in delineating various criteria to help determine the legitimacy of resorting to armed force. These criteria include just cause, correct authority, right intentions, proportionality, and the use of force as a last resort.[65] Other exercises have identified the circumstances under which a given agency (World Vision and CARE are examples) in their humanitarian activities will collaborate with military forces. Even though the criteria may be highly situational, require judicious application, and be agency-specific rather than community-wide, guideline exercises are a good investment.[66]

Fourth, all parties involved must move beyond the stereotypes of swift and efficient humanitarian action by the military as contrasted with amateurish bungling by civilian aid organizations or, conversely, of highly skilled humanitarians as contrasted with clueless troops. The standard dualisms are equally unhelpful: that coercive humanitarianism in the form of economic or military sanctions is inimical to humane values, or that coercion will by its very nature escalate the levels of general civilian pain.

The experience of responding to recent conflicts confirms certain commonalities across such dualisms. The schizophrenia of humanitarians caused by association with military force and economic sanctions is well documented. However, military personnel themselves are somewhat schizophrenic as regards the tensions between their succoring and fighting roles. Defense planners struggle with the question of whether training for emergency relief compromises the war-making capacity of the military.

Military and humanitarian personnel also share a common frustration with politicians and diplomats who avoid the kind of decisive political action needed to address the underlying causes of conflict and suffering. Both sets of institutions bristle at being kept on a short leash that inhibits their abilities to do their respective jobs professionally and effectively. In this regard, our conclusion from the Rwanda study has broader relevance:

> One element in a wider institutional universe, military forces are no substitute for effective policies geared toward conflict prevention and conflict resolution, development and peace. In that respect, they are like humanitarian action itself, which has an indispensable but at best partial contribution to make to a more just and secure world.[67]

7

Humanitarian Architecture

The year 1992 saw major crises on many continents. Large UN oper-
ations were under way in Iraq, Somalia, and Cambodia, while ethnic
tensions in the former Yugoslavia were on the rise. "The end of the Cold
War has hit like a hurricane, pulling many communities and nations
apart with almost centrifugal force," observed U.S. Congressman Bill
Emerson, Republican of Missouri, in convening a September hearing
entitled "Humanitarian Intervention: A Review of Theory and Prac-
tice." "This rapid global realignment [has] challenged our thinking on
issues of sovereignty and the protection of human rights.... [R]elief
agencies and political leaders have been forced by circumstance to
make up the rules of this new humanitarian game as they go along."[1]

Invited to speak at the hearing were UN Under-Secretary-General
Jan Eliasson, five months into his duties as the UN system's first under-
secretary-general for humanitarian affairs; an ICRC representative and
an NGO official; and Thomas G. Weiss and myself, codirectors of
the Humanitarianism and War Project. We were all asked about the
adequacy of the response to the proliferation of emergencies. Arti-
cles in the Washington Post *on "The UN Empire" had portrayed an*
incompetent world body fumbling badly in Africa and beyond.

Having offered testimony in July 1991 on strengthening UN co-
ordinating machinery, we identified what we believed should be the
priorities of the Department of Humanitarian Affairs, created in April
1992.[2] *"Today's darkening humanitarian landscape," we observed,*
"illuminates the limitations of the current humanitarian regime and
seems to be encouraging a hunt for villains," with aid agencies them-
selves heading the Most Wanted list. "[I]t should be remembered,"
we said, "that aid agencies are often confronted with situations which
have so deteriorated that their options are few indeed."[3] *While aid*
agencies are clearly accountable for their actions, they also share
responsibility for failures with states, politicians, and other key actors.

This chapter sketches the architecture of the humanitarian enterprise of
the future: that is, the institutional framework within which humanitarian

activities will be pursued. The chapter pulls together specific proposals made over a period of years in our individual studies, providing a conceptual framework and advancing a number of structural recommendations for the enterprise both in its own purview (building on the analysis of chapters 2–4) and in its interactions with political and military actors (chapters 5–6). The chapter thus needs to be read in conjunction with the chapters that precede it. Chapter 8, which follows, identifies the tools of the trade needed to enable the enterprise to function effectively.

A Conceptual Framework

A clear understanding of the nature and dimensions of "humanitarian action" provides the foundation for the humanitarian edifice. "Humanitarian" needs to be understood both broadly and narrowly, with careful distinctions also drawn between the humanitarian and the political-diplomatic-military spheres.

Broadly speaking, humanitarian action encompasses a range of activities that affirm the essential humanity and dignity of humankind. They include not only the provision of emergency food and medicine but also the reconstruction of war-torn societies and the building of just structures of international law and trade. More specifically, humanitarian action includes activities to provide emergency assistance and protection to civilians or to former soldiers no longer in combat. Under international humanitarian law, such activities are to be without extraneous agendas, political, religious, or otherwise.[4]

Although its decisions have addressed humanitarian issues, the International Court of Justice has yet to provide a precise definition of the concept. The absence of such a definition is evident in the case that Nicaragua brought in the mid-1980s against the United States. The Nicaraguan government charged that so-called "humanitarian" assistance that the United States provided to the Nicaraguan insurgents in the form of tents, boots, and communications equipment was a violation of Nicaragua's sovereignty. The court found that the aid was indeed not humanitarian. Rather than offering a definition, however, the court said somewhat elliptically that "humanitarian" *is* what the ICRC *does*. That is, humanitarian assistance must meet strict tests of neutrality, impartiality, and independence.[5]

Humanitarian action is thus at one and the same time expansive and delimited. Organizations face the challenge of contextualizing their activities within a broad framework geared toward promoting justice and human security while at the same time tackling the specific challenges of responding to life-threatening suffering and abuses of fundamental human rights. Organizations that take a narrow view are like the stonemasons, who, asked what they were doing, replied that they were cutting stone. Agencies that see their work in broader perspective are like stonemasons who view their task as building a cathedral. Both perspectives, of course, are legitimate and contribute to the edifice.

Within the humanitarian community and the framework of its common commitment to humanitarian values, managing the interactions among multiple moving parts — UN organizations, bilateral aid agencies, nongovernmental relief and rights groups, and the international Red Cross movement — involves challenges of coordination, integrating relief and rights, and strengthening local institutions. While acknowledging the importance of coordination, the perceived interests of individual agencies work against ceding the necessary authority to an effective focal point. While sharing a common commitment to international law and basic human rights, tensions divide relief and rights groups at the level of strategy and tactics. While affirming the importance of strengthening local capacity, ongoing tensions persist between international and indigenous organizations regarding agendas, decision making, and accountability.

One of the discoveries of the decade has been that respecting the "specificities" of each actor is key to maximizing the effectiveness of the enterprise as a whole. Within the humanitarian "project," as the British call it, there is room — and need — for diverse institutions. Yet despite substantial progress in each of the three areas examined, major structural dysfunctions remain largely unaddressed.

In broader compass, international humanitarian actors are a single element in a multifarious cast of characters engaged in responses to crises. The institutions with which humanitarian enterprise interfaces have their own agendas — none of them exclusively humanitarian — and their own constraints, yet each institution also has a potential contribution. Managing the dilemmas of humanitarian action is about orchestrating the interface with divergent institutions — political and diplomatic actors as well as the military and the media. Since humanitarian organizations tend to view the agendas of other actors as antithetical to their own interests and, conversely, since political and military decision makers often subsume humanitarian considerations within their own frameworks, a clear concept of how such institutions relate assists each in playing its complementary role.

Among the discoveries that provide a foundation for an improved humanitarian edifice is the realization of shared values between the humanitarian community and other actors. In the Rwanda crisis, humanitarian and military actors found ways of working together cooperatively. In fact, they discovered that the effectiveness of both aid-givers and troops was limited because of the short leash held by member UN states and the UN Security Council. One lesson identified as a result was that "to achieve their full potential, military assets, like humanitarian resources themselves, need to serve effective strategies not only of rescue and relief but also of conflict prevention and conflict resolution, reconstruction and development, reconciliation and peace."[6]

Economic sanctions, too, may involve converging as well as divergent interests. The tensions between the objective of protecting humane values through economic pressure and the inhumane impacts of sanctions on civilians are undeniable. Sanctions targeting governments that violate human rights and frustrate basic human needs may harm vulnerable groups and complicate humanitarian initiatives. Yet economic coercion can also serve humanitarian purposes, sparing civilians the ravages of war and, in unfortunately rare cases, bringing about positive political change.

So, too, with international military forces. Left to their own devices, humanitarian interests may be overwhelmed by the prevailing insecurity within which they seek to mount relief and rights operations. Yet in relying on military actors for increased security, they may compromise their own *bona fides*. Applying military force to gain access to civilians in distress can subvert and politicize the humanitarian imperative, but it may also promote and advance it.

A clear concept of institutional mandates and interests thus forms an essential underpinning of efforts to manage the dilemmas created by at once converging and conflicting objectives. "In its intense preoccupation with immediate pressures," comments Jonathan Moore, editor of a volume appropriately entitled *Hard Choices: Moral Dilemmas of Humanitarian Intervention,* "political decision making cannot afford to leave out moral energy and insight; neither can its inclusion be simple-minded."[7] For its part, the humanitarian enterprise ignores at its own peril the political terrain upon which it functions.

In the humanitarian community and throughout the wider family, the improvisational nature of responses to major crises has been the distinguishing feature of the decade. In the words of General Roméo Dallaire, the Canadian general who commanded UN peacekeeping forces at the time of the Rwandan genocide, it has been "a decade of adhocracy."[8] Successes have often been the result of circumstances rather than of coherent policies. The challenge of the future involves establishing structures that will help make effective responses expectable rather than serendipitous, the rule rather than the exception.

The Humanitarian Community

The experience of the first post–Cold War decade demonstrates the need for significant changes in the structure of the humanitarian enterprise itself. The distinctive features of the edifice of the future include more clear-cut authority for coordination, a more apolitical nexus for humanitarian action in conflict settings, greater consistency in responses to humanitarian emergencies wherever they occur, more effective management of the heterogeneity of the humanitarian family, reduced externality in humanitarian activities, and more synergistic relief and rights work. Each of these elements is examined individually.

Assertive Coordination

Our discussion in chapter 2 reviewed three models of coordination — command, consensus, and default — and recommended that a greater command element be incorporated into the UN's humanitarian apparatus. The UN has resisted such an approach, both at the global level and, for the most part, in individual crises.

Several recent reorganizations of the UN machinery have not moved beyond the coordination-by-consensus approach that characterized most first-decade responses. Our 1990 review of Operation Lifeline Sudan recommended establishing the new position of under-secretary-general and institutionalizing coordination arrangements modeled on the UN's Office of Emergency Operations in Africa (OEOA) in the mid-1980s.[9] We took this recommendation forward in testimony before the U.S. Congress in 1991 and in discussions with U.S. and UN officials over a period of years.[10] Despite improvements in some largely technical aspects of coordination and in reaching out to non-UN institutions, the UN's humanitarian agencies remain largely autonomous actors, marching to their own respective drummers. A recent study commissioned by OCHA contrasts the "resounding consensus" about the need for strengthened coordination and "the continuing ferocity of the debate" about what specific improvements should be made.[11]

The UN Department of Humanitarian Affairs (DHA) was created in 1992 as an outgrowth of dissatisfaction with the lack of coordination in the UN's response to the crisis in the Persian Gulf. Yet the emergency relief coordinator who headed the new DHA was given only limited authority vis-à-vis the UN's operational agencies. DHA's replacement in 1997 with the Office for the Coordination of Humanitarian Affairs (OCHA) *reduced* its size and, after a withering assault by the agencies against the expanded coordinating authority proposed by Secretary-General Kofi Annan, essentially reaffirmed the existing coordination-by-consensus model. Individual UN agencies retained full control of their respective mandates and activities, a preferable outcome from their perspective to a power-sharing arrangement that offered less certain benefits.

Each successive effort to create a more authoritative coordination nexus has met resistance not only from operational agencies fearing a loss of autonomy but also from donor governments favoring a business-as-usual approach. Although famous for beating the coordination drum and leading the coordination parade, donors have traditionally been loathe to fund coordinating mechanisms, slow to honor funding priorities that coordination processes identify, and unwilling to moderate entrenched bilateral instincts that subvert joint initiatives. A stronger case needs to be made for the value-added element that coordination-by-command injects, even though the merits of the argument themselves may not bring donor or practitioner agencies on board.

Coordination-by-command, however, is no panacea. More decisive authority needs to be matched by greater respect for those agencies that, for reasons of sound policy and practice, choose to operate on their own. Our earlier discussion reviewed how the tightly coordinated operations in the southern Sudan, insisted upon by both the Khartoum authority and by UNICEF as lead OLS agency, hamstrung the ability of some NGOs to fulfill their humanitarian mandates. The need for both greater authority and greater flexibility is at once generic and difficult to accommodate.

In addition, more clear-cut coordination authority and more decisive structures at headquarters do not necessarily translate into greater effectiveness in the field. Nor does disarray in headquarters disable creative problem-solving on the ground. Significant strides in in-country coordination in individual crises have even led to complacency, with some practitioners now dismissing coordination as no longer a major problem. But each new major crisis — witness the discussion in the epilogue regarding Afghanistan — will surely confirm that declaring victory and moving on to another issue is premature. Reported UN agency jockeying for position in the Democratic Republic of the Congo in 2001 — resulting in the public undermining of the credibility of an agency's staff person, with potentially life-threatening consequences — underscores the urgent need for change.

Beyond systemwide restructuring of humanitarian coordination, institutional reforms in agency headquarters are needed that will support creative in-country efforts to achieve coordination on the ground. The results in Ngara, Tanzania, illustrate what dynamic aid officials can do when given proper reinforcement by headquarters and host government authorities. The problems in Sierra Leone, by contrast, suggest that strong individuals in the field will be hard-pressed to overcome headquarters and systemwide confusion and disarray. As the principals contemplate their next steps, the recent comprehensive UN interagency review of coordination offers a useful starting point for concerted action.

Apolitical Functioning

The cumulative experience of the decade calls into question the prevailing assumption that the focal point for humanitarian action should be the United Nations. "There is no reason," concluded former UN World Food Program Executive Director James Ingram in a 1993 essay, "why a coordinated international humanitarian response should be built around the

United Nations."[12] Indeed, for the UN system to exercise a focal point role for humanitarian activities when the world body itself, as noted in chapter 5, remains the principal bastion of state sovereignty is difficult — perhaps altogether impossible.

The UN and its operational entities have had recurring difficulty functioning apolitically in highly politicized circumstances. In emergencies such as those in Chechnya and Nagorno-Karabakh, the UN failed to perform key coordination functions such as gathering data, managing information, and negotiating access with the authorities. With such experience confirmed in other settings of contested sovereignty in which the authority of a UN member state is challenged by insurgents, the conclusion seems clear: the assumed model of a UN-centric humanitarian apparatus requires reconsideration.

One alternative, offered in the context of the Sudan experience, is that the terms of reference of the UN's humanitarian organizations specifically stipulate that "data gathering or assistance in insurgent-controlled areas does not imply recognition of the legitimacy of the insurgency."[13] An alternative suggested in the Karabakh experience is that "In situations in which assessment and programming functions cannot be carried out by the United Nations, other organizations such as the ICRC, NGOs, and the OSCE should be encouraged to play an expanded role."[14]

Some analysts have concluded that attempts to insulate humanitarian action from politics are unrealistic. Intergovernmental organizations will always, they say, be subject to political pressures from member states, their stakeholders and their points of accountability. Even when the concept of sovereignty is infused with positive humanitarian responsibilities, nation states may continue to hamstring the functioning of intergovernmental institutions when doing so serves their perceived national interests.

What alternative structures, then, are available or might be created to provide a more apolitical institutional anchor for the humanitarian enterprise? Based on Ingram's view that the UN is "above all an organization of states, and even its humanitarian agencies are not apolitical," the former UN executive offered several options for anchoring the humanitarian enterprise in settings of civil strife. The first would create a new UN agency to manage aid operations in such situations. "The existing agencies would carry out operations at a later stage, after the situation has settled down, much in the way that ICRC sometimes looks to WFP to take over feeding responsibilities after the initial crisis has been surmounted."[15]

A second Ingram proposal would involve context-specific selection of the particular NGO most suited to serve as systemwide anchor in a given setting. While some people would dismiss this role as inappropriate for a nonstate actor, Ingram views the political and diplomatic reinforcement that states now provide to bilateral or multilateral initiatives as transferable to whatever NGO is thus deputized. The choice of an NGO would acknowledge the need to reach beyond not only the UN but other state-centric organizations, which carry similar political baggage.

Ingram's preference, particularly as regards the altogether critical function of negotiating with the belligerents to ensure humanitarian access, is the ICRC. Its custodial role over international humanitarian law and its Swiss identity, he believes, make it well suited for an expanded role, particularly now that it has a more thoroughly internationalized staff.[16] The ICRC plays its custodial role well and has enjoyed far greater access to victims of civil strife than has either the UN system or NGOs. Yet the ICRC would surely be reluctant to assume the pivotal task on behalf of the more heterogeneous humanitarian enterprise in which consistency of approach and adherence to principle are often conspicuous in their absence.

Apart from promoting discussion of innovative institutional arrangements such as these, we have not endorsed a particular proposal. We expressed the view at mid-decade that "the integrity of humanitarian action would be best served by abandoning the effort to incorporate such action fully into the political-military United Nations."[17] Years later, a strategy that is more frankly insulationist from the UN at some points and altogether independent of it at others still seems desirable. However, determining the best configuration of institutions — existing and new — requires additional research and analysis.

As with other dilemmas, each option has assets and liabilities. In my judgment — and this judgment separates me and some of my colleagues from many other analysts — the politicization of UN-associated humanitarian undertakings is sufficiently fundamental and recurrent as to require structural remedy. Within our research group, however, we differ about the degree to which structures require reform and recurrent problems may be resolved. If the causes of humanitarian emergencies are political, points out one colleague, why should political institutions not be vested with their resolution? Trying to create a structure that provides a less political nexus for the humanitarian enterprise, counsels another, is a mission impossible.

Consistency of Response to Need

One of the recurrent weaknesses of the enterprise lies in its imbalanced allocation of resources among crises. At issue is the core humanitarian principle of impartiality, which requires that responses be based strictly on incidence and severity of need. "Is Humanitarian Assistance allocated on the basis of need?" asks a recent UN-commissioned review. Answering in the negative, the study notes that "global donor response to emergencies is heavily skewed towards situations that have a higher profile."[18]

Resource allocations of international aid vary widely according to crisis. Some emergencies "can command almost 100 percent of whatever funds are requested and spending of $200 or $300 per head; others are lucky to get a third of what they need and spending per capita will be a tenth or less of that in more popular emergencies."[19] The dismay of aid workers in Sierra Leone in 1999 at the enormity of the resources lavished onto the Kosovo crisis is an example of the often-inverse relationship between extremity of need and size of aid flows. Seizing the opportunity in that instance, a number of agencies paired fund-raising appeals for Kosovo in 1999 with requests for funding for more urgent but less-headlined emergencies. The Swedish government has an explicit policy of funding emergencies that don't attract much international attention.[20]

Many humanitarian organizations affirm as a matter of principle the importance of proportionality. At the same time, they concede that media coverage and donor government priorities heavily influence their responses. As noted earlier, many factors influence media coverage of complex emergencies, including the presence of international military forces, imbalancing responses further still. Current allocations tilt not only against silent or forgotten crises but also against civilians in countries on which sanctions have been imposed. Although sanctions often increase human need, donor governments generally have difficulty simultaneously punishing a regime and providing assistance to its citizenry.

Some improvements have resulted from the UN consolidated appeals process (CAP), an instrument designed and improved during the decade to encourage coordinated planning at the country level and greater consistency in international responses among countries. More rigor is still needed both in establishing priorities within countries and, on the part of donors, in supporting CAP requests.[21] Based on the core affirmation that all human lives are equally precious, an effective humanitarian enterprise would consign no emergency to the "forgotten" category. Suggestions such as the creation of a global trust fund that would allow UN organizations greater discretion in allocating resources among crises have unfortunately not taken hold.

Acting on their own, NGOs should also take steps to moderate the continuing disproportionality in global resource deployment. To protect their integrity and independence of action, private relief and rights groups might attach higher priority to cultivating a base of support among private constituents. Such an approach would give new integrity to the term "nongovernmental." At present, the concept is quite misleading since, as noted earlier, many of the larger NGOs receive more than half — some of them more than three quarters — of their resources from governments and intergovernmental agencies. Surely a lesson can be learned from the fact that many of the NGOs currently doing humanitarian work in "forgotten" crises such as North Korea, Iraq, and Somalia have significant funding bases among private donors. Agencies receiving ample government funding for a given crisis often also feel constrained from directing those resources to their own identified priorities.

Respect for Heterogeneity

Another necessary feature of a more effective humanitarian edifice is the ability to harness the heterogeneity of its component parts. From the standpoint of coordination, the heterogeneity of the organizations that respond to major crises can be problematic. A profusion of agencies can create confusion within the host country and in the humanitarian enterprise itself, undermining synergies and even the businesslike conduct of activities. Properly orchestrated, however, heterogeneity may bring depth, dimensionality, and synergy to the humanitarian response.

The presence of multiple organizations enhances the possibilities for multiplier effects, particularly if comparative advantages are respected. Bilateral aid activities from individual donors offer a case in point. In Mozambique and Haiti, respectively, Finnish and Canadian bilateral aid activities brought something distinctive to the mix.

In Mozambique, the Finnish government aid agency FINNIDA provided the continuity of support needed for serious institutional change by making a fifteen-year commitment to supporting health sector institutions. The longevity of its approach contrasted sharply with the shorter time frames of other bilateral actors, UN organizations, and NGOs. In fact, the absence of reinforcing change in other sectors by other donors has limited the constructive change that FINNIDA has been able to nurture in the health sector.[22] Periodic progress reviews allow the agency to monitor developments and encourage course corrections as warranted.

As described earlier, the Canadian bilateral agency CIDA supported activities in Haiti redesigned by the local staff of a Canadian NGO after the Canadian staff had left the country for security reasons. While most donors require on-the-ground presence of their own nationals as a condition for ongoing funding, the Canadian government underwrote continued humanitarian activities during the coup period after the expatriate staff of the Canadian NGO and many other international personnel had departed. Haitians applauded the qualitative differences in approach between Canadian and other bilateral assistance. More recently, however, some in Ottawa have questioned whether the low-profile institution-building support that CIDA provided in Haiti runs counter to the need to have identifiably Canadian projects to publicize for the Canadian public back at home.

Heterogeneity may also offset the routinization of humanitarian action, as demonstrated within the NGO sector. Some NGOs are international bureaucracies with multimillion-dollar budgets; indeed, some have resources exceeding those of the host government ministries with which they work. Others are ad hoc undertakings: the handful of women from Dortmund, Germany, who traveled to Bosnia to establish counseling services for women, or the one-woman effort to transport Sarajevan children across active battle lines in central Bosnia to surgical facilities in Britain.

Large NGOs have the capacity and expertise to respond to major emergencies, but sometimes bureaucracy seems to obscure a sense of humanity. Smaller NGOs often bring greater creativity and resourcefulness to their task, but lack resources. "Mom and Pop" NGOs are often impelled by humanitarian urgency but short on the necessary wherewithal, savvy, and staying power. After an initial year, the Dortmund women left their Bosnian colleagues without resources as their own fund-raising and energies ebbed. Even more well-established agencies and their donors have been known to change their funding priorities abruptly or pack up and move on to the next crisis.

Thus while managing the panoply of relief and rights groups acting in specific crises has its difficulties, the humanitarian edifice needs to enlist and respect the comparative advantages of each particular kind of agency. An apparatus that draws on the respective strengths of a wide array of members and respects their individual "specificities" is arguably the stronger for doing so. This perspective is important to keep in mind when, in the exigencies of hot war situations and amid the maelstrom of agency disarray, the strategy of letting the proverbial thousand humanitarian flowers bloom seems patently counterproductive.

Reduced Externality

The humanitarian enterprise remains predominantly expatriate in design, culture, and accountability, almost irrespective of the particular state of local organizations in crisis countries. While individual foreign agencies may give lip service to strengthening indigenous capacity, local counterparts are more often treated as means to an end than actors in their own right. The reality that local institutions are the first line of humanitarian defense and the ultimate solution to a country's social and economic problems does not change this deeply ingrained reflex of the international aid apparatus.

A fundamental rethinking of relationships between external and indigenous actors is necessary. That shift was one of the themes of an April 2001 workshop in Ottawa on local capacity building through humanitarian action cosponsored with CARE Canada. In one particularly charged exchange, a Sierra Leonean who in 1999 had been an employee of an indigenous aid agency recalled how expatriate NGOs had disappeared overnight, taking with them the keys to warehouses stocked with food desperately needed in Freetown.

He did not fault his northern counterparts for their assessment of the security situation or quarrel with their desire to avoid having their food fall into the wrong hands. He was critical instead of the complete lack of consultation in the circumstances. "You don't abandon your partner in the midst of a crisis without a dialogue," he observed with evident passion and hurt. His observation is one element in a broader critique of the humanitarian enterprise on grounds that, beneath a rhetoric of partnership, its local members are treated as errand boys. The recurrence of this problem in Afghanistan, described in the epilogue, confirms the urgency of reform.

Giving overdue attention to local capacity building would have major structural implications for donors and aid agencies alike. If higher priority were placed on strengthening local institutions vis-à-vis the alleviation of suffering, the fabric of relationships between foreign and indigenous actors would change. Local NGOs (and, in some instances, local government officials) would become involved in the design and implementation of emergency programs. Greater attention would be given to long-term strategic planning at the country level, before as well as during crises. Shared decision making and accountability would become standard operating procedure.

Some analysts have pointed out that, realistically speaking, the amount of change that may be expected in this area is limited. "NGOs are answerable to the funder, not the beneficiaries," notes one research group in pointing out "a contradiction at the core of humanitarianism."[23] Analyst Mary B. Anderson has noted the stark inequality between those with resources and those with needs. In her judgment, while the imbalances in power are inevitable, "the tensions inherent in the giving and receiving of aid need not be antagonistic and destructive." Her larger point is equally essential: that "international aid is fundamentally about relationships," which provide the essential context within which resource transfers can be used productively.[24]

Reflecting this growing sense of the importance of relationships, the time is ripe for change. Indeed, the early fruits of such change are beginning to be felt. The architecture of the future humanitarian enterprise will require a larger and more diverse role for indigenous agencies, with decision-making structures, programming, and accountabilities reshaped to support the assumption of greater responsibility locally. More candor regarding structural inequalities between foreign and indigenous institutions can also promote a greater sense of humility on the part of external actors.[25]

Synergistic Relief and Rights Activities

Long-standing tensions between relief and rights groups have begun to give way to greater mutual respect and collaboration. Traditional dichotomies have eased between the delivery of emergency assistance and the protection of basic rights; between economic, social, and cultural rights and civil and political rights; and between acquiescing in rights violations as the price of maintaining access and the "naming and shaming" of rights violators. Both relief and rights groups face common problems such as gaining and maintaining access and finding and nurturing appropriate local partners. Neither relief nor rights agencies gain from association with the political agendas of donor states, though each set of organizations may benefit from resources of governments and political reinforcement by international institutions.

A vision that views assistance and protection as complementary aspects of the humanitarian imperative provides the basis for managing the unavoidable tensions. As noted by a CARE field worker, "Fulfilling the humanitarian imperative is to some significant degree fulfilling our obligation to secure the rights of those persons we are seeking to help."[26] The desideratum is not to have relief agencies become rights advocates, or for rights agencies to tackle the distribution of emergency food and medicine. Rather the two groups should work to understand and respect each other as component parts of a joint effort. There is space for both under a common humanitarian umbrella.

In the light of this conceptual discovery, the action now shifts to the operational level. In the struggle to manage the tensions between relief and rights, creative synergies are beginning to be realized. Growing out of a 1995 report by the Lawyers Committee for Human Rights on refugee protection in Africa and of workshops in 1997, 1999, and 2000, a network of indigenous human rights and humanitarian organizations in 2000 formed a West African NGO Refugee and Internally Displaced Persons Network (WARIPNET). With members drawn from ten West African countries and working in partnership with the Lawyers Committee and several international agencies, the network has developed policy papers on the economic, social, and cultural rights of refugees and carried out advocacy with governments and UN agencies.[27] The humanitarian architecture of the future will need to build on and incorporate such innovations.

In the coming years, headquarters discussions are likely to be upstaged by — or, preferably, reenergized by — breakthroughs at the field level. That said, more serious engagement with these issues at the interagency level is needed from the UN Office of the High Commissioner for Human Rights and the Office for the Coordination of Humanitarian Affairs. Ironically, more creative synergies seem to be taking place outside the two headquarters entities tasked with orchestrating the interaction than within. The widely shared consensus that both offices need to step up the resources committed and the priority attached to promoting synergies provides a starting point for action.

Other Actors

Beyond reforms within the humanitarian enterprise itself, recent experience also highlights the need for reconfiguring interactions between the humanitarian community and the wider set of nonhumanitarian actors. Here the areas of reform include restructuring relationships between humanitarian and other institutions, more consistent Security Council responsiveness to humanitarian crises, clearer terms of reference and division of labor between humanitarian actors and international military and peacekeeping forces, more discriminating use of economic sanctions, more proactive relations with the media, and the creation of a new capacity for humanitarian action in hot war situations.

Restructuring the Interface

In the discussion of humanitarian action and politics in chapter 5, various approaches for managing the inevitable tensions were identified. The project's case studies suggested that a delimited partnership was more satisfactory than a relationship that subsumed humanitarian action within a political rubric, or vice versa. With respect to the creation of a humanitarian architecture that allows the evident tensions to be managed, discussions within the UN over the past decade have advanced three approaches for structuring humanitarian and political-military relationships: integration, insulation, and separation of humanitarian from political-military actors.

The *integration* approach positions humanitarian work — along with other activities in the fields of development, trade, conflict resolution, and the like — as one among many means for advancing international peace and security.[28] The *insulation* approach protects the humanitarian enterprise from the more political aspects of the United Nations but affirms its essential complementarity with those areas. The *separation* approach seeks to isolate the functioning of humanitarian activities from association with the international political-military apparatus altogether.

A 1994 UN interagency paper vetted over a two-year period, "Protection of Humanitarian Mandates in Conflict Situations," illuminates these approaches. The Mandates paper embraces the *integration* approach. "Given the interrelated causes and consequences of complex emergencies, humanitarian action cannot be fully effective unless it is related to a comprehensive strategy for peace and security, human rights and social and economic development." Reflecting the perceived need for "integrated and unified operations," the paper proposes operational guidelines "to provide a framework for reconciling these objectives."[29]

The paper also articulates, however, the views of proponents of *insulation*. Because "humanitarian and political objectives do not necessarily coincide," UN humanitarian agencies should "maintain a certain degree of independence from UN-authorized political and/or military activities.... Humanitarian organizations are responsible for and should enjoy autonomy in accordance with their mandates."[30] Can such autonomy be accommodated within an integrated approach? The paper stops short of endorsing insulation, although acknowledging the desirability of preserving some distance between the UN's humanitarian and political activities. As noted earlier, the effort of UN agencies to insulate themselves from an encompassing political and policy framework leads to a schizophrenia that plays itself out in one crisis after another.

The third approach — full *separation* of humanitarian activities from the UN's political-military apparatus — would hardly be reflected in a UN document. Yet some agencies hold that humanitarian principle and practice alike require complete independence for assistance and protection activities from the prevailing UN political framework. What chance is there, they ask, of realizing the proposed "autonomy" for humanitarian work, given the heavy political-military context in which such activities are framed by the governments that make up the boards of UN agencies? In their view, the difficulties encountered in maintaining neutrality point toward devising structures altogether outside of the UN system and freed from its political-military baggage.[31]

The policy articulated in the 1994 Mandates paper was revisited in 2000 with the issuance by the secretary-general of a Note of Guidance, vetted again over a period of years with the agencies. He clarified the responsibilities for humanitarian coordination in any given crisis among three officials: the special representative of the secretary-general, the UN resident coordinator, and the UN humanitarian coordinator. The long-awaited pronouncement affirmed that the overarching framework for UN activities within a given country is indeed a political one, with the resident and/or humanitarian coordinators functioning within that framework. The note essentially restated the problem rather than mandating a solution.[32]

A decade-plus into the post–Cold War era, the three approaches to structuring humanitarian interactions with other actors enjoy anything but peaceful coexistence. Integration, insulation, and separation each has its own strengths and weaknesses. Each reflects indisputable realities: that effective humanitarian action may contribute to international peace and security; that to be fully effective such action requires independence from political agendas; and that in highly politicized settings, humanitarian action may require autonomous structures outside the UN system to preserve its integrity. Once again, each of the above may have its place, depending on the circumstances.

Most diplomatic-military actors advocate integration, subsuming humanitarian action within a broader political framework. The view of most of their humanitarian counterparts is that of insulation, viewing humanitarian activities as complementary to, but requiring a certain independence from, that broader political framework. A small number of humanitarian agencies take the more radical position that effective assistance and protection work requires full separation from the prevailing political framework.

Diplomatic-military actors buttress their views by citing circumstances in which the integrationist approach has enhanced the effectiveness of relief and rights work. Humanitarian actors counter by noting instances in which integrationist assumptions have harmed the independence of humanitarian action. One such instance was the suspension of UNHCR airlifts of material aid into Sarajevo in early 1993. The high commissioner acted after Serbian forces had prevented aid trucks from reaching Muslim villages, in response to which Muslims had boycotted the incoming airlift. Following the suspension, she later recalled, "Debate erupted in the Security Council. 'This will set back the peace negotiations,'" some said. UNHCR later resumed aid deliveries after the Bosnian authorities lifted their boycott.[33]

The project's research and analysis suggests that although humanitarian action may indeed contribute significantly to international peace and security, such action is unlikely to do so when harnessed tightly to an all-encompassing political framework. The patchy track record of the international community on peace and security issues itself strengthens the case for greater independence for humanitarian action. My own view is that as a result of recurring problems with the options of integration and insulation, the separation alternative deserves more serious consideration. Situating humanitarian action outside the UN altogether would reduce its politicization, although such repositioning would have other drawbacks, including the need for a clear distinction between emergency and reconstruction work.

At the end of the day, designing a structure for all seasons is probably impossible. A time and a place may well exist for integration, insulation, and independence. In any event, discerning judgments are needed to chart a discriminating course in each particular set of circumstances. At mid-decade, we observed that understanding and structuring the relationships between the humanitarian and the political-military spheres represented major unfinished business.[34] As of 2001, the relationships are better understood but structural accommodations have yet to be made and strategic choices yet to be determined.[35] The issue recurs in Afghanistan, where, as noted in the epilogue, agencies have struggled with the question of where to position themselves in relation to the antiterrorism rubric that frames many international humanitarian presence and activities.[36]

Capitalizing on Security Council Interest

During the first post–Cold War decade, the UN Security Council has become more seized with humanitarian issues than before. This new level of engagement, evolving along lines noted above, followed years of silence on relief and rights issues. The council has also become more accessible to input from the humanitarian enterprise itself, not only from the UN's own organizations but also from NGOs.[37] Advocacy efforts have helped promote the perception that issues of human security deserve higher visibility in the council's overall efforts to protect and enhance international peace. Indeed, threats to survival and violations of human rights are now often mentioned prominently to justify council actions.

The council's attention is still selective, however, giving highest priority to areas of perceived political importance to council members, particularly the Permanent Five. That said, initiatives by other council members during their terms and their presidencies — Sweden and Canada come particularly to mind — have succeeded in upgrading the profile of humanitarian concerns. During the years 1998–99, for example, one such initiative was the council's review, at the urging of the Swedish government, of the issue of the protection of humanitarian assistance personnel; another initiative was its examination of the protection of civilians in situations of armed conflict, initiated by the government of Canada.

Discussions of necessary reforms in the Security Council range well beyond the humanitarian sphere. With reference to the council's humanitarian agenda in particular, however, a number of changes have been suggested. One specific recommendation, growing out of our Sudan review, was designed to offset the selectivity of the council's attention to humanitarian crises. We suggested a humanitarian "trigger mechanism" that "could automatically bring an acute civil war situation to the attention of the Security Council through the Secretary-General under Article 99 of the Charter."

Indicators that might require council review could include the number of persons affected, the severity of the threat to human life, the uprooting of substantial populations, and a pattern of significant human rights abuses. Although such a provision would counteract the reluctance of member states or the UN secretariat to act, the provision would not compel the council itself to take action, thus respecting the council's need to reach its own judgments. The requirement that situations crossing a specified threshold be reviewed might, however, reduce the lack of evenhandedness in the council's current attention to crises.[38]

In a broader sense, other council reforms — for example, increasing the number and makeup of Security Council members — might also bring enhanced credibility to its review of humanitarian issues. Yet in addition to making the decision-making process more universal and representative, they might also make it more unwieldy. To the extent, though, that state sovereignty is viewed as one of the remaining protections of the weak against the strong, a less politicized approach from the council would help reassure governments wary of interventions in their internal affairs masquerading as humanitarian undertakings.

To expect to harness the Security Council to an exclusively humanitarian agenda would of course be unrealistic. At the same time, a more principled and consistent approach to humanitarian issues, beyond its benefit to the humanitarian enterprise, would reap dividends in the area of international peace and security, the council's primary charge. The secretary-general has challenged states to take a broader approach to defining their national interests, reminding them that "in a growing number of challenges facing humanity, the collective interest is the national interest."[39]

More Circumspect Relations to Military Forces and Force

International military forces are a fact of life in today's complex emergencies. For the wider family to clarify the areas of respective comparative advantage and for individual humanitarian agencies to specify the terms of their own collaboration is therefore essential. In the absence of more probing discussions of the pros and cons of the increased role of the military and of creative alternatives to its deepening involvement, many humanitarian agencies are accepting the militarization of the humanitarian enterprise as the inevitable price to be paid for working in insecure areas.

The experience of the decade suggests that from a humanitarian viewpoint, the military should concentrate on providing security for civilian populations, with assistance to humanitarian operations and direct aid to civilians of secondary and tertiary importance. Although forbidding outright civic action activities by the military may be unrealistic, time and again such hands-on help in local communities has distorted the comparative advantage of the military and duplicated the work of humanitarian organizations. Throughout the decade, longer-term problems associated with the military's aid efforts have offset the immediate value of hands-on assistance.

In the case of Kosovo, the involvement of multiple military configurations, some of them also engaged in NATO's action as a belligerent in the war, created confusion among humanitarian agencies and with the general public. In East Timor, the military's performance of civic action work, undertaken at the initiative of the military without consultation with aid agencies, was an irritant to the humanitarian enterprise.[40]

The clarification of functions in NATO's new policy and doctrine represents a major step in the right direction, and may influence other military groupings as well, including UN peacekeeping operations. NATO's primary focus on security-related tasks and discouragement of civic action, except in exceptional circumstances, reflect what most aid agencies would like to see. Unchanged, however, and unlikely to change, is the fundamentally political nature of the military's mandate and of its framework for civil-military cooperation (CIMIC).

The framework within which governments provide troops and humanitarian organizations use them is political and military rather than humanitarian. A draft statement of doctrine, expected to be approved by mid-2002, affirms that "NATO conducts CIMIC in support of a military mission."[41] Already approved policy upon which this doctrine is based specifies that "The long-term purpose of CIMIC is to help create and sustain conditions that will support the achievement of Alliance objectives in operations."[42]

The fact that CIMIC activities are "a key strand of the overall [NATO] operational plan and not an activity apart" means that humanitarian organizations, to the extent that they collaborate, run the risk of sacrificing their neutrality. That possibility exists despite NATO's specified commitment that "All practicable measures will be taken to avoid compromising the neutrality and impartiality of humanitarian organizations."[43] As noted earlier, political pressures of the moment can override written policy — whether produced by NATO, the UN, or national military forces — that delineate more circumspect engagement with humanitarian organizations.

Experience in a number of recent crises suggests the value of having military assets more responsive to humanitarian needs and priorities. While "control" would of course need to remain with the military, the possibility of placing UN peacekeeping personnel under the "command" of a ranking UN humanitarian official deserves consideration. A 1992 report by then-Secretary-General Boutros Boutros-Ghali based on the work of UNPROFOR in the former Yugoslavia moves in that direction. Reflecting on the experience in that theater, the secretary-general proposed that the military provide such protection "at UNHCR's request, where and when UNHCR considered such protection necessary." The commander would retain responsibility for "operational decisions relating to a protected convoy."[44] Some such shift in authority is necessary if the military is to be of genuine utility to the humanitarian enterprise in its own terms.

For their part, humanitarian actors need to reflect more seriously on their experience with the military and to become clearer regarding the policy options available to them. The disarray mentioned earlier among NGOs on the question of requesting assistance from the U.S. military to deal with the insecurity in Somalia in 1992 should serve as a learning experience. Military officials with responsibilities for interfacing with humanitarian agencies are understandably frustrated at the confusion they encounter among relief and rights groups on these issues. Whom shall we deal with, they frequently ask, and what do they want of military forces?

In fairness, NGOs have sought to clarify these views. The International Council of Voluntary Agencies (ICVA) at the international level and Inter-Action in the United States have affirmed the importance of protecting the integrity of humanitarian activities.[45] ICVA has been more circumspect than InterAction in its embrace of humanitarian roles for the military. ICVA views as a "dangerous" development discussions in the UN's Military and Civil Defense Unit that would transform the Oslo guidelines for natural disaster response into a framework for using the military in complex emergencies. ICVA reads the Kosovo experience as a troubling harbinger of things to come, fearing that governments will again fund military units to accomplish tasks that are properly the purview of humanitarian agencies.[46] ICVA has a point: creating a humanitarian architecture that embraces collaboration with the military while preserving the apolitical nature of humanitarian action is difficult, perhaps impossible.

Many national military forces are now more willing to take on humanitarian support missions (the United States is something of an exception). Conversely, many humanitarian actors are now prepared to enlist the help of the military in specified areas. Yet the collaboration usually takes place on the military's terms and encounters recurrent problems. The experiences reviewed point toward elaborating ground rules that provide for a more focused use of the military in future crises. Emphasis should be given to strengthening protection functions and discouraging hands-on aid. Such ground rules are needed not only for UN peacekeeping troops but also for other proposed configurations, including UN standby forces and the European Union's proposed rapid-reaction force.

On the broader issue of the stepped-up use of military force in support of humanitarian interests, serious questions of policy and practice have yet to be resolved. The integrity of UN enforcement action has been called into question as driven by the interests of key Security Council members rather than by universal norms. Indeed, the council's imprimatur on military action over Kosovo was not sought in order to avoid vetoes. As humanitarian objectives come to play a larger role in Security Council deliberations, enforcement action deserves and requires protection from politicization.

Based on the Kosovo experience, we recommended reviving a proposal first offered by Secretary-General Dag Hammarskjöld in 1958. He urged that UN-associated military forces not be drawn from the ranks of the Permanent Five (P5) members of the Security Council, nor from "any country which, because of its geographical position or other reasons, might be considered as possibly having a special interest in the situation."[47] Such an approach would help delimit disproportionate P5 influence in defining peace and security issues.

Because it would eliminate the contribution of influential countries, this proposal has been dismissed as further reducing the UN's already weak capacity to conduct multilateral military and peacekeeping undertakings. Yet stepped-up contributions from smaller countries that are already actively engaged in such undertakings could help to fill the gap. In any event, the distorting effect of P5 involvement needs review as a serious policy and institutional issue. In weighing options, the pros and cons of various ways of managing the dilemma require attention.

It would also be helpful for NGOs to clarify their views, both individually and community-wide. They need to distinguish between the utility of military force to their own conduct of relief and rights operations, on the one hand, and to the interests of civilian populations, on the other. Humanitarian actors also need to be aware of the extent to which belligerents may view them as message-transmitters to international political arenas rather than, in the first instance, as providers of assistance and protection. To the extent that they are seen as channels through which belligerents may mobilize pressure for military engagement on their behalf, humanitarian organizations may be drawn into a questionable political role.

More Humane Economic Sanctions

Sanctions often place civilian populations at grave risk, notwithstanding their laudable political objectives and the concerns articulated by those who impose them for the welfare of civilians. The impacts of sanctions on the humanitarian enterprise itself can also be sharply negative, in terms both of higher caseloads and of greater difficulties in functioning. At issue is not the objective of bringing about changes in the policies of regimes or in the regimes themselves but rather the acceptable level of pain that civilians should have to endure as part of the larger effort to produce political gains.

Based on our review of recent experience, we recommended that the UN Security Council "affirm, as a matter of principle, that vulnerable populations should be spared adverse consequences from economic sanctions." Affirmation of the legitimacy of international humanitarian activities in countries upon which sanctions have been imposed is also essential.[48] As with military coercion, sanctions represent an area in which, despite clear tensions, both political and humanitarian interests may be served. Yet the association may also be perilous for humanitarian actors.

In addition to clarifying ground rules for the imposition of sanctions, the use of the instrument itself needs refinement. Various approaches to exempting humanitarian essentials need to be examined and standardized. The credibility of sanctions in political as well as humanitarian terms requires that similar situations be treated similarly. True to the nature of the dilemmas that face policy makers, each of the three available approaches — institution-specific exemptions, item-specific exemptions, and country-specific exemptions — has advantages and disadvantages.[49]

From a humanitarian standpoint, the three options exhibit decreasing degrees of desirability. Exempting all items that specified agencies (e.g., the ICRC, UNICEF, and WHO) wish to introduce is preferable to enumerating each such item (e.g., baby food, textbooks, and kidney dialysis machines), which is in turn preferable to an itemized list country-by-country (e.g., for Iraq as distinct from Haiti or the former Yugoslavia).

A number of positive changes have occurred at the political and the humanitarian levels. The Security Council is now proceeding with greater caution and consultation in invoking sanctions. An informal council working group was created in 2000 to develop recommendations for improving the effectiveness of sanctions.[50] A subgroup on sanctions of the UN Inter-Agency Standing Committee has mounted a number of missions and is discussing recurring methodological and monitoring issues. However, the momentum for reform generated in the mid-1990s when many sanctions were in place has ebbed and needs to be reenergized.[51]

Both the progress and the problems are exhibited in the recent UN sanctions against Afghanistan. In imposing sanctions in 1999 and 2000 against international air travel by Afghan airlines aimed at forcing the Taliban to turn over Osama bin Laden and halt poppy cultivation, the council consulted humanitarian organizations in advance. The council also requested regular reporting of the sanctions' impacts on the civilian population. An OCHA report on behalf of the IASC established a vulnerability baseline for monitoring sanctions impacts, utilizing the health, economic, displacement, and civil society indicators suggested in our earlier study.[52] Resolutions included exemptions from the flight ban for recognized humanitarian organizations, certain chartered relief flights, and medical evacuations. In a distinct improvement over earlier sanctions regimes, OCHA found the exemption procedures "operating smoothly and without undue delay."[53]

Negatives were present as well. Sanctions disrupted aid operations, although many of the UN staff who were withdrawn when sanctions were being considered had returned in the subsequent months. While their impacts on civilians were limited, sanctions contributed to the "sense of isolation and the lack of confidence about the future felt by Afghans."[54] On the political side, the parties to the conflict, which is itself "the primary cause of human suffering in Afghanistan...do not appear to have altered their military stance, or their willingness to continue fighting."[55] Taliban authorities, while opposing sanctions, continued to cooperate with the UN's humanitarian agencies.

While the humanitarian pain seemed manageable, the political gain remained elusive. "Imposing sanctions in a bid to root out suspected terrorists," observes ICVA, itself a member of the IASC, "is doing little to help the Afghan population. Perhaps the time has come for the international community to rethink radically its approach to Afghanistan."[56] The same could be said of Iraq and other countries where sanctions have brought unconscionable civilian pain in relation to political gain.

As part of new humanitarian architectural arrangements, economic sanctions should be used in a far more limited and focused way than in the past. The late James P. Grant, executive director of UNICEF, aptly framed the management challenge in a statement to the UN Human Rights Commission in 1994. "We recognize that sanctions are a necessary tool for international action, occupying the middle-ground between rhetorical resolutions and the use of armed force. Sanctions must, however, be applied in a manner in which children of poor families — the most vulnerable and, I might add, the most innocent in a society — do not suffer most cruelly." He concluded, "Without renouncing the non-military mechanisms of international pressure wisely provided in the [UN] Charter, it should be possible to refine our existing tools — or to develop others — so that children are not major and unintended victims of particular sanctions."[57] That refinement process needs to be expedited if sanctions are to regain their credibility.

More Proactive Relations with the Media

A recurring leitmotiv of humanitarian action has been the influence of the media on the nature and scale of the relief and rights activities undertaken. Massive responses to the high-profile humanitarian emergencies of the 1990s coincided with a technological revolution in the news media. The media is now a more major actor in the wider group of institutions to which humanitarian organizations relate, although neither humanitarian crises nor their reporting is new to the post–Cold War era. Indeed, "the proliferation of both in an era of high-speed communications has led to widespread speculation about the influence the media may exercise" over humanitarian action.[58] What role does the media play in determining the timing, shape, and duration of humanitarian responses and to what extent may the humanitarian enterprise influence this situation for the better?

A broader question arises inasmuch as the media is also now playing an increasing role in the deliberations of the UN and governments. At mid-decade, then-Secretary-General Boutros Boutros-Ghali described CNN as "the sixteenth member of the Security Council."[59] The extent to which the media is implicated in the actions of the council and perhaps also in the selectivity and other problems associated with council actions bears review. The issues are explored in the project publication *The News Media, Civil War, and Humanitarian Action.*

Based on a 1996 review of the media's role in the crises in Liberia, northern Iraq, Somalia, former Yugoslavia, Haiti, and Rwanda, we proposed the concept of a "crisis triangle" as a device for analyzing and interpreting the media's impacts on various emergencies. The triangle is composed of the news media, governments, and humanitarian organizations. Confronted with humanitarian emergencies, each of the three institutions has its own interests and limitations; the international response in each instance reflects their dynamic interaction.

The case of Somalia demonstrates the interplay in all its complexity. Media coverage was minimal during the anarchy of 1991–92 that set the stage for widespread starvation and military intervention. Minimal, too, was involvement by foreign governments and humanitarian groups. By July 1992, aid agencies and some policy makers had wrested greater attention from governments and the media, but a U.S. military airlift of food from Kenya — designed specifically to catch the media's eye — engaged the media more fully. The media were also on hand to record U.S. troops coming ashore in December 1992. The arrival of the troops in the early morning hours, noted the *International Herald Tribune,* was "perfectly timed to reach the afternoon peak television audience in the U.S., and hundreds of well-briefed reporters were on the beach and at the port."[60] Yet by then, "the worst of the famine had passed and the most vulnerable already had died."[61]

Having played a role in the introduction of U.S. troops, the media also influenced their extraction. Coverage of the worsening security situation and of faltering aid operations during mid-1993 probably "contributed to the pressure that something be done about the strongman Aidid." Certainly the loss of lives of U.S. Rangers in their search for Aidid in October spurred pressures to withdraw American troops. "Network broadcasts of Somali video pictures showing dead U.S. marines being dragged ignominiously through the streets of Mogadishu at the very least hastened — and perhaps also drove — a policy reversal by the administration." President Clinton's National Security Advisor Anthony Lake confirmed that the television "pictures helped us recognize that the military situation . . . had deteriorated in a way that we had not frankly recognized."[62]

While Somalia demonstrates in a broad sense the "push-pull of television," the dynamics of the interaction within the crisis triangle were far more complex. "[T]he correlation between media attention on the one hand, and action by policy makers and humanitarian agencies on the other, followed a series of peaks and valleys. At some stages, media interest (itself reflecting goading by aid actors) preceded policy initiatives; on other occasions, media involvement followed."[63] The Somalia experience, confirmed in other crises elsewhere, suggests that the importance of the so-called CNN factor may well be overstated. While playing a key role in influencing humanitarian action, the media does so in tandem with government and humanitarian institutions.

Like the military, therefore, the media has claimed its own place in the humanitarian architecture of the future. Like the military, the media requires skillful cultivation by the humanitarian enterprise as an actor in its own right whose own constraints and agendas must be recognized. Relief and rights groups have already made major strides in managing media relationships more effectively. For individual agencies and the humanitarian enterprise as a whole to refine such strategies is an important agenda item for future action.

More Realistic Scenarios for Extreme Insecurity

Current difficulties in providing humanitarian assistance and protection in volatile settings are well documented. Agencies have become more circumspect in their approach to their missions; witness the release form that some agencies now require personnel to sign confirming their understanding that in the event they are taken hostage, their organization will not pay ransom. Precautions notwithstanding, humanitarian action involves risks. Agencies and personnel remain prepared to take such risks, and do so regularly.

Given the risks that unarmed relief and rights personnel experience, a prudent move for the UN (another entity might also be a possibility) would be to develop a new institutional capacity to provide assistance and protection in extremely insecure circumstances. Such a cadre of personnel, operating under terms of reference that provide for bearing arms, could be activated when military enforcement or economic sanctions are carried out under Chapter VII of the UN Charter. Such a unit would recognize the special skills needed to provide effective assistance and protection during hot war situations or in sanctions settings. Traditional aid personnel would be reintroduced after the situation had stabilized.[64]

Originally offered among the recommendations in our case study of the former Yugoslavia, this proposal met resistance from UN officials, who believe that as a matter of principle their agencies belong where people are the most imperiled, risks notwithstanding. Security officials within the UN, however, already bar UN aid personnel from high-risk areas, and their performance in such settings, however heroic, has often proved patchy. Whether or not a military cadre for short-term humanitarian deployment is created, aid agencies themselves are well advised to develop expertise within their ranks to cope with hot war and sanctions settings.

Short of withdrawing humanitarian organizations from some crises altogether, a case may be made for rotating out their normal personnel and rotating in some more seasoned experts. "In highly politicized settings where extraordinary measures such as international economic sanctions have been imposed," we concluded in our Haiti study, "consideration should be given to removing existing international personnel and inserting specially trained international teams for the duration of the crisis." As with other policy choices, however, this one involves dilemmas. "Such an approach would come at the expense of familiarity with the local context, but it would free organizations whose impartiality and effectiveness may be impaired by existing relationships and would recognize the special skills needed to respond effectively."[65]

Dilemmas and Discoveries

The effort to design an architecture for the humanitarian enterprise of the future confronts a series of dilemmas. In fact, issues of structure and policy may be even more difficult to manage than the more operational challenges reviewed earlier. The can-do pragmatists who make up the humanitarian breed tend to downplay the significance of fundamental issues such as how the humanitarian edifice should be structured, only to be brought up short by their recurrent relevance in each new major crisis.

Indeed, perhaps the most obvious dilemma concerns whether structural questions are worth seeking to address and resolve at all. The issue arises particularly given the culture of humanitarian institutions, which values leadership over structure, people over process, and improvisation over routine. There is, it seems, never an ideal time for reflection and follow-up action. The agencies are either putting out the latest fire or catching their breath from having done so.

The fact that there is a continuing lack of consensus on the structural reforms needed does not change the reality that the humanitarian enterprise is living on borrowed time in getting its act together. That sense permeates the early phase of the response to the Afghanistan crisis, as noted in the epilogue. It is high time to break the recurring impasses and tackle the management of recurrent dilemmas in serious and innovative ways.

The proposals highlighted in this chapter address issues that have demonstrated dogged resistance to change. That is the case within the humanitarian community, where consensus remains elusive with respect to more assertive coordination, more apolitical functioning, greater proportionality of response to need, greater respect for the distinctive contributions of individual agencies, reduced externality, and greater synergies between relief and rights actors.

The dilemmas vis-à-vis other actors have proved equally resistant to change: managing the interface with the political, capitalizing on newfound interest by the UN Security Council, finding a modus vivendi for relating to the military, reducing the inhumane impacts of economic sanctions, nurturing more productive relations with the media, and functioning in situations of extreme insecurity.

To be sure, these issues surface regularly in coordination meetings at the international level and in this crisis or that, and are the subject of discussion in the conference rooms and around the water coolers of individual agencies. Yet the structures that make up the humanitarian enterprise have changed surprisingly little during the past ten years. There is now greater interaction among the actors, but progress in identifying and making structural changes has remained patchy. It is discouraging in the extreme to hear observers compare the disarray of the agencies in Afghanistan in 2001–2 to the confusion that existed in Somalia ten years earlier.

The major structural discovery of the decade is that a serviceable humanitarian architecture for the future needs to position the work of the humanitarian community as a significant investment in wider international peace and security. To make its own distinctive contribution to the international political realm, however, humanitarian action must protect its integrity through careful insulation from the political arena. In fact, it may even benefit in certain settings from structural independence from the prevailing UN political framework. In a larger sense, politics more infused with humane values will produce benefits for all concerned: the political, military, and humanitarian spheres alike.

8

Equipping the Enterprise

*In mid-1972, Church World Service (CWS), a U.S. NGO, appointed
me to manage its reconstruction program in the southern Sudan. In
a fast-paced orientation, I learned about CWS's policies and procedures, discussed its earlier involvement in the Sudan, and read several
articles about the country. I met some of the church executives who
would provide funds, did a whirlwind tour of colleague agencies in
England and on the continent, visited the World Council of Churches
in Geneva, and touched down in Khartoum. I was thrilled to take
up my first overseas post but quite unprepared for the task. My only
previous trip to Africa had been as a tourist; my academic studies had
included no courses on economic development or on Africa or, for that
matter, on project management.*

*Responsible for modest amounts of food and other material aid,
I knew little about their potential impacts on the local economy, exchange rates, or wage scales. Though part of an international effort
mounted through the Sudan Council of Churches (SCC), I had given
little thought to the relationship between outside resources and local
capacity. While I sensed the urgency of using the opening provided by
the ecumenically brokered peace accords to create visible changes on
the ground, I had no inkling that a decade later the war would rekindle
and continue with horrific consequences for years to come.*

*By the time our aid operation in Juba had moved from tents into a
new office block, I was a bit more familiar with the region and the players, but hardly with the underlying policy and political issues. When
I returned home a year later, my debriefings were pro forma and my
successor was soon on his way. As an aid worker, I was probably typical of many humanitarians: well-meaning but superficially informed
and operating out of my depth.*

What does it take to function effectively in the conflict-related settings of
the post–Cold War era? Humanitarian personnel, observed analyst Susan
George in 1985, in something of a caricature, "must take graduate degrees in
social anthropology, geography, economics, a dozen or so difficult languages,

medicine, and business administration. Second, at a slightly more practical level," she continued, "they must demonstrate competence in agronomy, hydrology, practical nursing, accounting, psychology, automotive mechanics and civil engineering. In addition," she concluded, "they must learn to give a credible imitation of saintliness, and it would be well if they could learn sleight-of-hand as well, since they will often be called upon to perform feats of magic."[1] In the post–Cold War era, expectations have hardly dwindled.

This chapter examines the tools of the humanitarian trade, including the skills needed to deliver aid in conflicts without exacerbating them. The chapter draws on the Humanitarianism and War Project's policy dialogues, held twice a year with senior officials of North American NGOs, which confirmed data gathered in interviews conducted in the field with a wide array of humanitarian personnel and agencies. The chapter analyzes present trends and highlights dilemmas and discoveries.

The Changing Scene

My selection and training was probably fairly typical for the 1970s and 1980s. Agencies took freshly minted generalists, briefed them on responsibilities and reporting requirements, and dispatched them to a crisis. For NGO personnel, the cardinal virtues then, as now, were responsiveness, flexibility, collegiality, presence on-the-ground, a can-do spirit, and a no-frills approach to expenditures. Matters of broader agency policy — to say nothing of more generic relief and development issues — did not loom large. While bilateral and multilateral agencies were more policy oriented and provided more rigorous training and orientation, their personnel, too, had a lot of on-the-job learning to do upon arriving in their new environments.

As in my own case, most aid personnel during the Cold War years led charmed lives. Their missions were accepted, their resources put to use, their staff welcomed, their security assured. UN and bilateral agencies established working relationships with host governments, which also signed agreements with NGOs. The emphasis was on natural disasters and, where conflicts were concerned, on providing assistance and protection to refugees in neighboring countries rather than in hot war zones. The welcoming surroundings changed, however, with the passing of the Cold War.

The alterations in the landscape and their impact on humanitarian operations are evident in the Sudan, a country not on the front lines of East-West conflict. Years of energetic resettlement and reconstruction in the early 1970s gave way to drought-induced famine (1983–86), which segued into conflict-related famine in 1987 and then into resumed civil war. Agencies responding to the drought encountered severe logistical difficulties, north and south, which the UN's Office of Emergency Operations in Africa (OEOA) struggled to overcome. The suffering embedded in the civil war, as in other civil wars toward the end of the century, heightened the difficulties for aid agencies further still, even after Operation Lifeline Sudan extracted access agreements from the two warring parties. The presence of armed conflict and the need to deal with two sets of political authorities accentuated the humanitarian challenges and dilemmas that the agencies faced.[2]

The contrast between aid agencies' well-meaning efforts of earlier years, often conducted in a policy and political vacuum, with the more recently acknowledged need for greater savvy on matters of policy and politics does not hold uniformly for any and all crises. Earlier on, some agencies had sent highly informed experts to the field, while reflexive humanitarian impulses continue to drive some initiatives today. In general terms, however, the contrast is both true and telling.

The nature of the new environment for humanitarian action was sketched in chapter 1. Among the major factors that have contributed to the current debate about competency and skill sets are the increasing complexity of the political landscape, the rapid growth of the humanitarian enterprise, the higher profile role of humanitarian initiatives, and the agencies' loss of immunity to criticism from governments, the public, the media, and belligerents. What is taking place in this changed context is, in essence, "a fundamental reappraisal of the relief worker's essential identity" and a consequent "re-skilling in certain key areas."[3]

The Ingredients

The current debate about the nature of humanitarian professionalism provides an illuminating point of entry into a discussion of skills and competencies. For many agencies and staff, the humanitarian enterprise is like other sectors that receive government grants and contracts and that solicit public support. The enterprise needs to be conducted according to established management practices, embrace clear and measurable objectives and outputs, and be accountable to its stakeholders. Experiencing massive growth during the 1990s, many NGOs brought on board people from the corporate sector with strong managerial skills.

For others, however, the special nature of the humanitarian mandate and the circumstances in which it is implemented make standard business practices inadequate — necessary, but not enough. These agencies stress the special nature of their task: a common commitment to universal rights, the uniquely voluntary rather than for-profit aspects of the undertaking, and the need to develop systems that are less Western in concept and execution and that involve greater power-sharing and mutual accountability. As a result of the emphasis on growth and management, suspects Peter Walker, a senior official with the International Federation of Red Cross and Red Crescent Societies, the balance between "effectiveness/efficiency and commitment/passion, between humanitarian ideas and institutional survival and growth" may have become distorted. "Why and how we do things should be as important as what we do," he says.[4]

Both viewpoints acknowledge four ingredients that contribute to effective humanitarian action: management capacity, technical expertise, contextual knowledge, and interpersonal skills. These four elements constitute what one NGO chief executive, Ron Mathies of the Mennonite Central Committee, has called the "core competencies" of the profession. His organization attaches special importance to the latter two.

Management Capacity

In its most basic and generally accepted form, competent humanitarianism means the conduct of humanitarian activities according to established Western business management practices. The need to be perceived as functioning according to standard commercial procedures has involved something of a change for private relief groups, many of which were borne of a particular crisis, a particular person's passion to alleviate suffering, or a particular parent organization's interest in carrying out such activities.

Largely gone are the days when well-meaning do-gooders simply gather up resources and head for the latest emergency. With the advent of new agency leadership and a broader array of country challenges, adhocism and informality are giving way to more standardized approaches. Indeed, some agencies have made the exponential growth of the industry during the 1990s as the occasion for adopting long overdue and more businesslike management procedures.

Improved managerial competence enables agencies to operate according to standards of efficiency and financial accountability applicable in the for-profit world. Key aspects include improved human resource planning, management, and development, supported by information systems to identify skill availability within the organization and to train and track personnel. The complexity of crises, including elements of scope, venue, duration, and institutional relationships, is mirrored by greater complexity in the management of humanitarian organizations.

Donor insistence on better performance, on keeping administrative costs to a minimum, and on greater financial accountability has played a reinforcing role. In an example mentioned in chapter 2, a senior official of a major donor stipulated that her government would entertain no funding proposals for a particular emergency from NGOs that failed to mention the word "coordination." She was taking a tough line with certain NGOs that were prepared to commit themselves only to "interagency consultations." An increasingly crowded marketplace of agencies, governmental and nongovernmental alike, has also heightened competition for resources and constituency. Reaping the advantages of a funder's market, donors are now better positioned to insist on — and to define — well-managed aid operations.[5]

Technical Skills

Technical expertise is now also viewed as indispensable to effective humanitarian operations. A trend has emerged, particularly among NGOs, away from reliance on generalists and toward greater utilization of specialists. With the expansion in numbers and size of humanitarian organizations in the 1990s, some agencies have concentrated activities in sectoral areas of perceived comparative advantage such as public health, shelter, microcredit, or programming for women. Other agencies, continuing a broad spectrum approach, have augmented their expertise across the board. Various codes of conduct approved by the agencies during the past decade specify minimum standards of acceptable performance in identified program sectors.

Whether narrow or broad-gauged in approach, each agency needs access to the technical capacity to plan, mount, and monitor programs in its chosen areas. Here technical expertise and management capacity overlap. Some agencies develop that capacity in-house; others prefer to retain consultants from outside to fill their needs. Oxfam-UK is known for its work in potable water, MSF in emergency medicine, the IRC in refugee relief. The ICRC has the world's most extensive cadre of international humanitarian lawyers, available to backstop its country delegations when they need special technical assistance. Whether the humanitarian enterprise as a whole is becoming more segmented and specialized, however, is unclear.[6]

Today's emphasis on the development of technical skills is as welcome as it is novel. Agencies managing food aid programs now possess greater ability to monitor the impacts of the efforts, and donors that provide food aid resources now insist on such capacity. Yet many agencies, along with the academic and other training institutions that provide resources, believe that additional technical expertise is still needed, particularly in such areas as public health and nutrition, microcredit, conflict management, and human rights and humanitarian law. The importance of improving skills that have broad relevance to all humanitarian activities such as gender awareness and poverty analysis is also now widely accepted.

Contextual Knowledge

Beyond expertise of a technical or sectoral nature, the modern humanitarian needs contextual expertise. "Today's international relief professional," observes analyst Hugo Slim, "is like the multinational executive who feels able to operate in any part of the world because she knows the way the firm works. However, she very seldom knows the way the country works."[7] A map of Brussels is of little utility in navigating the streets of Bujumbura, an organization chart of a North American corporation little help in understanding the structure of a counterpart humanitarian agency in Central America.

Agencies have come surprisingly late to the realization that differing country situations require different approaches. In the 1970s, one American NGO that used U.S. food aid in dozens of countries acknowledged without apology that it employed essentially the same strategies wherever it managed Public Law 480 programs. One NGO involved in programming substantial tonnages of food aid in India in the 1980s had nobody on its field staff with the skills necessary to monitor impacts on the local economy. While the commodities that my program in the southern Sudan provided to returning refugees were modest in scale and temporary in nature, I myself had no way of determining — and little awareness of the importance of doing so — whether the stop-gap food aid we provided discouraged farmers who were returning from exile in Zaire, the Central African Republic, Uganda, and Kenya from growing their own food once back at home.

Today, widespread agreement exists on the need to move beyond good intentions and cookie-cutter formulas to undertake planning, programming, and implementation that are context-specific and circumstances-knowledgeable. Practitioners are now aware that the effectiveness of relief activities often depends on understanding local social, economic, political, and cultural forces and factors. Accessing and integrating this knowledge into program activity in a systematic way, however, remains an often largely unmet challenge.

The challenges of functioning effectively in complex political emergencies are formidable. One review, confirmed by our own research, sees these challenges as including "assessing, understanding and monitoring the situation, . . . matching types of intervention to the various priorities of affected populations, . . . minimizing the risk of benefits being swept away by renewed violence or manipulated in favor of belligerents [and] ensuring the safety of staff." The review concluded, and again our work offers corroborating evidence, that sometimes humanitarian workers "get it wrong, and when they do it is often because they fail to grasp the political complexities of the context in which they are working."[8]

Interpersonal Skills

A fourth element in effective humanitarian action involves interpersonal or "people" skills. Personalities often upstage managerial expertise and training in contributing to success, particularly in field operations. The earlier discussion of coordination documented the importance of dynamic individual leadership in UN agencies in Tanzania and Sierra Leone. In one of our policy dialogue sessions on professionalization, an NGO official noted the indispensable contributions of persons with strong "soft skills" but without adequate technical or contextual backgrounds. He gave particularly high marks to two of his agency's then-current country program directors. Before being hired, one had just completed a tour as a rock band sound engineer; the other was a volcanologist.

While many professions require solid people skills, "soft skills" are particularly important for humanitarian organizations. At the field level, staff confront difficult problems on a daily basis, interacting in different languages and cultures with different groups and individuals. They struggle with the dilemmas of applying humanitarian principles to operational options, each with its own liabilities. Human rights monitors have a dicey job of gathering data, negotiating access to victims of abuse, and engaging political authorities when abuses are encountered. Insecurity involves its own set of challenges, as dramatized in an interview in the Mogadishu compound of the International Medical Corps in 1992. A bullet hole in the office wall behind the director's head had resulted, he explained, from a shot fired by an employee disgruntled at having been dismissed.

At the headquarters level, interactions within and across organizations require careful management of interpersonal and institutional relationships. Outsiders would be astounded at the amount of time that headquarters staff — and for that matter, field personnel — spend in meetings, sharing information, building consensus, strategizing, trouble-shooting, and making decisions. As a result of the importance of such interactions, agencies are now paying more attention to people skills. NGO managers are developing more explicit career pathways and criteria for internal promotion, based on a combination of education, training, and experience.

The four sets of competencies are, to an extent, overlapping and mutually reinforcing. The challenge of functioning in countries upon which international economic sanctions have been imposed illustrates the need for a skill set that embraces management, technical, contextual, and interpersonal skills.

Our studies of the impact of sanctions in countries such as Iraq, Haiti, former Yugoslavia, and Burundi found aid personnel in a unique position to monitor those impacts on vulnerable populations, though they often lacked the *technical expertise* or agency mandate to do so. *Contextual expertise* was needed to track the impacts of sanctions on the country's political, economic, and social institutions. *People skills* were needed to relate to government officials and populations whom the sanctions affected and to colleagues in other humanitarian agencies. *Management skills* were involved in keeping headquarters apprised of the situation and ensuring the smoothest possible flow of agency resources despite embargoes. Sanctioning authorities needed to approve individually humanitarian items, while arranging shipment and clearance on the receiving end created delays and gaps in the supply and programming chain.

The demands of functioning effectively in sanctioned countries would likely overmatch the generalist aid worker of yesteryear. In fact, the recurring use of sanctions as an instrument and the recurring humanitarian impacts associated with their use point to the utility of developing a specialized cadre of experts who bring accumulated experience and expertise to the specific operational challenges encountered. Such a cadre might avoid the current temptation of concerned staff persons to equate their personal discomfort with sanctions as their agency's disapproval. Moreover, seasoned personnel could assist agencies in articulating legitimate humanitarian concerns about the often disproportionately negative impacts of sanctions on civilian populations. They could also help them develop and utilize the institutional memory now often lacking.

What is true of the special demands of sanctions holds in a broader sense for implementing a humanitarian mandate in every highly conflicted setting. Subsequent case studies bore out our 1992 assessment of the demands on staff functioning within the politicized environment of Central America. "Constraints on access demanded the highest levels of professionalism. Yet even the most seasoned humanitarian organizations and officials were often unable to succeed in the face of events frequently beyond their abilities to control. More often than not, the ability to get things done depended as much on interpersonal skills as on technical competence."[9]

Yet people skills in the absence of contextual expertise can also offer a recipe for disaster. In many settings, relief and rights personnel have demonstrated the difficulty of striking a proper balance between identification with suffering and cultivation of the ability to see the larger picture. Many people find themselves caught up in the injustices experienced by those whom they seek to assist and protect, to the detriment of their own sense of balance and judgment. A special breed of person is required to avoid becoming preoccupied with the frustrations of day-to-day program management at the expense of charting a discerning longer-term course.

Various humanitarian agencies have developed comparative advantages in specific competencies. Governmental and intergovernmental organizations often place a high premium on management expertise and demand it of their collaborators. Technical expertise in specific programming sectors has been cultivated in accordance with their mandates by UN agencies and NGOs (e.g., in food, health, children, and refugees). Private agencies are known for the importance they attach to interpersonal interactions. The ICRC has cultivated an impressive degree of contextual knowledge, negotiation skills, and country-specific contacts. While different genres of agencies may attach different degrees of importance to one skill set or another, a solid and serious commitment to the importance of succeeding at the tasks at hand characterizes the enterprise as a whole. The diversity of competencies provides a persuasive case for orchestrating joint action across the length and breadth of the enterprise.

Conflicting Views

Despite emerging agreement on the four core competencies, differences remain about using the concept of "professionalism" to describe the tools of the humanitarian trade. Many agencies are quite comfortable with the expectation that their employees should function according to established business management procedures. Indeed, agencies receiving significant amounts of government grants and contracts have little choice. Other agencies, however, would prefer to scrap, or at least to modify, the prevailing concept of professionalism. The reasons for doing so include the special nature of the humanitarian imperative, the partnership style of program implementation, and the predominantly Western orientation of accepted business standards.

The humanitarian enterprise, they argue, is not simply another business. Yes, the proliferation of need and of agencies in the post–Cold War era makes it reasonable to speak of the sector as an "industry," with organizations competing in emergencies for market share and in the labor market for staff. Yes, there is a "contract culture" in which NGOs vie with other nonprofits and with for-profit groups for financial and personnel resources. Yes, the political economy of the enterprise injects considerations of agency self-preservation into decision making about humanitarian need. Like their business sector counterparts, humanitarian organizations undeniably have fundamental economic and other institutional interests as well as noble purposes and altruistic values.

Yet the humanitarian enterprise is about more than delivering relief materiel at the lowest per-unit cost. The humanitarian imperative requires relieving suffering wherever it exists, regardless of expense. In complex emergencies, indispensable humanitarian operations mounted in perilous settings may be completely untenable from a business point of view. The neediest people are often isolated in settings where economies of scale and cost per unit do not apply. When human lives are at stake, no expense should be prohibitive. Agency personnel are committed to doing the job well, quite apart from financial incentives and often at great personal risk. The bottom line should be human and not economic, although cost considerations admittedly play a role.

Another set of factors calls into question the embedding of Western management procedures within the prevailing concept of humanitarian professionalism. Humanitarian action in its broadest sense ranges well beyond service delivery. Commitments to building transformative relations with local communities, to empowering people and respecting and promoting diversity, and to addressing root causes of poverty and conflict are not matters of the economic bottom line. Effective personnel find ways of realizing such objectives. They are best selected, equipped, supported, and evaluated not by standard inventories or checklists but with special training, reflective exercises, and ethical accounting procedures.

The partnership approach to implementation provides a case in point. Many NGOs that in an earlier era operated their own overseas relief activities — Lutheran World Relief, World Vision, and Oxfam-US are examples — now seek out implementing partners with local roots, indigenous decision making structures, and accountabilities within their own societies. Such partners — for example, in Mozambique, Zimbabwe, or Guatemala — are anything but analogous to wholly owned subsidiaries of multinational corporations based in Europe or the United States. The "partnership connection" affects — and complicates — everything. For example, staff must nurture the processes of indigenous decision making rather than exercising direct line authority over far-flung field operations.

A related point of tension exists between some approaches to humanitarian action and assumed parallels in international commercial endeavors. Images of professionalism based on models from the Western business sector assume that outsiders know what is best for a country in crisis. "Providing specialist people-services," notes one study, "necessarily implies that [outsiders] have the expertise which the people lack and must transmit it to the people. So the people 'to be developed' [in this instance, to be assisted] start out on an unequal footing." As a result, "the fairly strong human bias towards authoritarianism is legitimized and reinforced through the explicit authority of professional expertise."[10]

The emphasis on technical expertise generated from outside a given conflict mirrors and reinforces the heavy externality of the international humanitarian enterprise itself. Yet this emphasis runs counter to the more mutual approach to decision making and shared responsibility that some agencies seek. A division of labor rebalanced to give more weight to indigenous mechanisms would take the approach suggested in "capacities and vulnerabilities analysis." That approach is based on the affirmation that "outsiders cannot develop others but can help to create an environment and processes that help people on the path to their own development."[11] Traditional Western models of business management, by contrast, assume a more directive approach and impose standards that represent, in essence, a form of control.

Research at the country level has underscored problems associated with a Western-driven approach. Based on a review of the experience in Sri Lanka, our researcher concluded that "The failure of imported accounting and reporting systems in a given community is a failure precisely of these systems and not of the community's ability to use them." The analyst, a Sri Lankan national, made the further provocative observation that once the inappropriateness of the prevailing procedures is acknowledged, "Reinventing these systems can be a powerful exercise in capacity building."[12]

Efforts to make management and organizational structures more "businesslike" encounter resistance from another quarter. Some agencies with roots in the voluntary sector sense a threat to their authenticity as charitable organizations, particularly in the eyes of their donor base of private contributors. Faith-based organizations, for example, have built their philosophy and identity around notions of voluntary service, drawing heavily on the contributions of unpaid or nominally paid — but eminently qualified — personnel.

While "private voluntary organizations" may legitimately be expected to manage their affairs efficiently, the recommendation that humanitarian institutions become more "professional" seems to undercut this core ethos. That expectation is particularly an issue for organizations whose donor base has trouble identifying with agencies that seem big and bureaucratic. NGOs that largely receive their funds from bilateral donors or that function as UN subcontractors are, of course, more comfortable with the mainstream assumptions of professionalism. Tensions between voluntarism and those expectations are clearly less of an issue for bilateral and multilateral agencies as well.

Divergences in the approaches to the requisite tools of the trade are evident in the current debate over accountability. Mainstream humanitarian organizations in recent years have embraced standards of conduct that help ensure basic accountability. These standards are now reflected in such codes as the Sphere Project's Humanitarian Charter and Standards, which provide certain minimum standards in each of "the five basic life-sustaining sectors of disaster response: water and sanitation, food aid, nutrition, shelter and site selection, and health."[13] Such standards represent a positive evolution in the humanitarian enterprise from the former basically live-and-let-live approach to one of agreed industrywide expectations of performance.

Yet the standards remain essentially devoid of a regulatory or enforcement framework. Although the heterogeneous nature of private nonprofit organizations makes them reluctant to move beyond a voluntary and self-policing set of standards, a business model would find the present "accountability of embarrassment" lacking in necessary rigor. Some agencies have also challenged the Sphere approach, fearing that minimum standards will discourage them from doing whatever they can to save lives on the assumption that their best efforts in difficult circumstances may not meet minimum expectations. These agencies are also concerned that failure to meet such standards will give governmental donors a weapon to punish them for problems beyond their control or a smokescreen for politically inspired decisions to withhold funds.[14]

Functioning amid Conflicts

During the past decade, humanitarian organizations have been sharply criticized for contributing to the very conflicts within which they work. The critique raises an analytical question about the extent to which relief and rights activities have indeed fueled the intensity and duration of conflicts to the detriment of their humanitarian purposes. The perceived connection with conflict has also surfaced a policy question regarding the appropriateness of embracing as an explicit humanitarian objective the avoidance of the worsening of conflicts or, more positively, promoting their alleviation or resolution. The debate about humanitarian action and its "conflict connection" has tested the analytical and programming skills of practitioners, challenged social science researchers, and whetted the appetite of critics.

The link between humanitarian activities and the duration of conflicts is not a new one. During World War I, the Belgian Relief Commission was viewed askance by some among the Allied forces who feared that aid provided to civilians in Belgium and German-occupied France would fall into the hands of the German military.[15] Relief flights into Biafra in the 1960s were criticized for keeping alive the Nigerian civil war and extending the suffering of Biafrans. Cold War humanitarian assistance from the United States and the USSR enhanced the capacity of their respective proxies to pursue their often inhumane military and human rights strategies.

If humanitarian action has always had an uncomfortable association with the trajectory of conflicts, only in the 1990s have the specific linkages become a policy issue of ongoing debate. Until perhaps mid-decade, humanitarian actors tended to dismiss such criticisms out of hand, offering humanitarian motivations as an all-purpose defense against any and all conflict connections, real or alleged. As individual conflicts have continued in tandem with humanitarian assistance, however, the question of complicity in such wars has become unavoidable and, indeed, is now part of a far broader critique of humanitarian action.

How is it possible, critics properly ask, to bring international resources into war-torn and resource-poor environments without having any impacts on the conflicts themselves? Faced these days not with short-term crises that respond to in-and-out remediation but rather with complex political emergencies that last for decades, humanitarian actors acknowledge the need to understand and to minimize whatever harm may be associated with their involvement. Developing the competency to chart a discerning course at the nexus with conflict, however, has proved difficult.

The need to develop this competency is evident from the evolution of Operation Lifeline Sudan. At its outset, OLS promoted a ceasefire during which aid was delivered to civilians on both sides of the conflict. By the time of a major UN review in 1996, the initial access agreement had been renegotiated six times and aid had become deeply implicated in the strife.[16] Despite fifteen diplomatic missions, the pattern established in 1989 — generous aid but secondary priority for conflict resolution — became entrenched over time. With war once again engulfing the south, the burden of proof for continuing assistance had shifted. People who claimed that Lifeline had *not* become a prisoner of the war were compelled to demonstrate that the relief effort could accomplish its objectives in such fraught circumstances.[17]

Our own studies confirm that humanitarian action has had a decided impact on the conflicts in which suffering is set. The linkages are reviewed in *Humanitarian Action: The Conflict Connection.*[18] The issue, as we see it, is not whether humanitarian action influences conflicts but to what extent and in what ways. Available data suggests a dynamic interaction between humanitarian programming on the one hand and, on the other, the nature, causes, scale, and particular stage of a specific conflict.

Humanitarian action may exacerbate conflicts through providing resources that are diverted to military purposes or through freeing up local assets that are then committed to military uses. External aid can strengthen the hand of economic actors with criminal agendas or with vested interests in sustaining a particular conflict. Protection of humanitarian operations purchased locally can fuel a conflict and lend an imprimatur to violence as a means of social problem-solving. Outside aid may fan tensions between beneficiaries and nearby local communities that are often excluded from emergency help.[19]

Negative impacts notwithstanding, the criticism of humanitarian action for playing a substantial role in sustaining or exacerbating armed conflicts has been substantially overblown. Indeed, we concluded that "humanitarian aid is seldom a determining factor in the calculations of belligerents." Even in the relatively few situations in which the impacts have been major, whether the alternative of humanitarian disengagement would have had the desired effect of banking or terminating the conflict is unclear. In the final analysis, we found, humanitarian action represents "a rather small element in the complex dynamic of conflict."[20]

How can humanitarian actors develop the tools necessary to understand these conflict connections and adjust agency policy and programs accordingly? Many aid organizations have underwritten and participated in the work of the Local Capacities for Peace Project (LCPP), under the direction of development economist Mary B. Anderson. Her influential book *Do No Harm: How Aid Can Support Peace — or War* has been at the center of efforts by the humanitarian enterprise — and its critics — to understand and address the conflict connection.[21]

Since its inception in 1994, LCPP has sought to answer the question, "How can humanitarian or development assistance be given in conflict situations in ways that, rather than feeding into and exacerbating the conflict, help local people to disengage and establish alternative systems for dealing with the problems that underlie the conflict?" Based on extensive reviews of field experience, LCPP provides aid personnel with practical assistance in accomplishing their humanitarian objectives "without inadvertently undermining local strengths, promoting dependency, and allowing aid resources to be misused in the pursuit of war."[22] During 2001–2, LCPP has helped agencies "mainstream" the lessons identified from recent experience into policy and operations.

The fact that Anderson's signature "do no harm" approach has sparked controversy confirms the sensitivity of the issues and their importance to the future of the humanitarian enterprise. Proponents of the methodology, which seeks to design aid interventions that maximize the "connectors" that continue within societies even as conflicts rage, have found that aid can broaden and nurture indigenous constituencies for peace. Critics have faulted the methodology for oversimplifying the complexities of conflicts, for focusing too narrowly on microlevel action, and for harnessing humanitarian work to broader and ultimately political tasks such as conflict resolution. In addition, critics fear that underscoring the possibility of doing harm may provide a pretext for donors or agencies to reduce life-saving efforts.[23] The LCPP conclusion that "there are always options" to withdrawal of assistance, while heartening from a humanitarian viewpoint, also strikes some as politically naive.[24]

Controversy notwithstanding, many humanitarian organizations are now taking steps to identify and limit the potentially negative impacts of their interventions on conflicts. Strategies for minimizing the conflict connections include selecting relief commodities that are less desirable to belligerents, distributing food in cooked rather than raw form, locating refugee camps away from borders, enlisting widespread participation of beneficiaries in relief programs, and including assistance for local communities not directly victimized by conflicts. On occasion, aid agencies have threatened to withdraw or suspend assistance, although they have seldom followed through or, when they have, succeeded in achieving the changes necessary to allow their activities to resume.

Beyond seeking to avoid negative impacts, some agencies are taking the additional step of designing programs to maximize their contribution to peace and reconciliation. One example is the initiative to reconstruct the town market in Tskhinvali, South Ossetia, where the resumption of trade has had positive spinoffs for both the Georgian and Osset populations in the area.[25] Another example, at a higher level and involving reconstruction rather than emergency aid, is the funding of national Bosnian railway and power grids on the condition that representatives of all three ethnic groups jointly administer the grids.

To date, the most positive synergies between humanitarian action and peace appear to have come at the local rather than national level. The record suggests that "relatively small-scale and contextually sensitive efforts to adjust humanitarian programming in active conflicts may have a positive effect in mitigating the impacts of aid on war. Moreover, carefully delivered transitional assistance may assist in building sustainable peace."[26]

The experience in Central America provides perhaps the best example of positive synergies at the macro level. Our review concluded that "Beyond its immediate benefits, humanitarian action has the potential to contribute to creating a climate in which negotiated settlements to conflicts are possible."[27] This potential was particularly evident in El Salvador but was also true to one degree or another for Nicaragua and Guatemala. By contrast, a worst-case example comes from Nagorno-Karabakh, where there was "strong reason to believe that the lack of [humanitarian] assistance to Karabakh itself reduced the international community's credibility and influence there."[28]

Many humanitarian organizations remain wary, however, about positioning their activities as part of broader efforts to prevent, resolve, or transform conflict. They sense a danger that political conditionalities — for example, tying aid to changed behavior on the part of the belligerents — will intrude on their own mission of providing assistance and protection without extraneous agendas. Organizations acknowledge that the single most important humanitarian contribution to civilians caught in conflict is often resolving the conflict that generates the suffering to which they respond. Still, conflict resolution is rightly viewed as a political process in which humanitarian organizations often play at best an indirect, climate-setting role rather than a direct, mediating one. Conflict resolution requires different skills from those necessary among relief and rights groups seeking only to minimize the conflict connection.[29]

Obstacles and Incentives

Our research to date has identified a number of major obstacles to enhancing the competencies of humanitarian personnel. They include the culture of the organizations, the complexity of the humanitarian enterprise itself, and the uncertainty regarding the payoff in program effectiveness to be gained from achieving higher levels of professionalism. These obstacles, and some corresponding incentives to change, were the subject of discussions convened during the years 1997–99 and reviewed in *Humanitarian Action: Social Science Connections*.[30]

Perhaps the most basic obstacle to nurturing the four core competencies is the ethos of the organizations themselves. The enterprise has traditionally placed a premium on fast-paced responsiveness, rewarding offices and personnel that are engaged in the direct alleviation of suffering. For decades, the "tyranny of the urgent" has been the principal enemy of a more thoughtful approach to the humanitarian task. "In the heat of a crisis, aid workers are hard-pressed to bring their institution's wisdom to bear on a particular challenge. When 'crisis X' is followed in quick succession by 'crisis Y' and 'crisis Z,' retrospection and the implementation of lessons learned remain more or less permanently on the back burner."[31]

One NGO official has criticized his colleagues as "acto-maniacs." NGO staff in particular chafe under institutional priorities that stress delivery of the goods rather than understanding of the context. The premium placed on emergency life-saving action is reinforced by the absence of adequate funding from government underwriters and the public for staff training, policy development, and evaluation. Yet although the "action orientation of humanitarian organizations is unlikely to change significantly, ... it can be balanced by a more reflective approach."[32] In 1993, our *Handbook for Practitioners* suggested a new humanitarian motto: "Don't just do something. Stand there!"[33]

There are indeed some encouraging straws in the wind. "A working assumption behind many aid activities is that crises are short-term and in-depth analysis not possible." In reality, however, as relief and rights groups now acknowledge, "Evidence increasingly contradicts prevailing assumptions. Crises routinely become extended, along with humanitarian activities." The time horizons of agencies and their supporters are beginning to change. If its elapsed time on the ground in a given crisis now exceeds three years, as one relief group has reported, "should activities not be based on more carefully gathered and context-specific information?"[34] The humanitarian challenge is, in the end, more akin to a marathon than to a series of sprints, with the best agencies and individuals pacing themselves in the manner of long-distance runners.

In taking the long view, the humanitarian enterprise can learn something from the U.S. military, which sends military historians along on new deployments of forces. Their presence lays the groundwork for discussions of lessons to be learned upon conclusion of the mission and places personnel on the ground with experiences from other crises. Similarly, the "learning office" proposal of the Active Learning Network for Accountability and Performance in Humanitarian Action (ALNAP) would deploy in an evolving crisis a small cadre of persons familiar with lessons from other contexts that might be applied in the new setting.

A second obstacle to enhancing the competency of the enterprise involves the multifaceted nature of the activities involved. Differentiation of functions within a given agency often results in varying valuations of competencies required of people engaged in policy and operations, at headquarters and the field, and in relief and development units. In ways reminiscent of medieval distinctions between the professions and the trades, relief logisticians are sometimes viewed as "hewers of wood and the drawers of water," in contrast to more senior staff from whom higher levels of "professionalism" are required.

As activities have become more complex, some agencies have had difficulty conveying throughout their ranks that effectively managing a livelihoods program in Somalia requires skills no less important to the humanitarian enterprise than does offering recommendations to the UN Security Council or to a national parliamentary committee. The upsurge of funding available in the 1990s for emergencies, much of it at the expense of longer-term development programming, has also fueled tensions within individual agencies between emergency and development desks. The notion that success requires effective performance by all staff in their respective functions is sometimes lost in the organizational shuffle.

What incentives exist to overcome invidious distinctions? The major one is the value of a cohesive agencywide response in particular circumstances. An MSF press conference in Skopje, Macedonia, on April 9, 1999, challenged UNHCR's request for help from NATO on April 3 in dealing with the outflow of refugees from Kosovo. "NATO is first and foremost a military organization which is currently involved in the conflict and . . . not a humanitarian actor," observed the MSF spokesperson. "Protection and assistance for refugees is the responsibility of the UNHCR."[35] The statement represented an agencywide position, reflecting, staff confirmed, input from headquarters as well as field offices, from advocacy as well as operational units.

Many individual humanitarian organizations are seeking to familiarize far-flung personnel with each other's work and to cultivate more agencywide team effort. Modern computer-based technology has facilitated information flow among staff, wherever they are located and whatever their function. Some senior agency executives based in headquarters have spent countless hours on the road visiting and supporting staff. Training sessions at headquarters and in the field have drawn together persons with differing responsibilities. Rotation policies that set limits on the number of years that a person may remain in headquarters before returning to the field have made a contribution. Some agencies and staff, however, still find the pace of change disappointingly slow.

A third obstacle to enhancing performance concerns the perceived uncertainty regarding the payoff in effectiveness from greater competency. The prevailing tendency — witness the comment of a senior official in one of our debriefing sessions at the UN secretariat in New York — is to approach every crisis as unique. While each new crisis does have idiosyncratic elements, the latest emergency is likely to confront a standard set of actors with a recurrent set of humanitarian challenges.

Treating each crisis as unique also undermines the possibility of applying lessons from one to the next, reinforcing the traditional undercurrent of anti-intellectualism and adhocracy in the humanitarian enterprise. "There is a perceived anti-research environment in many aid agencies. They devote only minimal expenditures to the social science research that might better ground and inform their activities."[36] The lack of serious interest in hardheaded policy analysis and evaluation led one Ph.D. employed by a UN agency to conceal his advanced degree credentials from his colleagues.

In the prevailing culture, thoughtful staff do not feel encouraged to raise knotty policy questions that might slow down emergency response. Their hand would be strengthened if significant evidence were marshaled to demonstrate that "context-knowledgeable programming" is more effective than traditional approaches. Although social scientists and aid personnel charged with lessons-learning activities believe in a positive correlation, evidence that contextual analysis of individual crises results in more effective programming is still fragmentary.[37]

From conversations with humanitarian practitioners, however, have come specific examples of positive links. One Mercy Corps International official noted the contribution of its demographers, who had interviewed refugees at the North Korean border to determine the location and extent of famine in that isolated country. A CARE U.S. official recalled the contribution of a conflict resolution workshop in Sri Lanka to siting new wells in locations that would bridge rather than exacerbate intercommunal tensions. CARE has also incorporated the insights of economists into its livelihoods programs among refugees in Guinea. Casting a retrospective look, the agency has reviewed the extent to which the incorporation of human rights considerations into its work in Afghanistan, Rwanda, the Sudan, and Peru made — or might have made — a positive difference.

Our study on gender, *War's Offensive on Women*, also makes a strong connection between overall program effectiveness and the implementation of policies that are sensitive to women's needs and that enlist them in humanitarian work. "Whenever women gain influence in humanitarian activities, the net result is, at a minimum, a favorable adjustment in the power relations between men and women and an incremental advancement of equality, at least in the short term."[38] Moreover, "Humanitarian organizations have begun to realize that involving women in programmatic activities is 'not solely a matter of equity but, as far as projects are concerned, a condition of their success also.'"[39]

Yet the balance sheet on the linkages between technical expertise and contextual analysis, on the one hand, and effective programming, on the other, includes a negative column as well. Some agencies have stopped short of taking the steps necessary to correct problems documented by inside or outside studies. In one example from the 1980s, two Northern NGOs, having received a painstakingly detailed and overwhelmingly critical review of the negative impacts of donated food and used clothing on the spirit of self-help in two Asian and Caribbean countries, declined to phase down aid shipments as recommended. The principal deterrent was the importance of the support in many U.S. communities generated by material aid donations and collections and the perceived embarrassment to the groups that a course correction would have entailed.

Each of four papers presented at a conference and compiled in *Humanitarian Action: Social Science Connections* confirms the proposition that the professional insights of demographers, anthropologists, and public health specialists can improve the effectiveness of humanitarian activities. One chapter concludes that more accurate estimates of refugee numbers could improve the basis for anticipating major refugee movements, calling forward relief materiel, and planning durable solutions. Yet the most significant constraints to improved enumeration, our analyst concluded, are "less methodological than institutional.... In addition to improving technical training and increasing capacity, a change in attitude and institutional culture among practitioner organizations and donors is essential."[40]

In a chapter on "The Politics of Numbers," another analyst examines the reasons that accurate estimates of refugees are difficult to obtain. His review points out that refugee-sending and -receiving countries have their own reasons for deflating and/or inflating tallies. He concludes that despite recent improvements at UNHCR, "refugee statistics will always be a source of controversy and dispute." Rather than taking the politics out of the enumeration process altogether, he found that the UNHCR approach of increased "professionalization" in dealing with such statistics had improved the agency's effectiveness.[41]

One of the reasons for the lack of conclusive data regarding the link between available knowledge and improved effectiveness is that the agencies do not put such knowledge to good use. Based on his extensive anthropological research that penetrated the secretive world of young Burundian Pentecostals in Dar es Salaam, a third analyst concluded that traditional aid agency programming often neglects the needs of a significant sector of modern African society, urban refugees. Unless international actors adapt their programming, "alienated African youths will continue to pose a serious threat to peaceful, civil, and truly inclusive societies."[42]

The perils of inadequate contextual awareness are also highlighted in the Mozambique experience that a fourth researcher chronicles. An examination of the involvement of humanitarian agencies in the return of Mozambicans from Zimbabwe and South Africa to the Machaze district following the conclusion of the country's civil war in the early 1990s illustrates "how the exclusion of sociocultural factors in humanitarian analysis resulted in significant misinterpretations of data and a failure to understand the demographic distribution and the patterns of refugee return."[43] UNHCR had planned for some two hundred thousand men to return from South Africa to Mozambique, only about a sixth of whom actually did so. Agencies involved in the repatriation failed to understand how prolonged residence in South Africa had changed the economic strategies and social organization of

Mozambican refugees. Many had taken South African spouses and reconfigured their economic life so as to maintain residence in both Mozambique and South Africa, making them uninterested in permanent return.

Available data thus tends to confirm the connection between knowledge of context drawn from social science analysis and effective humanitarian programming. The growing body of evidence about the links between the major competencies and effective humanitarian action is a contribution that analysts in research groups, think tanks, and universities are making. Major disconnects remain, of course, between academic institutions and practitioner organizations. This gap is being bridged, however, as common ground is explored and creative collaboration mounted, in particular between the more field research- and action-oriented people in academia and the more policy-oriented and analytical staff people in the aid agencies.

During the latter part of the 1990s, the field of humanitarian studies has begun to come into its own, its evolution somewhat paralleling the emergence of refugee studies as a discipline a generation ago.[44] Social science disciplines such as demography, anthropology, political science, economics, and public health are now seen as essential building blocks in a more comprehensive understanding of the multisectoral challenges of humanitarian action. Short courses resulting in certificates as well as lengthier degree-conferring programs are now available for practitioners who seek to reflect upon their experience and to design more serviceable frameworks and methodologies for their tasks. Courses in human rights and refugee law at Georgetown and Harvard have filled an important gap, as have initiatives in psychosocial evaluation at Oxford and the University of Pennsylvania.

Despite the favorable trend overall, serious funding issues constrain an increase in staff competence. Many humanitarian organizations have moved cautiously to expand their technical expertise because of the lack of funding for such purposes from bilateral and multilateral agencies and because of their perception that the publicly generated contributions are intended to go for direct relief. Despite the importance of contextual programming, one NGO official has noted, "doing a better job context-wise means little to donors. What counts is the financial books." In the view of another official, if NGOs "were audited on *context* to the same degree as we are on *finances,* we would fail." In recent years, foundation funding has picked up some of the slack, with major commitments from institutions such as the Andrew W. Mellon and Ford Foundations underwriting cross-fertilization between relief and rights agencies and academic institutions.

At the end of the day — and at the close of the fiscal year — people are the key element in the humanitarian enterprise and the most indispensable element in the world's response to suffering and abuse. The conclusion of our Rwanda study may be writ large over other settings as well. "Successful efforts are generally carried out by dedicated and energetic professionals who are well-informed about the complexities of a given situation and well-trained in their respective specialties, pragmatic rather than ideological in approach, and able to draw on institutional experience to adapt strategies and resources to circumstances."[45] This new breed of humanitarian deserves to play an increasingly important role in the enterprise of the future.

Susan George's earlier characterization of the competent humanitarian may not, after all, be an inappropriate model for the new breed, with two provisos. First, the multiple expertise and sensitivity she describes need to be characteristics of agencies rather than lodged in specific individuals. Second, while humanitarian action remains a special calling, dedicated staff should not be viewed as saintly "miracle workers" who perform sleights of hand in altogether impossible situations.

Dilemmas and Discoveries

In upgrading competence, humanitarian organizations face difficult choices. What should be the relative balance between well-informed generalists and technical specialists? Should agencies develop in-house competence or rely on outside consultants? What incentives would encourage seasoned officials to remain in field assignments rather than steering top talent into headquarters assignments? What can be done to develop institutional memory in the face of high rates of personnel turnover? Should an agency develop "signature" sectoral or geographic expertise or instead seek to become identified with more comprehensive and global competence? What data is needed regarding competition and market share to make such choices? What funds are available to upgrade staff functioning? How can greater competence within an international NGO "flagship" agency be transmitted to, and shared by, local counterparts?

Such choices involve dilemmas. Agencies that find relying on outside consultants more economical than developing capacity in-house may suffer on occasion from institutional memory lapses as a result. Also, while concentrating expertise and programming in a given region (e.g., in Africa) may be more cost-effective, stakeholders may still expect their agency to respond wherever an emergency erupts (e.g., in East Timor).

Many organizations are hard-pressed to nurture under their own roofs a full array of resident experts knowledgeable in such areas as gender relations, demography, community politics, household organization, and socioeconomic activity. Importing outsider consultants, even given the significant costs involved in orienting them to the agency, may be more cost-effective. Often agencies prefer to go back to consultants already retained to capitalize on their familiarity with the organization and its particular approach to the issues. University-based expertise may be less expensive than consultant firms, although university overheads may themselves be prohibitively high.

Similarly with respect to training, agency staff are more familiar with their own organization and how to get things done, though they may be less specialized in technical areas of competence. Conversely, outsiders may be more skilled — but also more lacking in a sensitivity to agency culture. Some NGOs have sought the best of both worlds by cultivating ongoing relationships with universities on whose faculties some of their former employees now serve. Some agencies have found that holding training sessions in the field where programming choices are faced have special relevance and utility.

Generally applicable expertise such as international human rights law or statistical analysis is easier to develop than context-specific knowledge, which requires familiarity with the complexities of particular settings. Some expertise has universal aspects, such as public health, microcredit, psychosocial intervention, and conflict resolution, but requires context-specific knowledge for application. Counseling rape and trauma victims requires both cultural savvy and highly skilled psychological training.

The prevailing emphasis on technical expertise, while a positive development, raises fundamental questions regarding a given agency's niche within the wider humanitarian enterprise. Is cultivating selected areas of programming preferable to functioning across a wider range of activities? Each option has consequences. While some agencies have narrowed their sectoral or geographic focus, others have affirmed their generalist orientation. "The competent generalist," observes one long-time practitioner, has "the wisdom to know when specialist skills are required and whence they can be mobilized."

The social sciences, a potential boon to agency operations, are no panacea, having their own sets of costs and benefits. Partnerships between practitioners and social scientists take time to nurture. There are areas of convergence between the two, but also tensions to be addressed. Academics often have little patience for the ground rules that humanitarian agencies impose on research, while the agencies return the favor with a lack of patience for detailed and nuanced reports. Even though some differences of agendas and approach may be resolved, expectations that relief and rights personnel should function as professional social scientists or that social scientists will become card-carrying humanitarians constitute a recipe for confusion and misunderstanding.

The steady stream of people moving into and out of humanitarian agencies from year to year and crisis to crisis, particularly at the field level, undercuts investments in staff education and training and undermines agency efforts to develop institutional memory. "Personnel turnover is extremely rapid and the majority of field-workers are young and have a relatively short 'lifetime' in the field," observes Danida's Niels Dabelstein, a longtime evaluator of UN, bilateral, and NGO work. "Hard-learned lessons are not passed on."[46]

The fact that experienced personnel often move on to other humanitarian agencies means that their experience and the training invested in them are not lost to the enterprise altogether. Yet individual agencies may still come up short in the skills necessary for mounting certain programs. While organizations may seek to retain their most capable staff, there are limits to incentives in the form of salaries, benefits, and working conditions to discourage personnel turnover.

While the expectation that headquarters personnel will rotate regularly through field assignments encourages greater mutuality and skill-sharing, the fact that many field postings are in settings where the presence of family dependents is not encouraged limits the value of the policy. The most experienced people are often not available when and where they are most needed: in volatile settings in the field. Meanwhile, headquarters officials, who march to different drummers — or, in the case of CEOs, beat different drums — are often inadequately aware of the dilemmas their colleagues face on the front lines.[47]

Seasoned people who can manage operations amidst insecurity are the backbone of effective humanitarian organizations and an agency's most precious resource. That said, "infatuation with experience" can represent a professional liability. Aid officials point out that involvement on the front lines of many previous crises does not automatically credential a person for coping with the latest emergency. Experience must be balanced with expertise, and the two are not interchangeable. In broad compass, one veteran of both UN and NGO tours of duty concludes, "good people have disproportionate influence."

Humanitarian action during the past decade has been a growth industry, with many new personnel joining the ranks. More recently, however, the availability of personnel in relation to positions to be filled has increased. It is not uncommon for several hundred people to apply for a single vacancy. In mid-2001, the Danish Refugee Council received 192 applications for the position of program manager in Angola, hardly the agency's most coveted assignment.

The current situation of apparent oversupply has its benefits to employers, who can insist on specific skill sets and may enhance organizational competence as a result of a newly selective process of hiring. From the standpoint of well-motivated but less experienced applicants, however, the hiring scene has its obvious frustrations. In a broader sense, the humanitarian enterprise has yet to come to terms with an ongoing structural problem: the alternation of rapidly expanding need for personnel, followed by reduced demand for humanitarian services. Developing rosters of people available on short notice and the signing of memoranda of agreement between UN agencies and NGO personnel suppliers are steps in the right direction.

Within a given agency, a certain circularity is involved in developing staff competence. On the one hand, seasoned field staff are essential; on the other, recruits without field experience will never become seasoned without being given operational responsibilities. Some NGO executives and agencies are known in the trade for providing opportunities for newcomers, gambling on good people without previous overseas experience.[48] Rejecting all persons without prior experience and professional credentials would, of course, make little sense. However, recalling the earlier discussion, neither would staffing an agency largely with ex-rock band engineers and ex-volcanologists trying their hand at humanitarian activities for the first time.

While developing sensitivity to a particular country context is necessary, familiarity may breed contempt rather than competence. Interviews with aid personnel in the Caucasus found staff so cynical about the ineptness of one or another government that they rejected out of hand the possibility of any new programmatic initiatives. Conversely, some personnel may develop such close working relationships with their local interlocutors that they lose the requisite objectivity and compromise their ability to make independent judgments. Cynicism and overidentification with the local scene alike correlate with personal burnout, questionable judgments, and uneven performance.

To counteract the loss of objectivity that working in highly politicized situations can exact, our Karabakh study recommended "the rotation of personnel within and across the region and the closer coordination of programs on a regionwide basis to enhance accountability and transparency."[49] Many humanitarian organizations now have policies that encourage or require staff rotation, exposing them to a variety of viewpoints on a given conflict. One international NGO found that although it was not able to include members of the respective minority on its indigenous staff in either Armenia and Azerbaijan, meetings held at the regional level offered the possibility of bridging such differences in a more neutral setting.

In sum, the tools of the humanitarian trade are increasingly well understood. The first post–Cold War decade has seen a promising beginning in developing these tools. The humanitarian enterprise of the future needs to enhance its competence in the areas identified as an investment in improved effectiveness.

9

The Dynamics of Institutional Change

In March 1996, the long-awaited five-volume multidonor review of the international response to the Rwanda crisis was released at a UN press conference hosted by the Danish government. Briefing the UN press corps earlier the same morning, the spokesperson for the secretary-general had summarily dismissed the study. The detailed report, the most extensive ever undertaken of a major humanitarian response, contained "some serious inaccuracies," she observed, "which lend [it] almost a revisionist flavor."[1] The ranking UN humanitarian official, Under-Secretary-General for Humanitarian Affairs Yasushi Akashi, later acknowledged that the report provided some "useful insights."

In 1999, an independent inquiry launched with the blessing of the Security Council by Secretary-General Kofi Annan, who had directed UN peacekeeping operations at the time of the Rwandan genocide, confirmed many of the earlier report's conclusions.[2] In accepting the findings of his own inquiry, Annan acknowledged the failure of the United Nations and its member states to prevent the genocide and expressed his "deep regret." He welcomed "the emphasis which the Inquiry has put on the lessons to be learnt from this tragedy, and the careful and well-argued recommendations it has made with the aim of ensuring that the United Nations can and will act to prevent or halt any other such catastrophe in the future."[3]

The dynamics of institutional change, a leitmotiv of research by the project during the years 1997–2000, is the subject of this chapter. Faced with events of major consequences, the humanitarian enterprise has, by and large, responded haltingly and inadequately. This chapter also reflects on the contribution of the project itself to the change process and identifies a research agenda for the future.

The Process of Change

Change within any given set of institutions — be they multinational corporations, the international Olympics, or the humanitarian enterprise — generally reflects a variety of influences. In the humanitarian sphere, reforms in policy and practice reflect such diverse elements as the demands of rapidly evolving emergencies, the leadership of individual agencies at headquarters and field levels, pressures from parliaments and public constituencies, the competition of a crowded aid marketplace, the recommendations of evaluations and policy reviews, and the scrutiny of the media. "Considering the extensive literature that has developed over the last decade on organisational learning," concludes one analysis, "there are surprisingly few previous studies of learning in the humanitarian sector."[4] As in other fields, the effort to establish cause-and-effect connections raises complicated methodological issues.

Is the perception that relief responses need to be placed firmly within a human rights context — one of the more far-reaching conceptual breakthroughs of the decade — primarily the result of the problems of delivering relief in the Goma camps in Zaire, of bruising public and private battles between relief and rights advocates about the relative importance of assistance and protection, of the UN secretary-general's mandate that human rights be mainstreamed throughout all UN activities, of new work done on international humanitarian and human rights issues by international legal experts, or of some combination of the above?

Is the more reflective and less reflexive approach to humanitarian action that has emerged during the past decade the result of the perils of ensuring the security of civilians and humanitarian personnel in volatile settings, the formidable task of choosing the least flawed among inadequate options, critiques by evaluation teams, a failure of nerve within the humanitarian establishment itself, and/or alleged "donor fatigue" among governments and the general public with recurrent crises? Once again, while contributing factors and forces can be identified, establishing the comparative importance of specific change agents is difficult.

The role of the oft-cited and oft-hyped "CNN factor" in selected crises offers an instructive case in point. Media coverage of major emergencies during the decade undoubtedly contributed to changes in humanitarian policy and practice. However, some caveats are in order as well. Our studies of Liberia, northern Iraq, Somalia, former Yugoslavia, Haiti, and Rwanda confirmed key media roles in establishing or changing the terms of humanitarian engagement. Yet media influence in each particular crisis was a function of a highly individualistic interplay between the media and two other institutional actors: government policy makers and humanitarian organizations.

Where policy directions were already fairly well set, as in former Yugoslavia in 1992–93, media influence was quite limited. In that conflict on matters such as stepping up the level of international military engagement, "Strategic policy...proved largely immune from media influence." However, "peaks of shocking news coverage...produced heightened international reactions that have influenced the tactics used by governments and the United Nations." "U.S. airdrops of aid, emergency medical evacuations from Sarajevo by the UK, and even NATO's protection measures for the Bosnian capital were all responses to well-televised predicaments. In retrospect, these actions appear to have been exercises in damage control in response to public exposure of governmental impotence instead of key elements in established or evolving policy."[5] While policy changed, the media was only one of several influences at work.

In other settings such as Somalia and Haiti, where greater confusion and uncertainty characterized the response of government officials and aid agencies, the media's influence proved more substantial. In Rwanda, a media blitz led to an aid crusade, but with the genocide taking by surprise policy makers and aid institutions as well as the media. In the case of Liberia, an absence of media coverage had no apparent effect on the ample levels of international assistance provided. The concept we proposed of the "crisis triangle" allows for a nuanced understanding of the dynamic relationship among the three sets of institutions, whether strategic or tactical, long- or short-term, and varying across the phases of an evolving crisis.

Reflecting the complex set of relationships, our recommendations for improving interaction with the media were addressed to each of the three sets of institutions individually and to the institutional triangle as a whole. Government officials can strengthen their hand by clarifying generic policies related to complex emergencies and by acting on the early warning signs of crises. Aid agencies may advance their interests through nurturing productive interactions with governments and the media. The media may strengthen its contribution by improving the quantity and quality of its coverage of humanitarian concerns. Improved management of the interactions may result in better policy, better action, and better coverage in, and public understanding of, humanitarian crises.[6]

In view of this experience, glib generalizations crediting the media with being *the* major factor in the response of the humanitarian enterprise, or *the* driving force in producing policy changes are not useful. The change process is indeed complex, with many currents and cross-currents. As a result, more may be said about the areas of institutional change than about calibrating the forces and factors that have produced it.

The Record

The first post–Cold War decade has been a time of challenge and reflection. The well-documented difficulties that the humanitarian enterprise has experienced have translated into a greater willingness to review policies and programs with an eye to improving performance. In fact, "One of the most notable features of the decade has been the effort to learn and the recognition of the importance of the role of information."[7]

The enterprise has made a variety of institutional changes to address the recurring challenges of the post–Cold War era. Already mentioned have been the framing of relief responses in terms of rights rather than needs, the more thoughtful and contextual approach to the conduct of humanitarian activities, and the greater attention to the media's potential contributions. Other changes include more regular information sharing and improved early warning mechanisms; greater clarity in terms of reference and division of labor among humanitarian agencies and between them and political-military actors; fuller understanding of the interplay among humanitarian action, politics, and conflicts; wider support for institutional advocacy on humanitarian issues; and greater attention to the competencies and performance of humanitarian personnel.

Changes such as these cover a wide spectrum, ranging from conceptual understandings to day-to-day activities, from agencywide policies to country-specific operations, from senior managers at headquarters to far-flung field staff. Some changes identified in earlier chapters — examples include affirming the importance of strengthening local capacity and framing claims on humanitarian action in terms of rights — have been embraced at the policy level but are only beginning to reshape operational activities. Other changes have been confirmed in new standard operating procedures and are reinforced in regular training events and individual performance reviews.

Looking back over the decade, however, the prevailing impression that emerges from our various studies concerns not the wide-ranging and thoroughgoing nature of institutional reform but rather its paucity and superficiality. The experience with issues of gender and participation offers something of a microcosm of the difficulties encountered.

"Some organizations have engaged in conscious attempts to learn from their mistakes and to develop tools for gender programming so that staff members do not continually reinvent the wheel," concludes Julie Mertus in *War's Offensive on Women.* "Agencies are also increasingly aware that they must listen to the needs of local populations and include both local women and men in the design of projects. The results in terms of inclusiveness have been uneven, however, and systematic feedback of gender programming has been, at best, inconsistent. Agencies continue to repeat the same mistakes even as they stumble ahead."[8]

That being said, relief and rights groups often express a willingness to change. Individual organizations have created "Lessons Learned Units," which have in turn commissioned "lessons learned" reviews. Such exercises, though, often simply identify lessons, which then require translation into revised policies and programs. Some analysts have even suggested that lessons-learned units work to defuse pressure for institutional change rather than focusing or orchestrating it. In any event, in the change arena, cosmetics often wins out over serious reform.

A case in point is the study that OCHA commissioned in 2000 at the request of the Inter-Agency Standing Committee, mentioned in chapter 2. *Humanitarian Coordination: Lessons from Recent Field Experience* was undertaken to "summarize the existing and considerable literature on the subject, examine the most recent efforts at humanitarian coordination, and make recommendations for the best ways forward." In reality, the eighty-nine-page study documents failure by the UN and the humanitarian enterprise to follow up on a host of earlier reviews, both global and country-specific.[9]

Indeed, the laconic reception of this latest study offers little hope that its recommendations will be implemented. The reception, however, reflects the larger issues besetting OCHA, the agency in which UN systemwide lessons-learning functions are vested. A full decade after the creation of the first UN coordinating office with global responsibilities, the Department of Humanitarian Affairs, its successor is still struggling with the tasks not only of orchestrating coordination but also of defining "coordination" itself.[10]

Resistance to change, whether by institutions or individuals, is by no means unique to the humanitarian sector, as students of the behavior of international corporations and the international Olympic movement can attest. Yet, as noted in the previous chapter, a number of elements quite specific to the culture of humanitarian organizations constitute significant impediments to learning. One obstacle is the fast-paced nature of the enterprise, which puts a premium on quick action rather than on analysis and reflection. Another is the tendency to approach every crisis as unique, devaluing earlier experience and leading to the repetition of earlier mistakes. A third is a certain defensiveness to criticism. Some criticism is legitimate, but some takes aid organizations to task for factors over which they have little control. Finally, there is a lack of clear accountability, even for factors over which a given organization or individual does exercise control.[11]

The dynamics of institutional learning among humanitarian institutions suggest the need for a concerted strategy of bringing about greater structural change. Recent successes achieved in human rights–based humanitarian action, IDPs, and land mines enlisted multiple players over an extended period of time in the pursuit of carefully identified goals. Effective strategies can provide incentives for overcoming structural constraints: for example, rewarding the application of lessons identified or encouraging more tough-minded and wide-ranging discussion of programming options.

Yet often, change comes about in quite idiosyncratic fashion. The decision by a large U.S.-based NGO to shut down its operation in the UN's Goma camps in late 1994 provides a case in point. Based on the Goma debacle, the role of relief organizations in "feeding the killers" has become perhaps the single most-examined episode in post–Cold War humanitarian action. Among the factors commonly viewed as contributing to the willingness to continue to provide relief have been the need for international visibility, ignorance of the fact that the camps were peopled with *genocidaires,* the influence of UNHCR and the "contract culture," the view that reducing aid would not reduce the level of conflict, and of course the evident needs of civilians in the camps for food.

Why did the NGO in question decide to remove its staff and suspend its Goma operations? Its president and chief of operations together reached a decision in a brief weekend phone conversation when they realized they could no longer answer the misgivings of their staff in the field. The decision, they explained later, was surprisingly simple and straightforward. The result reversed institutional momentum generated by months of high-profile relief activity that had mobilized many resources for the Goma operation. Neither before nor after the decision, however, did the NGO in question, or NGOs as a group, follow or develop any guidelines for disengagement. As a result, the decision remained highly circumstantial, offering little institutional guidance for the future.

Impetus for change, highlighted by major crises and illuminated by media coverage, soon gives way to institutional lethargy. In fact, the post–Cold War moment of opportunity to make serious structural reforms may have been lost as humanitarian organizations have somehow managed to muddle through one major crisis after another.

Kosovo provides an example. Despite serious problems such as the bilateralization of assistance at the expense of the United Nations and the use of military forces of NATO, a belligerent in the conflict, for humanitarian work, the Kosovo experience produced few fundamental changes in the humanitarian enterprise. Such issues have come back to haunt the enterprise in Afghanistan, as discussed in the epilogue that follows. Yet how essential is fundamental change, cynics ask, if time and again the enterprise somehow manages to avoid total disaster?

In putting the best face on unsuccessful operations, aid officials sometimes fall back on the nostrum that imperiled people usually manage to cope with difficult situations, with or without help from the international humanitarian apparatus. While they have a point, as confirmed in chapter 4, their approach risks denigrating the importance of the humanitarian enterprise. The situation highlights a recurring dilemma. Organizations must dramatize the reality of need in a given crisis so as to mobilize action without overstating the extremity of the situation. If they understate the need, the necessary resources may not be forthcoming; if they hype the situation, they are accused of having played fast and loose with the data.

Testifying before a U.S. congressional committee in September 1992, five months after taking charge of the newly created UN Department of Humanitarian Affairs, Under-Secretary-General Jan Eliasson pleaded for time to make the necessary changes and for political support from donor governments while doing so. "I hope you still give me the benefit of the doubt, and a grace period," he said, "because it is not easy to turn an ocean liner." To the amusement of the gathering, the committee chairman obligingly offered him two weeks to introduce the necessary reforms.[12]

Speaking with the benefit of hindsight, the good ship *Humanitarian Enterprise* has not undergone the fundamental course corrections that the changed circumstances in the wider world during the past decade have warranted. Meanwhile, the humanitarian community and the wider cast of diplomatic and military actors increasingly feel the onus of fashioning a system that more effectively addresses the world's assistance and protection challenges. The humanitarian apparatus is too massive and expensive to have only occasional successes to set against many neutral-to-negative impacts.

The Role of Policy Research

As social scientists, our research group has been particularly interested in the contribution to institutional change that studies and reports have made, whether by relief and rights agency staffs or by outside consultants and research groups.[13] In the case of IDPs, research carried out at the Brookings Institution by the UN secretary-general's special representative and his team played an important contributing role.[14] In the case of the land mines convention, the ICRC and Halo Trust studies on the actual impacts of mines in the field successfully undercut the credibility of high-level statements by government officials that minimized the human costs.[15]

Recurrent difficulties in functioning in internal armed conflicts have arguably contributed to a greater openness among relief and rights groups to input from research and evaluations. Serious institutional resistance has also been encountered, though, reflecting such factors as the risks of attempting new approaches, the need for persuading stakeholders and constituencies of the need for change, the difficulties of communicating new directions to staff and of training people with the necessary new skills, and of course bureaucratic inertia.

With respect to coordination, where institutional resistance to change has proved fierce, the latest UN-commissioned report "set out in some detail the recurring picture over a decade of UN humanitarian agencies whose governance structures, funding sources, weak management and institutional cultures all constitute obstacles to effective coordination."[16] The multivolume Rwanda evaluation also documented the internecine struggle: "agencies competed for the limelight, accusing others of poor performance and complaining that their agency did not receive adequate attention. When the draft report was presented, however, agencies — particularly those within the UN — closed ranks: co-ordination and co-operation problems...were down-played."[17]

In some instances, senior management has promoted change but field staff have resisted it. Such was the case with UNICEF's emphasis on the rights of the child and rights-based country programming. In other instances, pressure for change has originated on the front lines, only to encounter resistance from higher-ups in headquarters. A case in point involves efforts by some NGOs to devolve greater decision-making authority and accountability to their counterpart agencies in crisis areas.

Individual institutions have encountered their own internal obstacles to fundamental change. A UNDP official interviewed during the Iraq crisis in 1992 made the observation that "it is beyond the capacity of the United Nations to reorganize itself. But governments do not allow the UN to organize itself rationally either."[18] That is, change often requires the support of donors, who may or may not be so inclined. NGOs frequently speak of the perceived resistance they encounter to upgrading the quality of their programs from boards of directors, public constituencies, and donors. Managing such tensions requires strategies that engage progressive forces both within various organizations and beyond, an approach that has indeed been taken in a number of successful change initiatives.

In the broad process of institutional change, the role of evaluations and policy reviews is, on balance, quite modest. Even parties that carry out such studies caution against attributing too much influence to their handiwork. Task forces or working groups within or among agencies may play a more significant role in adapting policies and procedures to emerging needs. Managers, even at the most senior level — some would say, particularly at the most senior level — often do not have, or take, the time to ponder findings and recommendations presented to, and sometimes even commissioned by, them.

If the role of evaluations in institutional change is modest, even more so is the contribution of individual studies.[19] The multidonor evaluation of the international response to the Rwanda crisis to which the secretary-general's spokesperson responded so disparagingly in the opening vignette is doubtless the most comprehensive and detailed review ever conducted of a single humanitarian initiative.[20] The review's direct costs were some $2 million. (The price tag would be even higher if it included the costs of individual agency staff, whose time, travel, and support costs were underwritten by their own organizations.) Study 3 on emergency assistance, which cost $580,000, was "a veritable Rolls Royce of humanitarian evaluation with unprecedented resources available to it," commented team leader John Borton.[21]

Thirty-eight humanitarian agencies and coalitions were represented on the steering committee; some fifty-two consultants and researchers were engaged in the study itself. The report had five volumes, each the product of teams of highly skilled personnel. (The fifth, with which I was associated, provided an overview of the previous four.) The multidonor study was followed by a review of the changes that had taken place during the year after its unveiling in March 1996.[22] The wrap-up session of the steering committee in early 1997 highlighted the progress made, noting some of the methodological difficulties encountered in tracking impacts.

Of the thirty-eight UN organizations, government aid agencies, NGOs, and others comprising the steering committee, nineteen had responded to the request for information about the study's impact. They reported that their institutions had discussed or acted upon more than half of the report's sixty-four recommendations. More progress had been made on technical than on structural matters, some of it even preceding the release of the report itself. The joint evaluation, the group concluded, was "more a process than an event" or a product. Indeed, among its constructive contributions was to reinforce processes of positive change that were already under way.

Some observers credit the Rwanda study with more significant change than the data reviewed in 1997 might indicate. "The Joint Evaluation has influenced policy in UN forums, multilateral agencies, national governments and their official bilateral donors arms and individual NGOs," concluded one analyst in 1999. "All told the instruments created by the international humanitarian community in the wake of Rwanda cover everything from the proper methods of oral and intravenous rehydration to the appropriate ways to advertise for donations."[23]

The chairman of the study's steering committee, Niels Dabelstein, has remarked that the value of the study "lies in the comprehensiveness of its analysis and thus in the validity of lessons learned. . . . [It] showed the synergy which exists between different agencies cooperating, therefore amplifying the power of lessons and recommendations it documented."[24] The team leader for the emergency assistance volume, John Borton, calls its impact "considerable." In his judgment, "it was able to show that humanitarian aid had been used, in this particular case, as a substitute for more effective political and military action to confront the *génocidaires;* that the UN system for providing and coordinating international humanitarian assistance was structurally flawed; and that the accountability mechanisms within the international humanitarian system were extremely weak."[25]

Yet the Rwanda study has been associated with only limited structural reform in the international humanitarian apparatus and, as of 2002, momentum to implement its recommendations has waned. It did succeed in documenting many policies and procedures that are now accepted as requiring change. The current UN secretary-general has accepted many of the criticisms made in the original study, in marked contrast with the initial reception to the multidonor evaluation.[26]

Perhaps the most enduring outcome of this "mother of all evaluations" is the Active Learning Network for Accountability and Performance in Humanitarian Action (ALNAP).[27] An organization composed of representatives of government, UN organizations, NGOs, think tanks, and academia, ALNAP meets twice yearly to review developments, share proposed research undertakings, and promote greater accountability. Founded in 1997 and now emerging as a focal point for lessons-learning, ALNAP has developed a database on which evaluations of humanitarian programs are available, a template for conducting such studies, and training resources. ALNAP has also launched an annual review series that seeks to "advance understanding and thinking on learning, quality, and accountability issues."[28]

The Contributions of the Project

Following a discussion of the limited impacts of the mammoth multidonor Rwanda study, assessing the influence of the far more modest Humanitarianism and War Project may seem odd. Yet in such a book as this, asking about the project's role in promoting institutional change is fair. While in the grand scheme of things the project cannot claim to have played a major role, it has been associated with the general ferment of the decade on humanitarian issues in policy, practitioner, and academic circles and with several specific reforms.

A consultant retained in 1996 to evaluate our initial five years of work found that our stakeholders credited us with "raising levels of interest and discussion on the subject of humanitarianism and war. The Project is recognized for having called attention convincingly to policies, practices and performance of international 'humanitarian actors' in crisis situations and, in particular, on the often complex articulating of these policies, practices and performance with those of other actors."[29] A survey conducted in 2000 by the London-based Overseas Development Institute found the project's publications to be the single most recognized series of materials among humanitarian practitioners in both Europe and America.

Users of our materials have expressed appreciation for the effort to engage the views of practitioners, the timeliness of individual studies, and the nuanced formulation of issues. Some, however, have also taken exception to our "judgment calls." We have been challenged for expecting too much from humanitarian institutions, not acknowledging the dilemmas they face, overreacting to the problems of coordination, and overstating the effects of politicization on the integrity of humanitarian activities.

Throughout our work, we have sought to use the accepted principles of social science research and have introduced safeguards, described in chapter 1, to guard against bias. Yet we acknowledge that a process of selectivity is necessarily involved, affecting individual studies as well as the project as a whole. That selectivity has a bearing on our selection of crises for review (for example, Sierra Leone rather than East Timor); on our choice of issues (coordination rather than cost-effectiveness); and our identification of persons and organizations to be interviewed (more aid agency staff than refugees). Different choices would have produced different findings and conclusions. The credibility of our work among practitioners and policy makers is therefore probably a more telling characteristic than its objectivity.

On occasion we have been caught up in the politicization that affects the humanitarian activities we describe. Our review of the Nagorno-Karabakh conflict detailed the intrusion of politics into humanitarian action, including the influence of the Armenian diaspora on the ground rules for U.S. assistance to both Armenia and Azerbaijan. NGOs were particularly appreciative of this feature of the study. We also noted in our report that "in apparent retaliation for views expressed in earlier writings," the Armenian government had denied entry to one of our researchers.[30]

A review of our report in the *Journal for the Society of Armenian Studies* took us to task, both for our comment about the visa denial and, more broadly, for "a certain bias" favoring Azerbaijan over Armenia. "An occupational hazard of either working in the Caucasus or writing about it," commented the reviewer, "is the strong inclination to forgo scholarly objectivity and promote an agenda for one side or another."[31] We sought to set the record straight in the journal's next issue. "Objectivity in scholarship, like neutrality in humanitarian action," we wrote, "is as essential as it is difficult to achieve."[32] Indeed, highly politicized emergencies represent hazardous ground for researchers as well as for practitioners.[33]

Broadly speaking, the impacts of our work to date have been modest at best. We take some credit for having framed and promoted the concepts of humanitarian action and humanitarian space and for research detailing interactions with the military, media, and political spheres. The UN system now accepts a number of our recommendations concerning a methodology for assessing the impacts of economic sanctions. Our approach to policy reviews has, we are told, led to a broadening of the prevailing indicators used in evaluations, which now include such factors as coherence and connectedness as well as the more traditional categories of efficiency and impact.[34] We have also contributed to the evolving spirit of critical reflection within the humanitarian enterprise.

A distinction by ALNAP has a certain relevance here. In finding that "the behaviour of organisations is often not influenced by evaluations," ALNAP notes that "evaluation forms only one of the mechanisms by which humanitarian organisations learn. . . . Learning can and does take place separately from evaluation." In fact, while evaluations and policy reviews may serve to enhance accountability, the process of identifying and implementing lessons from experience is a more extended and complex process, with many parties involved. In that wider effort, the project has, by most accounts, played a positive role.

A Research Agenda for the Future

Reference was made earlier to a series of discussions among U.S. NGOs in 1985–87 on the politics of humanitarian action and the professionalism of the people engaged in humanitarian work. The conclusion fifteen years ago was that "Continuing attention to issues of humanitarian policy and practice constitutes essential unfinished business for the [humanitarian] community in the years ahead."[35]

In the intervening years, a veritable sea change has occurred in both policy and practice. Issues gingerly identified during the mid-1980s have received substantial scrutiny from an array of research groups and from an increasingly self-analytical humanitarian enterprise itself. In fact, one of the defining differences in the post–Cold War era is the new level of interest in the humanitarian enterprise: its mandates, organization, effectiveness, and accountability.

In the course of our research, a number of issues have emerged that bear further study. Here are some samples:

Principle and Pragmatism

Humanitarian organizations frequently debate the relative merits of pragmatic rather than principled approaches to the dilemmas confronted in the field. For the moment, pragmatists have the upper hand. The burden of proof is currently on those, for example, who caution against compromising neutrality and impartiality as the price for humanitarian access.

A study of the dilemmas that practitioners face in managing the tensions between principle and pragmatism would bring additional concreteness to the debate. Of the paradigms available for understanding the relationships between humanitarian action and politics identified in chapter 5, which have proven the most effective in terms of producing real gains in assistance and protection? Our own data, which remains uneven, points toward the longer-term value of adherence to principle, despite acknowledged short-term disadvantages in doing so. A review of the trade-offs could provide strategic guidance to the enterprise, although individual agencies would be free to continue to chart their own courses.

The Political Economy of Humanitarian Action

A subtext of the research conducted to date has been that the humanitarian enterprise has resisted a litany of changes, the need for which have been demonstrated in crisis after crisis, study after study. Improvements in coordination and in strengthening local capacity are cases in point. The political economy of humanitarian organizations plays a significant role in their resistance to change. The humanitarian enterprise reflects major imbalances of power between donors and recipients, between funders and implementers, between Northern and Southern institutions.

Research could help identify the relative importance in shaping humanitarian action of such factors as the competitiveness of the aid marketplace, the availability of donor funding for specific sectors and functions, the lack of funding for other functions such as evaluation and reflection, and the bearing of such factors on agency decision making and effectiveness. Realistic incentives to address the imbalances of power that distort effective programming and to promote change might then be fashioned.[36]

Support for Multilateralism

A recurring theme of our research has been that the politicized nature of internal armed conflicts in the post–Cold War era points toward the need for more effective multilateral humanitarian institutions and for a more thoroughly multilateral cast to the humanitarian enterprise as a whole. The data do not demonstrate, however, that multilateral mechanisms are inherently more effective than bilateral or nongovernmental channels, and indeed in some instances they may not be. The data do suggest that governments' prevailing "a la carte" approach to humanitarian response — using UN agencies, bilateral channels, NGOs, the Red Cross movement, and military troops here or there as they so desire — undercuts effective multilateralism.

Particularly troubling in this respect was the Kosovo experience and its self-fulfilling prophecy: that having retrenched for several years in their support for UNHCR and other multilateral instruments, donors found it necessary to deputize the military forces of NATO, a belligerent in the crisis, to fill emergency aid gaps in Macedonia and Albania. If it is true that "For the most part, donors get what they pay for," additional research might identify some of the benefits and costs of more consistent support of multilateral humanitarian action.[37] Given the tensions arising when an organization of nation-states functioning in politicized settings mounts would-be neutral and impartial humanitarian responses, multilateral solutions outside of the United Nations should also be explored.

The Nongovernmental Component

A mapping exercise would be useful to identify and situate the numbers and functions of NGOs — North and South, foreign and indigenous. Has there recently been an upsurge in the numbers of NGOs operating in humanitarian emergencies or a change in the market share controlled by a few major NGOs? Have NGOs developed greater geographical or sectoral specialization? Is the recommendation useful that a strictly limited number of NGOs, perhaps on a rotating basis, become active in any given crisis?

Research could also shed light on whether the receipt of funds from donors constrains or facilitates NGO advocacy, whether agencies that are more authentically nongovernmental have a comparative advantage operating in politicized conflict settings, and whether more limited acceptance of government funding by NGOs would have a liberating or constricting impact on the evolution of a more balanced and effective humanitarian enterprise.

Research to Support Innovative Programming

Two encouraging changes during the decade involve the use of rights-based programming in relief work and the application of knowledge of country contexts to framing program options. In each instance, although we have encountered examples that link these two approaches to more effective humanitarian action, the data remains sketchy. Additional research on the correlations would be helpful, even though more than social science data will be required to move programming further in those directions.

Comparative Cost-Effectiveness

Coordination discussions frequently affirm the importance of a division of labor in emergencies that respects the "specificities" of individual agencies. Researchers, however, have had difficulty establishing the differential costs and cost-effectiveness of multilateral and bilateral organizations, NGOs, and the Red Cross movement. In wider compass, the costs of utilizing military assets for tasks in the humanitarian sphere are often not available to the public nor calculated according to an agreed-upon framework.

"Attention to financial and cost-effectiveness analysis of humanitarian assistance has been limited due to 'ethical considerations,' particularly, given the difficulties in evaluating the benefits relative to costs," observes one seasoned evaluator. "There seems also to be a pervasive opinion that humanitarian aid is too important to take time out to record what you are doing, to look seriously at how much it cost, or to assess whether it could have been done more cost-effectively."[38]

Research to establish a template and provide data on comparative cost-effectiveness would lend additional concreteness to discussions and could enhance the efficiency of the enterprise. Such research would also be a point of entry into a larger discussion about the optimum shares of the action that the various genres of humanitarian organizations should assume.

Post–Cold War Lessons and the Israeli-Palestinian Conflict

Much of the reflection on humanitarian action during the past decade has focused on high-profile emergencies such as Central Africa and the Balkans; surprisingly little has been directed to the Israeli-Palestinian conflict. That anomaly reflects in part a UN bureaucratic quirk. Humanitarian activities in Israel and the Occupied Territories are the purview of the UN Relief Works Administration (UNRWA), which is not a member of the Inter-Agency Standing Committee. Only recently have those issues surfaced at all on the OCHA agenda.

As a result, many of the concerns that have preoccupied the humanitarian enterprise elsewhere have not been brought to bear on the Israeli-Palestinian conflict, or, conversely, have benefited from the experience there. The challenges are common: humanitarian access, the civilian vs. military character of refugee camps, the connection between humanitarian action and the exacerbation or amelioration of conflict, the influence of the diaspora on humanitarian action, the use of sanctions, and the relevance of international law and norms to the conduct of belligerents. There are many lessons to be learned and applied.

Research issues such as these deserve to be tackled, with findings encouraged and allowed to shape the humanitarian enterprise of the future. It is true that "at present the resources expended on evaluations are minuscule relative to the funds disbursed for humanitarian assistance."[39] At the same time, the cottage industry of humanitarian research that has burgeoned during the past decade does not correlate with commensurate improvements in relief and rights operations. This is the case if one looks at the funds spent on study after study of the Sudan, our own included. It is also the case, if a sweeping generalization be permitted, for the cumulative impacts of the many reviews that have been carried out during the decade. Indeed, "the range of humanitarian evaluation work is rapidly expanding and the gap between practice and guidance is growing."[40]

Our own work has identified a number of impediments to the realization of the institutional changes warranted in the circumstances. One problem is that research groups — for example, those based in North America and those located in Europe — often do not connect with each other. The result is duplication of work and denial of the necessary cross-fertilization of viewpoints and experience. Some of these communications gaps are now being systematically narrowed by ALNAP, as noted above.

A second impediment is the political economy of research itself. The sources of resources for evaluations and lessons-learning exercises influence the research agendas of humanitarian organizations. While the increase in government-funded research on humanitarian and related issues is welcome, a serious question arises as to whether such studies have adequate independence from the political agendas of funders. What government-funded research may gain in policy relevance, or at least in access to policy makers, may be lost in independence, objectivity, and candor.[41] In short, researchers and practitioners both need greater accountability for the impacts of their work on enhancing the effectiveness of the humanitarian enterprise.

Concluding Reflections

We conclude with some brief comments on the need for the more skillful identification and management of the dilemmas of humanitarian action, moving beyond the adhocracy of the 1990s toward a more structured and consistent approach. Greater humility in the process of humanitarian action and reflection is also required.

This ten-year review has sought to identify major dilemmas that relief and rights agencies face in functioning in post–Cold War settings of internal armed conflicts. The discoveries that have emerged involve the need to face rather than ignore tough choices, to assess the costs and benefits of available options, to anticipate consequences, and to make course corrections as necessary. Clear benefits would accrue from closer collaboration within the humanitarian community and more carefully delineated interactions with other actors. Given the dynamics that distinguish one crisis from the next, contextual decision making is essential. Yet recurring challenges faced by a consistent set of actors makes drawing upon past experience critical.

Some dilemmas require a clear choice of one option over others. In the case of collaboration with military forces, humanitarian agencies must choose. As noted by a senior ministry of defense official contributing troops to the NATO force in Kosovo, "Humanitarian organizations can't on the one hand be a beneficiary of military support and on the other hand keep a posture of studied independence."[42] Aid organizations may, of course, delimit their cooperation with the military to certain spheres: for example, accepting responsibilities for providing services in a camp run by the military or utilizing military escorts for aid personnel working in insecure areas. Even limited cooperation, however, has its consequences, which should be better understood from the outset.

Another forced-choice dilemma involves trade-offs between decentralizing authority so as to facilitate strengthening local capacity and ownership, on the one hand, and, on the other, retaining centralized control and accountability, thereby reinforcing the externality of the humanitarian enterprise. Agencies can't have it both ways. Authority is either centralized or decentralized. Authority cannot be decentralized for purposes of nurturing the development of an indigenous organization and centralized for purposes of accountability to Northern stakeholders. A strategy of phased decentralization is of course an option, but the authority must ultimately reside in one place or another.

Other dilemmas lend themselves to a both/and approach. UN agencies have struggled with the tensions between maintaining control in headquarters, thereby ensuring greater consistency and accountability, and devolving authority to senior staff in the field, which makes for more responsive programs. In Ngara, UNHCR enjoyed the best of both worlds, adapting headquarters policies and procedures to reinforce the creative leadership of frontlines staff.

Another dilemma involves the tensions between a rights-based understanding of emergency relief and the more traditional approach to the delivery of life-saving essentials. Aid agencies can utilize the access they enjoy to monitor abuses of human rights, providing the information generated to *bona fide* human rights groups for action. Assistance providers may become more sensitive to rights issues without adopting rights portfolios.

Although the performance of the humanitarian enterprise during the decade is disappointing, the record is not without successes. Highlights include UNHCR's programs for Rwandan refugees in Ngara, Tanzania, and repatriation into Cambodia as part of the UN peacekeeping operation; the negotiation and implementation of a ban on antipersonnel land mines and the expanded protections for IDPs; the initiative by Haitian staff of a Canadian NGO to reconfigure and continue programs, with CIDA's blessing, after the departure of their expatriate colleagues; and the reconstruction of a market town in South Ossetia, where the resumption of trade ameliorated tensions between Georgians and Ossets.

Successes were often the product of serendipities and circumstances, of creative individuals making the best of difficult situations, often without institutional support and stretching their mandates to the limit. Some are microlevel initiatives, with positive features that do not yet characterize broader efforts at, for example, strengthening local capacity or developing synergies between humanitarian assistance and the amelioration of conflict. Others involve changes of global impact and import.

The larger challenge is to follow the past decade of adhocracy with a period of institutional consolidation and reform. Innovation and success need to become the rule, not the exception. Ten years ago, humanitarian personnel often observed that they were functioning — in some cases, floundering — in uncharted waters. We recall one UN official who in 1990 approached Operation Lifeline Sudan activities in areas controlled by the insurgents as "a voyage of discovery." With an eye to tapping experience and regularizing practice, we proposed at a conference in 1991 creating a "checklist for practitioners" to help assure that "new relief efforts avoid past mistakes and do not reinvent discredited wheels."[43]

In our case study on Yugoslavia in 1993, we noted that "novel circumstances pushed many organizations, humanitarian, political, and military alike, beyond traditional missions and standard operating procedures and, in some instances, beyond expertise and comparative advantage."[44] It was here that UNHCR used bulletproof vests and armored vehicles for the first time in a major operation.

In 1994, the UN coordination office in Rwanda "suffered from the absence of a rule book, covering such basic administrative tasks as hiring and deploying staff, the management of funds, reporting requirements, and simple office procedures.... Consequently, much was left to improvisation."[45] Our Sudan study suggested developing "a protocol or checklist of essential components of successful relief or development activities in a zone of conflict."[46] One consistent theme of our recommendations has thus been to regularize the ground rules of agency functioning.

Ten years into the post–Cold War voyage of discovery, the waters are now more fully charted. Humanitarian agencies have developed greater familiarity with regions in which they had no prior experience (the countries of the former Soviet Union are a case in point) and with hot-war settings (Sarajevo and Dili come to mind). Agencies are proceeding with greater discipline, often avoiding areas where they lack comparative advantage and expertise. Many organizations now deal with insurgents as well as with government interlocutors. They have written, or updated, their manuals; their standard operating procedures now address the new challenges.

Humanitarian organizations are engaged in training programs to alert headquarters and field personnel to now-clarified agency policies and procedures. In the area of security, many groups now have standard training modules that address what to do and what to avoid doing when civil strife erupts and agency operations and personnel are endangered. Aid staffs now avail themselves of a wide array of field exercises with military forces. Relief and rights staffs are more in touch.

Some may read the data to suggest that the humanitarian enterprise is doing about as well as can be expected.

- Practitioners are more alert to coordination problems, but for reasons inherent in the institutions involved, coordination authority is unlikely to be expanded significantly. Therefore, the enterprise should do its best in each crisis within the constraints of the particular situation.

- The imbalance between the international humanitarian apparatus and local institutions is natural. If locals had the resources, outside help would not be required. The resources they need will create inequities in the relationship, which should be minimized. Yet humanitarian agencies shouldn't agonize about the intrusive nature of their activities, which are inherent in their task.

- Politics intrude on humanitarian action, distorting the proportionality of allocations and constraining the access that relief and rights personnel enjoy. That is to be expected, as assistance and protection take place on highly political terrain in a highly politicized world. Rather than lamenting the circumstances, humanitarian personnel should cut the deals that do best for their clientele in the circumstances.

- Humanitarian action is indeed becoming militarized, but that is the price for pressing the considerable assets of the military into humanitarian service. Denying the military a major role would do a disservice to people who need help.

- Humanitarian personnel should be trained to function in today's settings of internal armed conflict. People remain human, however, and for all of their dedication and energy, they make mistakes. The enterprise deserves support under duress rather than second-guessing with the wisdom of hindsight.

The data convince me, by contrast, that the humanitarian enterprise can do better in each of these respects. I believe in the need to embrace an approach to humanitarian action that provides clearer and more decisive coordination authority, frames activities more clearly in a legal rights rather a voluntary context, minimizes intrusiveness, seeks to maximize independence from political agendas, and welcomes a security-provision role of the military but not direct hands-on aid functions.

One of the overarching discoveries from the post–Cold War era involves the need for humility in the face of the dilemmas encountered. Humanitarian initiatives are often undertaken with a sense of high purpose and urgency, and indeed the end of the Cold War offered, according to the general view, a golden moment for humanitarian values. A decade ago, humanitarian imperatives enjoyed a new sense of promise.

Ten years later, however, relief and rights organizations have moved away from earlier delusions of humanitarian grandeur, whether their own or those of policy makers and the international public. Organizations now embrace a more sober assessment of their task and its obstacles. A recurrent theme of experiences in places such as Rwanda, Somalia, Cambodia, the former Yugoslavia, and the Balkans is that such crises "are generated by forces which, in the final analysis, respond to neither humanitarian nor military remedies. Understanding the limitations on coercion and kindness alike may be the beginning of wisdom in the post–Cold War era."[47]

That lesson is still being learned. Many humanitarian personnel still approach their next engagement with a mixture of commitment and hesitation, with personal energy but contextual innocence. Finding a balance that avoids triumphalism on the one hand and faintheartedness on the other is proving difficult. More difficult still is the process of making the structural changes needed in the architecture of the humanitarian enterprise to meet the claims for assistance and protection of civilians wherever they find themselves across the globe.

Humility is good advice not just for the humanitarian enterprise but also for people who study it. Thanks to thousands of interviews, visits to agency headquarters and field outposts, and participation in international gatherings, the Humanitarianism and War Project has developed greater appreciation for the difficulties that humanitarian actors face. We also have a deeper sense of the urgency of augmenting the capacity and deepening the competence of the humanitarian enterprise. In that spirit we offer this volume and pursue our ongoing work.

Epilogue

Humanitarian Action in a Time of Terrorism

Considerable time has elapsed since the completion of the foregoing narrative in early September 2001. As noted in chapter 1, momentous events have taken place in the interim. First, a terrorist attack on the United States led to the assembling of a U.S.-led global antiterrorism coalition. Second, the United States has mounted a military campaign against the al Qaeda network, its leader Osama bin Laden, and the Taliban government of Afghanistan. Third, a major effort has taken place to avoid a humanitarian catastrophe with winter approaching and widespread civilian displacement.

The response of the community of states and the humanitarian enterprise to the terrorist attack has been an all-consuming preoccupation since September 11, 2001. The attack and the response both highlight many of the dilemmas and discoveries identified and analyzed earlier. This epilogue retraces our steps through the substance of the volume, following the sequence of the nine themes examined earlier.

In one sense, these comments are freestanding; in another, they become more meaningful in the context of the foregoing analysis. Against that backdrop, the international response to this latest crisis is examined as something of a barometer of lessons learned in managing the dilemmas of responding to humanitarian extremity embedded in armed conflict.

Between the time of this writing in January 2002 and its publication in July 2002, the situation will undoubtedly have changed significantly. Even now, only four months into the crisis, too little time has elapsed to draw definitive conclusions. Anticipating whether, a decade from now, "Afghanistan" will rank with Somalia and Bosnia or with Burundi and Nagorno-Karabakh is difficult. One suspects the former, but only time will tell.

Given the circumstances, this concluding chapter is not only more anticipatory than its predecessors but also more opinionated. The epilogue also differs from earlier chapters, which conveyed an international perspective, by concentrating more on U.S. policy and practice, necessitated by the role that the United States is playing in the global antiterrorism coalition. What follows is not an epilogue in the dictionary sense of a speech by an actor after the play is over, but rather a search by the author for clues as to how the play may conclude.

Having closely monitored developments since September 11 and having interviewed a number of the organizations and officials involved, I offer my own assessments of the opportunities and the dangers. Endnotes are included less with an eye to documenting hypotheses or conclusions — the situation is too early for that — than to give the flavor of recent developments. The epilogue is organized topically according to the chapters that preceded it.

Because I view the effects of both the terrorism and the antiterrorism on the humanitarian enterprise as profoundly negative, readers may also sense a difference in tone from the preceding nine chapters. At a minimum, the difficulties experienced by the enterprise in Afghanistan confirm the consequences of not having acted earlier on some of the lessons identified from previous crises. Beyond missed opportunities, however, the early response to recurring dilemmas bodes ill for the future of the enterprise.

The *geopolitical setting* of the world's latest high-profile humanitarian crisis has a number of new and distinctive features. One is the acknowledgment of terrorism as a threat to global security. Another is the level of international political will manifested by a broadly united community of states, reflecting a new willingness to respond in concert to the September 11 events. The resulting agreement among the Permanent Five members of the UN Security Council is unusual, if not totally unprecedented.

In October, one UN spokesman proclaimed the crisis to be "the most serious complex emergency in the world — ever." His statement strikes me as hyperbolic — many crises appear intimidating in the early going until events come into focus and proper perspective is achieved. However, elements of the novel and the unprecedented certainly exist in the Afghanistan crisis.

For Americans in particular, a radical disjuncture distinguishes our world before and after September 11, which says something about the consequences of the events and about their perceived links to previous crises. Prior to September 11, the protection of the world's foremost military in history and the isolating effect of geography had largely sheltered the United States from direct attack and bred a sense of invincibility.

Sampling the public mood in Middle America after September 11, a British journalist found a people "whose faith in their invulnerability has been so badly jolted." Wrote Richard Tomkins in the *Financial Times* three weeks after the terrorist attacks, "[H]istory will record the existence of two Americas: the one that prevailed before September 11, in which America was America and the rest of the world was another place, and the one that will exist hereafter, in which America reluctantly becomes a part of that sometimes hostile and frightening world."[1]

With respect to *causes* of the crisis, however, as with the post–Cold War era itself, numerous commonalities exist between the Afghan situation and other emergencies to which the world had responded. As in Somalia and the Balkans, years of humanitarian desperation among civilian populations had preceded the dispatch of external military forces. Afghanistan was *in extremis* well before international political and military engagement — or, more precisely, reengagement — conferred "crisis" status.

As in Kosovo, prominent major donors — the United States contributed some 80 percent of the resources for emergency Afghan aid — were themselves belligerents in the conflict and dispensers through their troops of assistance to civilians. As in Kosovo, victorious militants may dictate the postconflict political structure, setting the stage for the next round of violence. Certainly the U.S. selection — by the Central Intelligence Agency, according to news reports — of Hamid Karzai as leader of the interim government does nothing to change the pattern, and the liabilities, of generations of outside manipulation of the Afghan players on the regional and international chessboard.

In the case of Afghanistan in particular, the crisis brings the Cold War legacy front and center. The recipients of highly politicized U.S. and international aid during the 1980s, now called warlords, have again assumed positions of authority. In what the intelligence community calls the "blowback" effect, however, figures like Gulbuddin Hekmatyar and Osama bin Laden himself, supported handsomely during the East-West confrontation from outside by U.S. or Pakistani agencies, have strayed from the reservation.

But there are humanitarian blowbacks as well. Aid agencies, many of which, as noted earlier, channeled highly political and largely unaccounted-for "humanitarian" assistance in earlier days to Afghan "freedom fighters," are back on the scene. Their former clients are quite familiar with how to manipulate outside aid. To guide U.S. policy, the Bush administration is appointing to senior foreign policy positions officials who had shaped U.S. policy in Afghanistan and Central America during the Cold War.[2]

Indeed, antiterrorism is already showing signs of becoming "the new Cold War," the world this time divided in Manichean fashion between terrorists and antiterrorists, good and evil, us and them, those who are "for us" and those "against us." As noted later, the Afghan crisis puts a premium on identifying the yet-unlearned lessons, political and humanitarian alike, from the Cold War, which the United States and its allies continue to pride themselves for having "won."

Even before the September 11 attacks, there had been harbingers of the key issues for the humanitarian enterprise of an emerging era of terrorism. The bombings of the U.S. embassies in Kenya and Tanzania in August 1998 led to reprisal U.S. bombings of Khost and Khartoum, causing severe hardships for civilians and for aid agencies and personnel. The destruction of a pharmaceutical factory in Khartoum, which supplied many of the nation's drug needs, conveyed that collateral humanitarian damage would not impede the sending of clear political-military messages.

In addition, the twin reprisals in East Africa, like the military strikes against Afghanistan that commenced on October 7, 2001, increased the possibility that violence against Americans and other aid personnel would ricochet around the world. At least, seasoned aid personnel in places such Indonesia, the Philippines, and Somalia interpreted events in that fashion and hunkered down in anticipation.

"Few in the humanitarian community would dispute that terrorism should be addressed as a matter of urgency," I wrote in an opinion piece reflecting in August 1998 on the bombings in East Africa and the U.S. response. "Yet, American foreign policy and practice should recognize that effective and durable humanitarian programs, in friendly and unfriendly countries alike, represent a counter to terrorist violence and an investment in a more just and secure world."[3] As I suggested then, a look at the humanitarian implications of antiterrorism as well as of terrorism is necessary.

In a more general sense, efforts to understand and address the root causes of terrorism in the wake of the September 11 attacks have been slow to take shape in the United States, but somewhat less so in Europe and elsewhere. Perhaps in part this is because the United States has taken longer to come to terms domestically with the stunning human and economic consequences of the attacks. Yet the time lag also reflects the greater willingness of others to acknowledge the realistic limits on the effectiveness of military force and nonmultilateral global problem solving. Bush administration policy in the early months has been notably unwilling to examine the roots of the latest violence in U.S. policies, whether Cold War or more recent.

The absence of a more probing and self-critical look at structural problems and the need for policy alternatives to address them, too, may be changing. One U.S. reporter in mid-January 2002 noted how in quiet corners of the State Department, "hushed voices are wondering...whether the greatest threat to world stability might not be nuclear proliferation but youth unemployment."[4] Meanwhile, European and other governments — not to say certain humanitarian agencies themselves — that signed on for the Afghanistan chapter of the antiterrorist campaign are exhibiting restiveness about the chapters that have yet to be written.

On a positive note, the early days of the mobilization of humanitarian resources for Afghanistan have witnessed an oft-expressed commitment by donors and practitioners to learn from past experience and "do it right" this time. The interest in learning lessons and avoiding past problems has been sufficiently novel to catch the attention of the press. One reporter, in a dispatch from an international aid meeting in Islamabad in November, noted that "the process of re-examining past relief efforts produced an unexpected result: aid officials criticizing themselves for their record."[5]

The humanitarian enterprise has a sense — quite accurate, in my judgment — that it is on trial and must acquit itself well in this crisis or face a serious and perhaps fatal loss of credibility. This onus makes it doubly necessary to learn from experience and introduce the necessary changes in strategy and architecture to deal with the immense challenges. As of early 2002, many lessons from the past have been identified. However, whether these lessons become the core of evolving humanitarian policy and practice in Afghanistan remains to be seen. On that subject, I have serious misgivings.

Coordination efforts in Afghanistan started out on a positive footing, with donors and agencies intent on avoiding the well-publicized disarray of earlier crises such as in Goma, Zaire. During November and December 2001, at various meetings of the United Nations, the Afghan Support Group, and other groups of actors in Islamabad, Bonn, Berlin, and Brussels, participants made many of the right noises. One of their objectives, they said in Brussels in December, involved "identifying a structure to coordinate the implementation of rehabilitation and reconstruction assistance." Plans were made for establishing a "single trust fund" and a "common database integrating all significant humanitarian, relief and reconstruction information." The group agreed to "monitor coherence of donors' activities within an integrated reconstruction and development framework."[6] In Berlin, several donors made a commendable proposal: that donors take a more rigorous approach to the selection of NGOs for operational work in Afghanistan.

In the first four months of the humanitarian operation, however, no single agency was given a mandate involving coordination-by-command. While information flow from the region through the UN's Integrated Regional Information Network (IRIN) and other sources was far more plentiful than in earlier crises, the process of strategic planning for humanitarian action languished. "We are taking part in a traveling circus of meetings," observed one bilateral aid official privately on December 18, with a mixture of frustration and amusement, "doing our best with some like-minded countries to make different processes [i.e., planning streams] meet at the high-level pledging conference in Tokyo in late January."

However, the Tokyo meeting was itself the subject of controversy. Much jockeying took place behind the scenes about the roles of the World Bank and the United Nations, the scale of need, and the relative obligations of various governments to make sizeable contributions. The U.S. government was anxious to keep the focus on reconstruction needs, while some other governments and humanitarian actors wanted to see simultaneous discussion of relief, recovery, and development activities. Innovative proposals for a single consolidated appeal and trust fund to bring more coherence to international funding at accountability were not considered.

In the early months, the changing military situation on the ground and a lack of clarity about the political and aid roles of the UN complicated the task of strategic planning by the UN secretariat. By year's end, however, some of the lines of authority had been clarified. In early December, OCHA opened a Humanitarian Information Center in Kabul and made plans for OCHA suboffices throughout the country. The delays, however, proved costly. The predictable procession of senior officials of UN and other agencies was already putting a strain on the Afghan interim authority and on their own aid staffs and resources. The main purpose of one such five-day visit by an agency head was "to see the situation on the ground."[7] By early December, one UN official in the region confided to "feeling swamped by visitors/missions/numerous planning exercises."[8] One of the major lessons of earlier crises — that institutional flag-flying impedes concerted action — had been lost.

Whether the perceived needs of individual agencies are allowed to sculpt the action of the humanitarian enterprise, as in the earlier experience in Tanzania and Sierra Leone, remains to be seen. No new Sadruddin Aga Khan or Sir Robert Jackson, drawing on their earlier Afghan and Cambodian experience, appears to be waiting in the wings to implement a coordination-by-command mandate. The mandate itself seems unlikely to be conferred on today's lesser luminaries.

Yet the absence of effective coordination among humanitarian organizations could well prove to be a make-or-break issue for the enterprise as a whole. The problem of warlordism and other centrifugal forces will surely pose a major challenge to the interim and elected governments and the task of nation building. Unless humanitarian agencies are able to approach their interlocutors with a consistent and concerted strategy, they may repeat the experience of the 1980s, again to be whipsawed and abused. Even the more recent dealings with the Taliban authorities in the 1990s confirmed the weakness of a live-and-let-live approach to coordination.

With respect to *human rights,* the early response of the humanitarian enterprise has been more positive. In the first days of the coalition's air campaign, a number of major human rights groups — Human Rights Watch and Amnesty International, for example — recalled past abuses by the Northern Alliance and the Taliban and flagged the danger that competing factions would use captured prisoners to settle scores. The threat to human rights of the uncontrolled flow of weapons from within and outside the region was also noted. Their advocacy exercised for a time a braking role on the policies of the antiterrorism coalition, although the thrust of the prevailing political-military policies and assumptions did not change.

From the outset, relief agencies sought to give higher priority to the protection of vulnerable civilian populations in relation to assistance, a lesson noted from Bosnia and the Caucasus. In one specific example, NGOs late in 2001 agreed to create a "focal point for protection," based in Kabul, which, modeled on a similar position in Kosovo, would seek to sensitize NGOs to the protection potential of their aid activities and encourage geographical coordination of NGO protection efforts.[9]

The human rights of women in particular have been an object of concern. The relaxation of strictures on women's dress, employment, and participation in civil society by the Northern Alliance was followed with interest and approval outside the country. Women in Afghanistan, however, were more cautious, noting that women had suffered abuse under all factions over an extended period of time. A reminder that gender and other human rights issues would not improve automatically was provided in late November when the Northern Alliance banned a women's freedom march in Kabul. One thorny issue still to be resolved is the extent to which reconstruction and development aid should be conditioned upon equitable gender policies.

Also evident in the opening months has been a constructive interplay between relief and rights advocates. Aid agencies have highlighted the special needs and resources of Afghan women, both during the bombing and in the time of reconstruction. Conversely, human rights actors have drawn attention to violations of economic and social rights. The UN special rapporteur on the right to food "condemned US airdrops of food rations in Afghanistan as a catastrophe for humanitarian aid and warned that the US was effectively feeding Taliban fighters."[10] High Commissioner for Human Rights Mary Robinson called for a pause in the bombing in mid-October, although she later, apparently under heavy political pressure, withdrew her suggestion.

Concern was also expressed for the rights and needs of persons within Afghanistan whom drought and conflict had dislocated. In mid-November, the representative of the secretary-general for internally displaced persons (IDPs), Francis Deng, and the UN's special coordinator on internal displacement, Kofi Asomani, called upon "all parties to the conflict to undertake immediate and sustained efforts to provide greater protection to the displaced and civilian population and to respect their rights as guaranteed by international humanitarian and human rights law."[11] These various initiatives confirm that the Afghanistan response may witness a potentially positive contribution by human rights institutions to the evolution of humanitarian norms, and vice versa. The initiatives also confirm the centrality and precariousness of human rights in conflict and postconflict settings.

The importance of *strengthening local capacity* also received greater attention from the outset than in many precursor crises. A steady drumbeat of official pronouncements has supported the "Afghanization" of the assistance effort. In late November an international conference in Islamabad sponsored by the World Bank, the Asian Development Bank, and UNDP sounded the essential note. "A genuine long-term and sustainable reconstruction and development effort must be led by the people of Afghanistan themselves through their legitimate and recognised leaders," said the conference spokesperson. "It is critical that the leadership which emerges for Afghanistan is in the driver's seat of this process."[12] "If the assistance community were to drive the rebuilding of Afghanistan," added a World Bank vice president, "we would merely become part of the problem, instead of part of the solution."[13]

Our earlier review of capacity building during the 1990s, however, underscores the mammoth difficulties of turning such rhetoric into reality. The rhetoric is as axiomatic as the reality is resistant. If past is prologue, international actors will soon be lamenting the absence of counterpart agencies with which to collaborate. Such an outcome would be the logical consequence of repeated references in late 2001 to Afghanistan as a "failed state," as if the Taliban had not been the governing political authorities. Even after twenty-plus years of internecine conflict, civil society organizations do exist, in Afghanistan, Pakistan, and the diaspora, with significant contributions to make. The issue first and foremost is not the absence of indigenous leadership and institutions but the commitment and resourcefulness of the aid apparatus and its political masters.

By early January when the apparatus was gearing up for operations, signs were already present of "business as usual." "The NGOs are playing the role of a new colonial administration," charged a Kabul academic. "They hand out flour, but don't build factories. They give oil, but don't create jobs. They manage the aid by themselves and prevent the creation of a strong state." His comments recalled the experience examined earlier in the so-called Donor Republic of Mozambique, where, given the distrust among donor governments of the political authorities, NGOs became the preferred and pliant channel of assistance. While using NGOs to detour around Afghan warlords and petty potentates has its appeal, such an approach ignores the paradoxical reality, noted in Mozambique, that state legitimacy must be reinforced first in order for external funders to cultivate a viable independent grassroots force that can itself then engage the state.[14]

Disconnects between the international aid apparatus and Afghan institutions, however, did not spring up overnight. A series of UN missions had regularly flagged the problem. One in which I was involved as early as 1997 cautioned that "the heavily western thrust, if not intent, of current efforts puts the assistance collectivity on collision course with the Taliban." A structural problem such as this could hardly be expected to evaporate simply with a change of political regime.[15]

Generic problems well-documented in other crises — expatriate-led operations competing with each other, bidding up the costs of indigenous personnel, housing, office space, and leaving little enduring improvement behind — are likely to recur here. Already, indigenous NGO employees are lamenting that over half the money donated for Afghanistan is either spent in neighboring Pakistan or for expenses of international staff. The irony is telling, inasmuch as senior UN officials have described as "a political and moral imperative" the need to "design future programs around as few international staff as possible, with extensive management and control by Afghans."[16]

The heart of the problem, clearly, is the political economy of the humanitarian enterprise itself. As concluded in our earlier assessment of strengthening local capacity, the apparatus is driven not by the needs of vulnerable civilian populations but by donor interests, heavily political in nature, and reinforced by the institutional dynamics of humanitarian organizations themselves.

The functioning of a primarily Western aid apparatus in a country with a predominantly Muslim population has raised special, although again not unprecedented, problems. Not only have outside agencies had difficulty identifying indigenous counterparts, but Afghan NGOs and their extensions in other countries have come under close political scrutiny for connections with terrorism. Pakistan has reportedly expelled expatriate staffs of several agencies thought to be sympathetic to the Taliban. The U.S. and Canadian governments have seized the assets of a number of NGOs with suspected terrorist links. On the same grounds, the United States has closed firms that send remittances from Somalis back to their homeland. UNICEF has come under pressure for funding certain Muslim NGOs in Asia.

The impact of politicizing humanitarian work in this fashion is likely to be wide-ranging and destructive. "As the war [against terrorism] turns truly global," notes one reporter, "we will confront a new challenge for which we are profoundly unprepared: Kalashnikov-toting terrorist groups that have earned large followings by providing basic social services, like medical care, to people the rest of the world has abandoned."[17] In fact, groups like Hamas and Hezbollah have gained legitimacy by stepping up the scale of their aid work in relation to their military activities.

The United States is in what may become an uncomfortable position: taking actions in the name of antiterrorism that cause wide-ranging humanitarian consequences without making provision to fill the humanitarian breach. Its current rhetoric of looking to other donors to play the lead in funding reconstruction and development activities will become even less tenable as U.S. policies, and U.S. pressures on allies, force cutbacks in human needs programs in numerous countries according to a terrorist/antiterrorist litmus test.

Again, the implications are wide-ranging. In an effort to pick up some of the slack, the United States and other donors may step up their own human needs activities. Already analysts have pointed out that setting up clinics and schools "in areas now controlled by terrorist groups would cost a fraction of fighting a guerilla war against them."[18] Yet competing for hearts and minds is alien to the humanitarian agenda, although some of the specific activities may parallel each other. Scrutiny of Muslim groups may also turn the public spotlight on Western and Northern NGOs, many of whom receive funds from donor governments and some of whom have implicit, if not explicit, political agendas of their own. At stake, in the end, is a humanitarian enterprise characterized by the hallmarks of independence, neutrality, and impartiality.

This discussion brings us to the broader subject of *humanitarian politics*. While all aid activities in armed conflicts are to one degree or another politicized, the new overlay of the war against terrorism is having a potentially deeper and more dramatic impact on the humanitarian enterprise than garden-variety post–Cold War politics.

In every complex humanitarian emergency, relief and rights work functions on highly political terrain. Our review of humanitarian activities in the 1980s and 1990s in Afghanistan itself confirmed as much.[19] Not only have recent events complicated the sociopolitical landscape, but they have also embedded humanitarian activities more firmly within it. With the political stakes higher, humanitarian space may be more constricted. The possibilities of conducting humanitarian activities outside of the overarching antiterrorism rubric are, in my judgment, likely to become increasingly scant.

I continue to use "politicization" in a pejorative sense, mindful that, as noted in the earlier chapter on the subject, some of my colleagues see the concept as neutral or even positive in connotation. The high political profile of the Afghanistan crisis has, to be sure, had a number of positive features. The military phase of the response has succeeded in replacing a repressive regime, opening the possibility of a more just and representative polity. The crisis has brought new international interest and energy to confronting the country's debilitating situation of the preexisting drought and conflict that the rest of the world had largely forgotten. A total of 20 percent of the UN's consolidated appeal for global humanitarian programs in 2002 is requested for Afghanistan — although some feel that the high percentage may penalize other settings of humanitarian extremity.

However, the international response to the crisis has failed to move the human being noticeably closer to the center of the political firmament. Had humanitarian factors been paramount, the Pentagon would doubtless have paid greater heed to the view of USAID, the humanitarian focal point within the U.S. government, and to the objections of UN humanitarian agencies that humanitarian daily rations (HDRs) should not be dropped in tandem with the bombing of the country. Similarly, the rationale for the targeting of first al Qaeda and then the Taliban had nothing to do with improving the lot of Afghan civilians and everything to do with reprisals for the September 11 events. This perspective was evident even before U.S. servicemen inscribed "FDNY," memorializing the heroism of New York fire personnel in responding to the World Trade Center disaster, on Afghan-bound missiles. The continuing of the bombing despite calls by other coalition governments, including the United Kingdom, and some humanitarian groups for its cessation risked wider civilian casualties without offsetting political-military gains.

In fairness, the longer-term impacts of the antiterrorism campaign may turn out to be positive for Afghan civilians. The jury will remain out until the effectiveness of reconstruction and development activities can be assessed. Yet long-term questions combine with short-term damages and dislocations to tip the early balance sheet. One tally puts Afghan civilian deaths at 3,767 through December 10, 2001, roughly the number of American and other lives lost in the September 11 events.[20] The loss of international aid assets, including personnel, as a result of wayward ordnance has also been significant, although paling by comparison with the expropriation of relief supplies by first the Taliban and then the Northern Alliance.

Many of the policies pursued by the United States as leader of the antiterrorism coalition have had ostensibly humanitarian elements. For example, President George W. Bush called on school children across the country to contribute to a White House fund for the children of Afghanistan. Humanitarian organizations, however, objected on the grounds that it is inappropriate for government authorities to be appealing directly to the public for charitable contributions. The more troubling issue, however, is the use of an ostensibly humanitarian undertaking to generate public support for broader U.S. policies in the crisis. "Why is the president asking us to help the children of Afghanistan," asked one seven-year-old in Massachusetts, "when he is bombing them?"

Again in fairness, the United States has been the world's preeminent donor to Afghanistan in recent years, and in the emergency phase of the latest crisis. In announcing a new U.S. contribution of $320 million in early October 2001, however, President Bush said, "We are a compassionate nation, but our compassion is limited."[21] If politicizing the instincts of the American public, including its next generation of leaders, violates the humanitarian ethos, tying the provision of life-saving essentials provided by the U.S. government to a political agenda is no less dangerous.

Many NGOs and UN agencies have sought to avoid too-close identification with the antiterrorism coalition and its heavily political mission and operations. In fact, during the bombing phase, the UN was reluctant to accept responsibility for assistance programs within the prevailing antiterrorism framework. But differences of view also prevailed among individual humanitarian actors about how to situate their own work, recalling our earlier discussion of humanitarian politics.

Some U.S. NGOs — the issue is somewhat less problematic for NGOs from other nations — are comfortable with, or at least resigned to, working within the prevailing political context. They acknowledge that the aid funds available to them and the humanitarian space within which they function reflect political givens. Those political realities are conveyed by the comment of U.S. professor Graham Allison, "American policy makers must not think of the humanitarian campaign as an afterthought or charity work. It should be regarded as a genuine second front."[22]

Other NGOs and the ICRC are keeping their distance. Some have opted not to seek or accept U.S. government funds for humanitarian activities in the region. Some are accepting such funds but using them — for the moment, at least — only among refugees outside the country. Some are relying on private donations, which come with fewer strings. Some are open to using funds provided by the UN or other governments, although the UN system and its humanitarian organizations are facing some of the same strategic issues relative to the antiterrorism initiative.

Groups that agree to function within the antiterrorism framework do not see U.S. policy and humanitarian principles colliding, at least for the moment. My own view is that the two are indeed on collision course, and that when the irresistible force hits the anything-but-immovable object, the damage to the enterprise will be far-reaching. The executive director of the International Council of Voluntary Agencies, Ed Schenkenberg, states the issue in stark terms: "During the days and weeks to come, political grounds and humanitarian goals will totally interfere with each other. Those who wish to offer aid in Afghanistan under American organisation will have to put aside the principles of independence and impartiality, recognised principles of humanitarian relief."[23]

In the early going, many humanitarian organizations have found little place for suggesting alternative approaches within the antiterrorist rubric. In a letter to President Bush dated September 19, 2001, InterAction spoke of "the balance and deft leadership required to right this wrong [the attacks against the United States] while also preserving the core values that define us as a people and nation." The coalition of 160 U.S.-based groups encouraged "a comprehensive approach to attack and weed out terrorism over the coming months and years through military, economic, legal, diplomatic, and other means."[24] A second letter from InterAction two weeks later urged an "ample" set-aside of funds for Afghanistan within the $40 billion emergency legislation for post–September 11 needs, representing "our government's recognition that innocent people are suffering greatly."[25]

Statements by smaller coalitions of U.S. NGOs and by NGOs in other countries have been both more circumspect and more specific. A group of five faith-based agencies in the United States cited three "long-standing principles of international humanitarian assistance as guidelines during the current and complex crisis in Central Asia": humanitarian aid must be provided on the basis of need, not as an instrument of political-military strategy; multilateral cooperation is critical for effective aid in Afghanistan; and military intervention must not exacerbate humanitarian crises.[26]

A statement from a group of nine Canadian NGOs urged that "as the Canadian government considers its participation in any international action, adherence to International Humanitarian Law must be given the utmost priority by all parties." The statement also noted that with Canadian international staff having been withdrawn from Afghanistan, "more than 1000 locally hired staff" were in place "to take up the challenge of managing these important assistance programs."[27] From a mixed group of nineteen agencies working in the region came an appeal to "the US and its allies, the Taliban and the Northern Alliance to formally recognise the need for an independent, non-political humanitarian action of massive proportions for Afghanistan."[28]

These statements are noteworthy for the nuanced differences in their messages. Not surprisingly, varying vantage points — agency headquarters or field, American or Canadian — influence agency perspectives. Those variations bring a certain richness and — one would hope, balance — to the advocacy. When NGO orientations give an implicit imprimatur to government policies, however, the cause of independent humanitarian action may be called into question. One NGO public information official, Jonathan Frerichs of Lutheran World Relief, describes "the incredible power of self-censorship among NGOs in the face of public opinion poll numbers that are 90 percent in favor of a U.S. policy that puts a low priority on human needs."[29]

Self-censorship may have taken its toll in other ways as well. Even after the discovery that the military campaign was causing substantial civilian deaths and casualties, many agencies were reluctant to advocate a pause or halt. My impression is that U.S. public opinion has been more committed to the bombing than European opinion. European aid agencies appear to have felt they had more scope for questioning the rationale for a heavily military rather than diplomatic approach to the crisis and the extent of damage to Afghan civilians. One international federation with national chapters in Europe and the United States found its non-U.S. members willing to question the rationale of the events, but its U.S. members reluctant, delaying its advocacy as a result.

The politics of the crisis is apparent in other ways as well. Some agencies deferred for a time their appeals for responding to the humanitarian crisis in Afghanistan, in part to avoid competition with appeals for the families of those killed in the World Trade Center and Pentagon incidents. One agency that advertised its work in Afghanistan received hate mail for the first time. The delicacy sensed by U.S. NGOs recalled the Iraq situation, where donor governments and their publics failed to sustain humanitarian programs in a country they were simultaneously trying to isolate through economic sanctions.

Coercive humanitarianism is back in action in Afghanistan. As in Kosovo, the United States is both cobelligerent and provider of humanitarian aid.

In this instance, humanitarian daily rations (HDRs) and cluster bombs both came in yellow packages. While the confusion was inadvertent, the highly publicized HDR initiative — that was no doubt in part its purpose — undercut more serious efforts by professional humanitarians to reach the vulnerable. In opposing HDR drops by the military, AID was told that they would continue until the danger of starvation was past and civilian agencies could meet the need. The double standard, however, was palpable: civilian agencies would doubtless have paid a heavy price for being a party to distributions of food that benefited opposition fighters as well as civilians and that attracted people into mined areas to retrieve the parcels.

Such confusion between military and humanitarian missions recalls the situation in Albania, where NATO planes in the Albania Force (AFOR), which had a humanitarian mission, shared the Tirana tarmac with U.S. Apache helicopters, on hand to prepare for a possible invasion of Kosovo.[30] However, illustrating the differences in transatlantic perspectives noted earlier, most of the criticism of the Defense Department's HDRs came from European rather than American agencies.

Better information-sharing seems to be taking place in the Afghanistan mobilization between the military and the humanitarian enterprise. Early on, the headquarters of the U.S. Central Command in Tampa established the Humanitarian Assistance Coordination Cell. Through it, representatives of OCHA and several individual UN agencies, along with InterAction, on behalf of U.S. NGOs, communicated on a day-to-day basis with senior U.S. military personnel. While the information flow was largely unidirectional, some humanitarian officials felt that the exchange was useful in avoiding the bombing of humanitarian convoys and personnel by alerting military planners to aid movements. Several of the agencies viewed the stationing of their staff in Tampa as somewhat controversial but on balance justified by the result.

Recalling differences in approach among humanitarian actors noted earlier, however, some agencies have expressed grave reservations about the propriety as well as the implicit message that such arrangements conveyed. What does the collocation and presence of humanitarian actors within the headquarters of a belligerent say about the independence and neutrality of the humanitarian enterprise? The ICRC took the issue seriously, opting not to station a staff person there but to make occasional visits instead. Several NGOs also kept their distance.

The dilemma recalls a similar situation during the war in Kosovo, which also divided the community. Although NATO had neither a mechanism nor an intention to systematically consult the agencies, some relief and rights groups felt "obliged as a matter of principle to engage with those planning diplomatic or military initiatives with humanitarian consequences." Otherwise, the agencies themselves "would have 'blood on their hands.'"

By contrast, one senior UN official "refused an invitation to meet with visiting U.S. Ambassador Richard C. Holbrooke at the time the Rambouillet peace process was floundering, fearing that such prior consultation would be invoked in justifying an eventual NATO decision to bomb."[31]

The reluctance among some humanitarian groups to be closely identified with military forces is also reminiscent of the Kosovo experience. "Agencies working under the Kosovo Force security umbrella were wary of too close an association because of the importance of their credibility among minority Serb and Roma population and even among Kosovar Albanians."[32] In Afghanistan, a discredited or unpopular international force could tarnish the credibility of humanitarian operations associated with it. The UN appears to have intervened with NATO at the highest level to discourage its involvement.

As to the roles of the military in Afghanistan, humanitarian agencies have supported the presence of a strong security force that would reestablish law and order throughout the country and provide a climate in which relief and rights activities could be carried out. The interim Afghan government initially insisted on a smaller force limited to Kabul and designed more to pacify international public opinion than to rein in a volatile countryside. Eventually, however, it pressed for more troops. Yet it seems likely that the mandate, size, and deployment of a security force, authorized by the Security Council and led by the United Kingdom, may not be able to provide the necessary security that humanitarian organizations desire. If that is the case — again now is too early to tell — one of the cardinal lessons of the peacekeeping and humanitarian debacle in Rwanda will have gone unheeded.

What of hands-on assistance activities by international military forces? As the air war winds down, signs are that U.S. policy makers, particularly in the Pentagon, will place greater emphasis on civil-military operations. If and when that happens, serious tensions are likely once again with humanitarian organizations. As of the turn of the year, isolated instances of "humanitarian" initiatives undertaken by the U.S. military without consultation with aid agencies had already occurred. At risk is the lesson identified from earlier crises: that distinctive contribution of international military and peacekeeping forces in the postconflict humanitarian sphere is the provision of security, not engagement in hands-on assistance activities.

The use of military force itself in the Afghan crisis has been the subject of considerable debate, both within the humanitarian enterprise and beyond. Some have applauded the use of force as the only language understood by terrorists, who certainly have no qualms in using it themselves. Others have argued that military force is likely to prove ineffective in stemming terrorism and may at the same time undercut the potential problem-solving contribution of international law, diplomacy, financial pressure, and economic sanctions.

My own reading of the results of the application of force is negative, both in the circumstances in Afghanistan and in the confrontation with terrorism in the wider world. While terrorism requires a firm response, the use of overwhelming force plays into terrorist hands, both the al Qaeda and similarly inclined movements elsewhere. As with the earlier critique of unsuccessful economic sanctions, military-led antiterrorism strategies offer the worst of both worlds: the failure to achieve stated political objectives while complicating the humanitarian challenge.

"Even before we have accomplished the single most important war aim — 'decapitating Al Qaeda,'" wrote analyst James Carroll in early 2002, "our war has transformed the meaning of conflict elsewhere and has forced other nations [he mentions India, Pakistan, Israel, and the Palestinians], in imitating us, to previously unimagined levels of bellicosity." I fear that Carroll is right in discerning "the shape of a world in which America's hyper-martial response to terrorism [has become] the new template for the exercise of power." He is doubtless also on target in seeing in American-led military action against Afghanistan the undercutting of the last century's "single greatest moral shift...the fragile, but precious idea of institutionalized international mutuality."[33] The selective and opportunistic use of multilateral channels and international law would also recapitulate the destructive bilateralism of the Kosovo initiative.

As regards other issues of *humanitarian architecture,* the experience of the first four months in Afghanistan confirms the need for a number of the structural changes identified in the earlier chapters. The most crucial change concerns the issue of how to situate the international humanitarian response in relation to its political-military framework, a challenge replete with structural difficulties.

The broad pattern established has been that the special representative of the secretary-general, Lakhdar Brahimi, has two deputies, one each for political and humanitarian affairs. How this arrangement will play out is not yet clear. However, the approach seems to integrate humanitarian action into the political framework rather than to insulate or separate such activities from that framework. As noted earlier, this option has both advantages and liabilities for humanitarian activities and actors.

Since 1997, the UN has sought to develop a "strategic framework for Afghanistan," not only to resolve the embarrassing lack of coordination among humanitarian organizations but also to situate the humanitarian exercise in relation to UN political and diplomatic objectives. I served as a consultant to a team that made recommendations on these issues in late 1997.[34] Neither the recommendations of that team nor the strategic framework methodology that was viewed as a possible prototype for other crises situations were implemented. Whether the arrangement with Brahimi and his deputies succeeds where years of laconic attempts at strategic planning have failed remains to be seen. More decisive action by the UN and member states in the interim since 1997 might arguably have positioned the system better to respond to the present crisis.

In fact, revisiting the issues in October 2001, a review of the Strategic Framework for Afghanistan (SFA) confirmed in painful detail the serious and unresolved disconnects within the humanitarian enterprise and, more importantly still, between it and the UN's diplomatic/political work. "The SFA embodies the possibility of greater coherence between aid, politics and human rights. However, among the UN agencies in Islamabad and Kabul the review team found that 'coherence' was a contested terrain of distinct institutional dynamics and contrasting positions." The team concluded that "the division between politics and aid in Afghanistan is essentially systemic rather than the result of personal differences, lack of administrative structures or institutional disconnect."[35]

As the international effort at relief and reconstruction goes forward, many of the other missing elements in the present humanitarian architecture may also become highlighted. These include:

- consistency of response to need, with the high-profile Afghan situation threatening to preempt resources needed in equally serious crises elsewhere;

- the need for sensitive management of the heterogeneity of the humanitarian actors, respecting the distinctive potential contributions of each;

- minimizing the externality of international presence and activities. Connecting with the Muslim population in Afghanistan is something of a test case for dealing with refugees more globally, some 80 percent of whom are Muslim.

- more circumspect relations between the humanitarian enterprise and international military forces, within the security framework that outside troops will hopefully provide; and

- more proactive relations with the media, encouraging it to play a more probing and contextually sensitive role.

With respect to some of the other structural problems identified earlier, the die is probably already cast. The NGOs are already flocking to the region, mooting our suggestion that they and the donors that underwrite them take a more disciplined — that is, rotational, or at least coalitional — approach. Our proposal for a 90- or 180-day moratorium on visits by UN and other agency heads to Afghanistan came too late and was not taken seriously anyway.

Events overtook our recommendation, drawn from experience in Yugoslavia, that special military contingents replace functions of humanitarian personnel in hot-war settings. The fact that expatriate aid staff had to be withdrawn from Afghanistan for an extended period of time, however, confirmed the need for provision for such circumstances. Indicative of the problem is the situation that developed in a camp of some 150,000 to 200,000 Afghan IDPs near Herat. A reporter noted that "a group of aid agencies working in the camp [to feed and shelter people has decided] to consider an offer from the United States Army to take over the entire relief effort if the situation demands."[36]

With the humanitarian mobilization at an early stage, I find it difficult to comment on the dilemmas raised in our earlier review of *equipping the enterprise*. While it is far too early to anticipate the quality of the performance of humanitarian institutions and officials, the spirit of the undertaking has been constructive, with everyone on best behavior. The interest in bringing to bear the lessons of the post–Cold War period, described in the following section, is also definitely positive.

There are some early straws in the wind. The first two chapters of a real-time evaluation by UNHCR of its performance at headquarters and in the region, completed before the end of 2001, have been quite positive. On the matter of leadership, however, UNHCR says, "While HCR has been relatively effective in deploying personnel to the field, some concern has been expressed in relation to the organizational structures within which those people must function. In this respect, more work is required in terms of developing model emergency staffing organigrams, prioritizing the staffing profiles required in different emergency scenarios and developing standard terms of reference for emergency deployments."

Differing assessments of the humanitarian situation have also cast some doubt on the credibility of the enterprise. At year's end, WFP Executive Director Catherine Bertini and USAID Administrator Andrew Natsios were stating that famine in Afghanistan had been averted, thanks in large part to massive delivery of food supplies in recent weeks. At precisely the same time, however, aid workers on the ground were citing serious impediments to food distribution, including threats by warlords and criminal elements and the previously looted aid infrastructure. On the broader question of whether the enterprise is better equipped now than in previous crises to meet the challenges it faces, only time will tell. Reports of humanitarian personnel lacking training or experience remain anecdotal.[37]

As regards *the dynamics of institutional change*, some quite positive developments are already taking place. Practitioner organizations increasingly accept the idea of "real-time evaluations." In addition to the UNHCR-specific evaluation mentioned above, the Strategic Monitoring Unit, based in Islamabad, has drawn up terms of reference for its own systemwide study, and OCHA itself reportedly has one on the drawing boards. "The history of evaluation over the past decade," observes one evaluation specialist, "shows a movement from resistance (pre-Somalia) to reluctant acceptance (around Rwanda) to a mature endorsement of the role of evaluation (Kosovo)."[38] The Afghanistan situation may carry the evolution to the stage of anticipation — with practitioners themselves welcoming real-time assessments with an eye to making the necessary course corrections sooner rather than later.

Less encouraging has been the failure to avoid recurrent tensions between humanitarian and military personnel in the Afghan theater. In early April 2002, sixteen agency executives flagged a specific concern in a letter to the Bush administration. The authorization of "civil affairs and Special Forces personnel to engage in humanitarian activities while dressed in civilian clothes and carrying weapons," they wrote, "risks confusing military and humanitarian personnel in the minds of local populations." It also "significantly increases the security risks of every humanitarian aid worker in that country." The NGOs pointed out that "this decision contradicts a consensus reached in years of discussions between American NGOs and senior American military officers, as well as practice in previous crises of the past decade in which we have delivered humanitarian aid in conflict or post-conflict areas where U.S. military forces have been present." In this particular instance, the Afghan response confirms that lessons identified have not been effectively institutionalized.[39]

On a more positive note, an ALNAP initiative in late 2001 provides some useful guideposts for determining the extent to which lessons learned from the decade's experience are incorporated into the evolving Afghanistan effort. At the request of the chair of the Working Party on Evaluation of the OECD's Development Assistance Committee (DAC), the organization in December drew together for application to the situation in Afghanistan nine key lessons, based on a review of more than fifty evaluation reports from various crises. The ALNAP review noted that "the current climate, characterized by a justified sense of urgency among aid agencies to maximize the impact of aid and avoid the recurrent problems of the past, provides a real opportunity to put into place effective mechanisms for getting the relief and rehabilitation effort right."[40]

Because of their convergence with the subject of this book, I list the nine lessons that are recommended to guide the Afghanistan effort:

- Develop a coherent policy framework that recognizes that humanitarian aid requires its own "space."

- Frame international engagement in long-term and inclusive perspective.

- Approach and manage the situation as a regional crisis.

- Establish firm coordination through clarity of structure, leadership and a willingness not to "fly national flags."

- Utilize external military forces for the provision of security and protection rather than aid delivery.
- Address the relief-rehabilitation-development transition through delegation of authority, flexibility, and strengthened monitoring.
- Strengthen, use, and support local institutional capacity.
- Control the "war economy" and confront the risk of entrenched chronic violence.
- Strengthen accountability and learning mechanisms of the aid system.

Our earlier discussion noted that many factors promote institutional change and that, on balance, the role of evaluations is modest. At the DAC meeting itself, attended by evaluation specialists from donor agencies, the paper identifying lessons was "well received" and plans are being made to disseminate it widely. How many of its recommendations influence policy and practice, whether in Afghanistan or beyond, is of course to be determined.

Despite the ALNAP undertaking and our own study by Antonio Donini, I continue to be struck by the lack of detailed review of the Cold War and post–Cold War experience in Afghanistan, which could inform current strategic planning. Many NGOs now concede that they played a highly political role in the area in the 1980s but without the necessary attention to the politics of the scene. "We thought we were doing humanitarian assistance," recalls one operations manager of a major U.S. NGO, but were "unaware of the political framework." Programming in a historical vacuum has been a problem in crisis after crisis, and Afghanistan appears to be not yet an exception.

The newfound awareness of the politics of humanitarian action is one of the discoveries of the post–Cold War era noted earlier. That awareness, however, has yet to translate into an Afghanistan-specific retrospective on the highly politicized and generally ineffective performance of the humanitarian enterprise there during the 1980s. A review of the impacts on humanitarian action of the Cold War itself would be timely, whether or not we are now entering a "new Cold War." One of the necessary lessons from such a review would be one cited earlier: that factors over which it has little control greatly influence the performance of the humanitarian apparatus in its own right.

In conclusion, humanitarian action in a time of terrorism is not a contradiction in terms but a necessity. However, such action requires historical wisdom, strategic insight, contextual savvy, independence, flexibility, and resilience to be effective: precisely the attributes associated with effective protection of and assistance to civilian populations in conflicts in nonterrorist settings.

Conversely, humanitarian action in a time of antiterrorism is not a contradiction in terms. Effective antiterrorist strategies involve not only responding to human need, whether in Kabul or New York, but providing protection and space for humanitarian activities characterized by independence, neutrality, and impartiality.

In retrospect, the events of September 11 highlight the impacts of both terrorism and antiterrorism on humanitarian action. Each of the twin realities in its own way gives new urgency to putting the human being and human security in the center of the international political debate. Each requires moving beyond cosmetic to authentic humanitarian action. Perhaps the horrendous events and the major loss of life in the September 11 events in New York, Washington, and Pennsylvania among people of many nationalities will spur a greater sense of international solidarity, expressed through a more effective humanitarian enterprise. Solidarity and its partner optimism are situated at the core of humanitarian action.

The terrorist attacks in the United States, and their ripple effects around the world, may hold promise of giving new and more personal meaning to a wider public regarding what humanitarianism is all about. An old Palestinian man, interviewed in Jordan late in 2001, told a reporter, "We feel pain and sadness for those five or six thousand innocents killed in the attacks [in the United States]. But you know, we lost many, many innocent people. Tens of thousands, hundreds of thousands of them. And no one felt our pain. And maybe what happened in the United States, this will teach the people of the United States on how people feel from a long time ago."[41]

The reporters who interviewed the gentleman, however, noted that "Traveling in the Arab world, you encounter this deepening sense of pessimism — among Muslims and Christians, rich and poor. The deaths in Palestine and Iraq pile up on television. National economies lie in the dumps. The suppression of speech and political opposition stifles hopes for democratic participation. The emotions of the street are rage and despair."[42]

After a quarter-century of work on humanitarian and development issues and a decade-plus of research into post–Cold War complex emergencies, I fear for the future of the humanitarian enterprise. More basically still, I fear for the future of the shared impulse to which organized humanitarian efforts attempt to give practical meaning. In my judgment, the humanitarian enterprise is living on borrowed time. The international response to the crisis in Afghanistan and to the broader global threat of terrorism has meaning far beyond Afghan borders. Practitioners and researchers, governments and beneficiaries, the military and the media must do their utmost to ensure the success of the humanitarian enterprise and the nurturing of the impulses on which it is based.

Appendix 1

Time Line of Recent Events with Significant Humanitarian Implications

This appendix contains a list of selected events since the end of the Cold War that have had major impacts on the understanding of humanitarian action and the conduct of the humanitarian enterprise. They range from UN Security Council and General Assembly pronouncements to operational initiatives in the field, from the evolution of international legal institutions to the launching of specific military and peacekeeping actions, from successful life-saving efforts to tragic losses of life, and from evaluations of past efforts to the creation of new institutions.

The list is not intended to provide a chronology of major humanitarian crises of the decade. More detailed time lines are provided in the project's individual case studies referenced in appendix 2. Some of the events listed in the time line are not analyzed in the present volume. Taken together, however, the events illustrate the broad context within which the humanitarian enterprise functioned during these years and which shaped its evolution.

1989

April	Operation Lifeline Sudan launched by the United Nations.
October 5	Fall of the Berlin Wall

1990

July	Massacre at Monrovia, Liberia, church kills 600 IDPs, highlighting deteriorating situation and flight of 250,000 refugees to Côte d'Ivoire.
August 2	Iraq invades Kuwait; UN responds on August 8 with Security Council Resolution 661 imposing economic sanctions.

1991

April 8	Establishment of a UN safe haven in northern Iraq to protect Kurds massed on the Turkish border seeking asylum.

September 30   President Jean-Bertrand Aristide of Haiti ousted in a military coup, leading to imposition of U.S. and OAS sanctions.

December 19   UN General Assembly adopts Resolution 46/182, leading to creation of Department of Humanitarian Affairs with a mandate to improve coordination of humanitarian responses.

1992

March   UN Transitional Authority in Cambodia (UNTAC) established, assuming key government functions through September 1993 when the Cambodian government resumed its roles.

    Bosnia and Herzegovina declare independence; fighting breaks out in Sarajevo and in the Muslim enclave of Gorazde. In May, the Security Council demands an end to the war and to ethnic cleansing, imposing economic sanctions on the Federal Republic of Yugoslavia.

June 17   UN Secretary-General Boutros Ghali publishes *An Agenda for Peace,* reflecting Security Council discussions on preventive diplomacy, peacemaking, peacekeeping, and postconflict peacebuilding.

December 9   U.S. Marines land near Mogadishu to restore order and safeguard relief supplies and personnel in Somalia.

1993

May 25   Security Council Resolution 827 establishes tribunal to prosecute violations of international humanitarian law in the former Yugoslavia.

September   Security Council Resolution 866 establishes UN military observer mission in Liberia (UNOMIL) to address perilous humanitarian situation.

October 3   Eighteen U.S. Rangers killed in Mogadishu, leading to evacuation of U.S. troops in early 1994. Twenty-two UN peacekeepers from Pakistan had been killed in June.

1994

February 6   Bombing in Sarajevo market kills sixty-six people and wounds more than two hundred, fueling international concern over vulnerability of civilians in the conflict.

April 6	Rwandan genocide unleashed, eventually killing over 800,000 Tutsis and moderate Hutus; 2 million Hutu refugees and Hutu militias flee to neighboring countries.
May 3	President Clinton signs Presidential Decision Directive (PDD) 25 restricting U.S. engagement in future peacekeeping activities.
September 20	U.S. troops land in Haiti when military junta refuses to step aside, paving way for the return of Aristide.
November	*Humanitarianism Unbound? Current Dilemmas Facing Multimandate Relief Operations in Political Emergencies*, published by African Rights, a U.K.-based NGO, sharply criticizing the tackling of political issues by humanitarian agencies. The critique is taken further in Alex de Waal, *Famine Crimes: Politics and the Disaster Relief Industry in Africa* (1997).
November 8	Security Council Resolution 955 establishes tribunal to prosecute violations of international humanitarian law in Rwanda.

1995

March	Seasoned U.S. relief expert Fred Cuny, his Russian interpreter, and two Russian doctors disappear on needs assessment mission to Chechnya; later found to have died in circumstances implicating Russian troops.
April 14	Security Council Resolution 986 authorizes sale of limited quantities of oil by Iraq, with proceeds to fund humanitarian activities and UN administrative costs there. The oil-for-food program continued into 2002.
April 18	Some 4,000–8,000 people killed by Rwandan troops when the government closes the Kibeho IDP camp in southwestern Rwanda in an effort to return Hutus to their communes.
July 26	Truth and Reconciliation Commission established in South Africa, facilitating the processing of the apartheid legacy.
July	Srebrenica, a UN-declared "safe area," falls to Bosnian Serbs after Dutch UN peacekeeping contingent overrun; an estimated 8,000 Muslim men killed. Gorazde and Zepa fall soon thereafter.

1996

March 13   Five-volume Joint Evaluation of Emergency Assistance to Rwanda released at press conference at the UN in New York and in London and Geneva; dismissed out of hand by UN spokesperson Silvana Foa.

April   Mary B. Anderson publishes *Do No Harm: How Aid Can Support Peace — or War,* stimulating wide-ranging debate among humanitarian practitioners and used extensively in agency training efforts; 2d edition published in February 1999.

April   Guatemalan government and rebels, in negotiations facilitated by outside governments and NGOs, agree to end 36-year civil war.

June 4   Three ICRC workers ambushed and killed in Burundi while returning from an aid distribution trip in a vehicle marked with the Red Cross emblem.

July 25   Arusha Regional Summit condemns military coup in Burundi, calls for imposition of economic sanctions by governments in the area. Seven countries do so, without exemptions for humanitarian essentials.

October   Responding to attacks launched from refugee camps in Zaire, Rwandan troops invade Zaire and attack Hutu militia to drive refugees back to Rwanda; refugees also forced to return from Tanzania.

December 17   Six ICRC workers — from the Netherlands, Canada, New Zealand, Spain, Norway, and Pakistan — murdered in their compound in Chechnya.

1997

May   The Revolutionary United Front (RUF) deposes Sierra Leone's President Kabbah, leading to widespread atrocities against civilians; amputations of limbs and use of child soldiers stun world public opinion.

June   First ICRC World Humanitarian Summit in Wolfsberg, Switzerland, analyzing the interface between humanitarian and political action; two annual summits follow.

June   Humanitarian Ombudsman Project launched by a consortium of U.K.-based NGOs.

December 4   139 countries meeting in Canada sign Ottawa Accord banning trade in antipersonnel land mines; treaty ratified by 109 nations. United States, China, and Russia refuse to sign.

1998

July 17   150 UN member states meet in Rome to negotiate treaty to establish an international criminal court; 120 members agree in principle. As of December 31, 2001, 140 had signed and 48 had ratified. One provision stipulates that attacks against humanitarian personnel constitute war crimes.

August 7   U.S. embassies bombed in Kenya and Tanzania; United States launches retaliatory missile attack on Khost, Afghanistan, and on a pharmaceutical plant in Khartoum, Sudan.

October   Multiyear NGO consultative process leads to publication of Humanitarian Charter and Minimum Standards in Disaster Response as part of the Sphere Project.

November 25   Pinochet verdict in London finds the former dictator lacking immunity from extradition and from prosecution in Spain on charges of murder, torture, and genocide. After 16 months in London, he is sent back to Chile because of his medical condition and in July 2001 found unable to stand trial there.

December 10   50th anniversary of the UN Declaration of Human Rights

1999

January   Rebels backing RUF seize parts of Freetown from the West African force ECOMOG; city devastated by weeks of heavy fighting with civilian population in jeopardy.

March 24   NATO launches air strikes against Yugoslavia military targets, continuing for 78 days; in Kosovo, thousands flee attacks by Serb forces; mass exodus into Albania and Macedonia, where NATO and other troops provide emergency aid.

June 10   Security Council Resolution 1244 authorizes international security and civilian presence in Kosovo to establish "a secure environment in which refugees and displaced persons can return home in safety . . . and humanitarian aid can be delivered."

August 12   50th anniversary of Geneva Conventions

August 31   UN-orchestrated referendum in East Timor preceded by violence perpetrated by pro-Indonesian militiamen in which countless East Timorese and five UN staff killed; Indonesian army joins postelectoral violence, with over 200,000 East Timorese fleeing to West Timor.

September   Regional peacekeeping troops arrive in East Timor and, in October, Indonesian government hands over control to the UN Transitional Authority in East Timor (UNTAET).

October   One WFP and one UNICEF worker killed in ambush in Burundi; Russian rocket attack on civilian and ICRC convoy in Chechnya kills two ICRC staff and scores of IDPs.

2000

April 3   UN Secretary-General Kofi Annan's Millennium Report contains an action plan for the new century that addresses issues of state sovereignty and international responsibility, conflict, and humanitarian action.

April/May   RUF abducts several hundred UN troops in Sierra Leone; 800 British paratroopers sent to Freetown to rescue British citizens and secure the airport for UN peacekeepers.

September 6   UN legal counsel completes formal discussions with Cambodian government to establish international tribunal to try Khmer Rouge leaders.

2001

March 4   Rebuffing international pressure, Taliban destroys historic Buddhist statues.

April 26   Six ICRC workers (two expatriates and four Congolese) are killed in Ituri Province, Democratic Republic of the Congo. Traveling in an ICRC-marked vehicle en route to a remote health center, the group is shot and hacked to death.

July 3   Milosevic appears before UN tribunal at the Hague to be tried for crimes against humanity.

August 2   In the first genocide conviction by an international war crimes court in Europe, the International Criminal Tribunal for the former Yugoslavia in the Hague found former general Radislav Krstic guilty for his role in the massacre of Muslim men and boys from Srebrenica in July 1995. He is sentenced to 46 years in prison.

August   Taliban authorities in Afghanistan arrest 24 aid workers
                  from a German NGO, Shelter Now, on charges of proselyti-
                  zation. Trials begin the following month. The group is later
                  freed as the Taliban flees coalition bombing.

September 11   Terrorist attacks in New York and Washington, D.C., kill
                  over 3,000 persons. Following Security Council condemna-
                  tion of the acts, the United States assembles a coalition of
                  nations to root out global terrorism, focusing on Al Qaeda
                  and the Taliban authorities thought to be harboring its
                  head, Osama bin Laden. The antiterrorism campaign leads
                  to the bombing of Afghanistan beginning on October 7. On
                  December 22 an interim government is installed.

Appendix 2

List of Project Publications

Humanitarian Challenges, Politics, and Intervention

Books

Minear, Larry, and Thomas G. Weiss. *Humanitarian Action in Times of War: A Handbook for Practitioners.* Boulder, Colo.: Lynne Rienner, 1993. In Spanish: *Acción Humanitaria en Tiempos de Guerra.* Boulder, Colo.: Lynne Rienner, 1993. In French: *Action Humanitaire en Temps de Guerre.* Boulder, Colo.: Lynne Rienner, 1993.

Minear, Larry, and Thomas G. Weiss. *Humanitarian Politics.* New York: Foreign Policy Association, 1995.

Minear, Larry, and Thomas G. Weiss. *Mercy under Fire: War and the Global Humanitarian Community.* Boulder, Colo.: Westview, 1995.

Smillie, Ian, ed. *Patronage or Partnership: Local Capacity Building in Humanitarian Crises.* Bloomfield, Conn.: Kumarian Press, 2001.

United Nations Volunteers. *Volunteers against Conflict.* Ed. Larry Minear and Thomas G. Weiss. Tokyo: United Nations University Press, 1996.

Weiss, Thomas G., and Cindy Collins. *Humanitarian Challenges and Intervention: World Politics and the Dilemmas of Help.* Boulder, Colo.: Westview Press, 1996.

Weiss, Thomas G., David Cortright, George Lopez, and Larry Minear. *Political Gain and Civilian Pain: The Humanitarian Impacts of Economic Sanctions.* Foreword by Lakhdar Brahimi. Lanham, Md.: Rowman & Littlefield, 1997.

Weiss, Thomas G., and Larry Minear, eds. *Humanitarianism across Borders: Sustaining Civilians in Times of War.* Boulder, Colo.: Lynne Rienner, 1993.

Research Monographs

Frohardt, Mark, Diane Paul, and Larry Minear. *Protecting Human Rights: The Challenge to Humanitarian Organizations.* Occasional Paper 35. Providence: Watson Institute, 1999.

The Occasional Papers published by the Humanitarianism and War Project are available in their entirety on the project's Web site at *hwproject.tufts.edu.* Commercially published materials are summarized on the Web site and available for purchase from their publishers. The Web site also contains reviews and other comments on project publications. A CD-ROM containing the corpus of the project's work is referenced in the final entry in this appendix.

Hubert, Donald. *The Landmine Ban: A Case Study in Humanitarian Advocacy.* Occasional Paper 42. Providence: Watson Institute, 2000.

Lubkemann, Stephen C., Larry Minear, and Thomas G. Weiss. *Humanitarian Action: Social Science Connections.* Occasional Paper 37. Providence: Watson Institute, 2000.

MacFarlane, S. Neil. *Humanitarian Action: The Conflict Connection.* Occasional Paper 43. Providence: Watson Institute, 2000.

MacFarlane, S. Neil. *Politics and Humanitarian Action.* Occasional Paper 41. Providence: Watson Institute, 2000.

Minear, Larry, David Cortright, Julia Wagler, George A. Lopez, and Thomas G. Weiss. *Toward More Humane and Effective Sanctions Management: Enhancing the Capacity of the United Nations System.* Occasional Paper 31. Providence: Watson Institute, 1998.

Minear, Larry, and Thomas G. Weiss. *Humanitarian Action: A Transatlantic Agenda for Operations and Research.* Occasional Paper 39. Providence: Watson Institute, 2000.

Minear, Larry, Thomas G. Weiss, and Kurt M. Campbell. *Humanitarianism and War: Learning the Lessons from Recent Armed Conflicts.* Occasional Paper 8. Providence: Watson Institute, 1991.

Smillie, Ian. *Relief and Development: The Struggle for Synergy.* Occasional Paper 33. Providence: Watson Institute, 1998.

Sommers, Marc. *The Dynamics of Coordination.* Occasional Paper 40. Providence: Watson Institute, 2000.

Articles

Chopra, Jarat, and Thomas G. Weiss. "Sovereignty Is No Longer Sacrosanct: Codifying Humanitarian Intervention." *Ethics and International Affairs* 6 (1992): 95–118.

Minear, Larry. "A Conceptual Framework." In *The Challenge of Development within Conflict Zones,* ed. Terrance Lorne Mooney. Paris: OECD Development Centre, 1995. Also available in French.

Minear, Larry. "The Evolving Humanitarian Enterprise." Pp. 89–106 in *The United Nations and Civil Wars,* ed. Thomas G. Weiss. Boulder, Colo.: Lynne Rienner, 1995.

Minear, Larry. "The Forgotten Human Agenda." *Foreign Policy,* no. 73 (winter 1988–89): 76–93.

Minear, Larry. "Humanitarian Aid in a World of Politics." *Lutheran Partners* 5, no. 2 (March–April 1989): 12–16.

Minear, Larry. "Humanitarian Intervention in a New World Order." Pp. 113–22 in *NGOs and Refugees: Reflections at the Turn of the Century,* ed. Morten Kjaerum, Klaus Slavensky, and Finn Slumstrup. Copenhagen: Danish Centre for Human Rights, 1993.

Minear, Larry. "Humanitarian Intervention in a New World Order." *Overseas Development Council Policy Focus,* no. 1, February 1992.

Minear, Larry. "Humanitarians and Intervention." Oslo: Norwegian Institute for International Affairs, 1994.

Minear, Larry. "The International Relief System: A Critical Review." Prepared for a meeting of the Parallel National Intelligence Estimate on Global Humanitarian Emergencies, Washington, D.C., September 1994.

Minear, Larry. "Learning the Lessons of Coordination." Pp. 298–316 in *A Framework for Survival: Health, Human Rights, and Humanitarian Assistance in Conflicts and Disasters,* ed. Kevin Cahill. New York and London: Routledge, 1999.

Minear, Larry. "Learning to Learn." Paper prepared for a seminar on Lessons Learned on Humanitarian Coordination, Stockholm, April 1998. Pp. 27–45 in UNOCHA, *Humanitarian Coordination: Lessons Learned.* New York: UNOCHA, 1998.

Minear, Larry. "The Morality of Sanctions." Pp. 229–50 in *Hard Choices: Moral Dilemmas in Humanitarian Intervention,* ed. Jonathan Moore. Published under the auspices of the International Committee of the Red Cross. Boulder, Colo.: Rowman & Littlefield Publishers, 1998.

Minear, Larry. "Notes from the Rapporteur." June 3, 1999. Third Wolfsberg Humanitarian Forum, Switzerland, May 25–27, 1999.

Minear, Larry. "Terms of Engagement with Human Need." *Ecumenical Review* 24, no. 1 (January 1990): 4–16.

Minear, Larry. "The Theory and Practice of Neutrality." *International Review of the Red Cross* 81, no. 833 (March 1999): 63–71.

Minear, Larry, and Thomas G. Weiss. "Do International Ethics Matter? Humanitarian Politics in the Sudan." *Ethics and International Affairs* 5 (1991): 197–214.

Minear, Larry, and Thomas G. Weiss. "Groping and Coping in the Gulf Crisis: Discerning the Shape of a New Humanitarian Order." *World Policy Journal* 9, no. 4 (fall/winter 1992–93): 755–88.

Weiss, Thomas G. "Principles, Politics, and Humanitarian Action." *Ethics and International Affairs* 13 (1999): 1–32.

Country and Regional Case Studies

Books

Deng, Francis M., and Larry Minear. *The Challenges of Famine Relief: Emergency Operations in the Sudan.* Washington, D.C.: Brookings Institution, 1992.

Minear, Larry, in collaboration with Tabyiegen A. Aboum, Eshetu Chole, Koste Manibe, Abdul Mohammed, Jennefer Sebstad, and Thomas G. Weiss. *Humanitarianism under Siege: A Critical Review of Operation Lifeline Sudan.* Trenton, N.J.: Red Sea Press, 1991.

Research Monographs

Aboum, Tabyiegen A., Eshetu Chole, Koste Manibe, Larry Minear, Abdul Mohammed, Jennefer Sebstad, and Thomas G. Weiss. *A Critical Review of*

Operation Lifeline Sudan: A Report to the Aid Agencies. Washington, D.C.: Refugee Policy Group, 1990.

Chopra, Jarat. *United Nations Authority in Cambodia.* Occasional Paper 15. Providence: Watson Institute, 1994.

Donini, Antonio. *UN Coordination in Complex Emergencies: Lessons from Afghanistan, Mozambique, and Rwanda.* Occasional Paper 22. Providence: Watson Institute, 1996.

Eguizábal, Cristina, David Lewis, Larry Minear, Peter Sollis, and Thomas G. Weiss. *Humanitarian Challenges in Central America: Lessons from Recent Armed Conflicts.* Occasional Paper 14. Providence: Watson Institute, 1993. In Spanish: *Desafíos Humanitarios en Centroamérica: Lecciones Aprendidas en los Recientes Conflictos Armados.* San José: Arias Foundation, 1993.

Hansen, Greg. *Humanitarian Action in the Caucasus: A Guide for Practitioners.* Occasional Paper 32. Providence: Watson Institute, 1998. *Gumanitarnye Dejstviq na Kavkaze: Spravohnik dlq Praktiheskovo Rabotnika.* Moscow: Watson Institute, 1999.

Hansen, Greg, and Robert Seely. *War and Humanitarian Action in Chechnya.* Occasional Paper 26. Providence: Watson Institute, 1996.

Hoskins, Eric, and Samantha Nutt. *The Humanitarian Impacts of Economic Sanctions on Burundi.* Occasional Paper 29. Providence: Watson Institute, 1997.

MacFarlane, S. Neil, and Larry Minear. *Humanitarian Action and Politics: The Conflict over Nagorno-Karabakh.* Occasional Paper 25. Providence: Watson Institute, 1997. For an exchange of views on this publication, see Section 8.

MacFarlane, S. Neil (team leader), Larry Minear, and Stephen Shenfield. *Armed Conflicts in Georgia: A Case Study in Humanitarian Action and Peacekeeping.* Occasional Paper 21. Providence: Watson Institute, 1996.

Maguire, Robert (team leader), Edwige Balutansky, Jacques Fomerand, Larry Minear, William O'Neill, Thomas G. Weiss, and Sarah Zaidi. *Haiti Held Hostage: International Responses to the Quest for Nationhood, 1986–1996.* Occasional Paper 23. Providence: Watson Institute, 1996. In French: *Haïti prise en otage: Les Réponses Internationales à la Recherche d'une Identité Nationale de 1986 à 1996.* Providence: Watson Institute, 1996.

Minear, Larry, U. B. P. Chelliah, Jeff Crisp, John Mackinlay, and Thomas G. Weiss. *United Nations Coordination of the International Humanitarian Response to the Gulf Crisis, 1990–1992.* Occasional Paper 13. Providence: Watson Institute, 1992.

Minear, Larry (team leader), Jeffrey Clark, Roberta Cohen, Dennis Gallagher, Iain Guest, and Thomas G. Weiss. *Humanitarian Action in the Former Yugoslavia: The U.N.'s Role, 1991–1993.* Occasional Paper 18. Providence: Watson Institute, 1994.

Scott, Colin, in collaboration with Larry Minear and Thomas G. Weiss. *Humanitarian Action and Security in Liberia, 1989–1994.* Occasional Paper 20. Providence: Watson Institute, 1995.

Articles

"A Case Study of Humanitarian Action in Chechnya, 1991–1996. Preliminary Report."

Hansen, Greg. "Displacement and Return." *Accord: An International Review of Peace Initiatives,* no. 7, The Georgia-Abkhazia Peace Process (October 1999): 58–63.

Hansen, Greg, and Larry Minear. "Waiting for Peace: Perspectives from Action-Oriented Research on the Humanitarian Impasse in the Caucasus." *Disasters* 23, no. 3 (1999): 257–70.

MacFarlane, S. Neil. "The Role of the UN." *Accord: An International Review of Peace Initiatives,* no. 7, The Georgia-Abkhazia Peace Process (October 1999): 36–41.

Minear, Larry. "Introduction to Case Studies." Pp. 43–66 in *Humanitarian Action and Peace-Keeping Operations: Debriefing and Lessons. Report and Recommendations of the International Conference, Singapore, February 1997,* ed. Nassrine Azimi. London, The Hague, and Boston: Kluwer Law International, 1997.

Minear, Larry. "Report to the Headquarters Colloquium on the InterAgency Strategic Framework Mission to Afghanistan." September 1997.

Minear, Larry. "Time to Pull the Plug on Operation Lifeline Sudan?" *Crosslines Global Report* (March–April 1997): 59–60.

Minear, Larry, and Randolph C. Kent. "Rwanda's Internally Displaced: A Conundrum within a Conundrum." Pp. 57–95 in *Forsaken People: Case Studies on the Internally Displaced,* ed. Francis M. Deng and Roberta Cohen. Washington, D.C.: Brookings Institution, 1998.

"Tbilisi Symposium on Conflict and Humanitarian Politics: Summary Record of Proceedings." Tbilisi, Georgia, October 7, 1998.

Weiss, Thomas G., and Amir Pasic. "Dealing with Displacement and Suffering from Yugoslavia's Wars: Conceptual and Operational Issues." Pp. 175–231 in *Forsaken People: Case Studies on the Internally Displaced,* ed. Francis M. Deng and Roberta Cohen. Washington, D.C.: Brookings Institution, 1998.

The Human Rights Interface

Books

Mertus, Julie. *War's Offensive on Women: The Humanitarian Challenge in Bosnia, Kosovo, and Afghanistan.* Bloomfield, Conn.: Kumarian Press, 2000.

Research Monographs

Frohardt, Mark, Diane Paul, and Larry Minear. *Protecting Human Rights: The Challenge to Humanitarian Organizations.* Occasional Paper 35. Providence: Watson Institute, 1999.

Hoskins, Eric, and Samantha Nutt. *The Humanitarian Impacts of Economic Sanctions on Burundi.* Occasional Paper 29. Providence: Watson Institute, 1997.

Kenny, Karen. *When Needs Are Rights: An Overview of UN Efforts to Integrate Human Rights in Humanitarian Action.* Occasional Paper 38. Providence: Watson Institute, 2000.

O'Neill, William G. *A Humanitarian Practitioner's Guide to International Human Rights Law.* Occasional Paper 34. Providence: Watson Institute, 1999.

Articles

Minear, Larry. "Partnerships in the Protection of Refugees and Other People at Risk: Emerging Issues and Work in Progress." *New Issues in Refugee Research.* Working Paper no. 13. Geneva: UNHCR Centre for Documentation and Research, 1999.

The United Nations and Humanitarian Action

Books

United Nations Volunteers. Introduction and Conclusion by Larry Minear and Thomas G. Weiss. Foreword by UNDP Administrator James Gustav Speth and Preface by UNV Executive Coordinator Brenda Gael McSweeney. *Volunteers against Conflict.* Tokyo: United Nations University Press, 1996.

Weiss, Thomas G., ed. *United Nations and Civil Wars.* Boulder, Colo.: Lynne Rienner, 1995.

Research Monographs

Collins, Cindy, and Thomas G. Weiss. *An Overview and Assessment of 1989–1996 Peace Operations Publications.* Occasional Paper 28. Providence: Watson Institute, 1997.

Donini, Antonio. *UN Coordination in Complex Emergencies: Lessons from Afghanistan, Mozambique, and Rwanda.* Occasional Paper 22. Providence: Watson Institute, 1996.

Kenny, Karen. *When Needs Are Rights: An Overview of UN Efforts to Integrate Human Rights in Humanitarian Action.* Occasional Paper 38. Providence: Watson Institute, 2000.

Articles

Minear, Larry. "The Evolving Humanitarian Enterprise." Pp. 89–106 in *The United Nations and Civil Wars,* ed. Thomas G. Weiss. Boulder, Colo.: Lynne Rienner, 1995.

Weiss, Thomas G. "Humanitarian Shell Games: Whither UN Reform?" *Security Dialogue* 29, no. 1 (March 1998): 9–23.

The Military and the Media
as Humanitarian Actors

Books

Minear, Larry, and Philippe Guillot. *Soldiers to the Rescue: Humanitarian Lessons from Rwanda.* Paris: Organization for Economic Cooperation and Development, 1996. In French: *Soldats a la Rescousse: Les Leçons Humanitaires des événements du Rwanda.* Paris: Organization for Economic Cooperation and Development, 1996.

The News Media and Humanitarian Action. Disaster Management Training Programme. Madison, Wisc.: Disaster Management Training Programme, 1997. A separate Trainer's Guide by the same name is also available to complement the training module.

Rotberg, Robert I., and Thomas G. Weiss, eds. *From Massacres to Genocide: The Media, Public Policy, and Humanitarian Crises.* Washington, D.C.: Brookings Institution, 1996.

Scott, Colin, Larry Minear, and Thomas G. Weiss. Foreword by CNN Correspondent Charles Bierbauer. *The News Media, Civil War, and Humanitarian Action.* Boulder, Colo.: Lynne Rienner, 1996.

Weiss, Thomas G. *Military-Civilian Interactions: Intervening in Humanitarian Crises.* Lanham, Md.: Rowman & Littlefield, 1999.

Research Monographs

Minear, Larry, Ted van Baarda, and Marc Sommers. *NATO and Humanitarian Action in the Kosovo Crisis.* Occasional Paper 36. Providence: Watson Institute, 2000.

Articles

Minear, Larry. "The Humanitarian and Military Interface: Reflections on the Rwanda Experience." *Hunger Notes* (summer 1996): 20–23.

Minear, Larry, and Thomas G. Weiss. "The Media as Humanitarian Factor." *Crosslines Global Report,* no. 12–13 (March 1995): 35–37.

Nongovernmental Organizations
and Humanitarian Action

Books

Minear, Larry. *Helping People in an Age of Conflict: Toward a New Professionalism in U.S. Voluntary Humanitarian Assistance.* New York and Washington: InterAction, 1988.

Articles

Minear, Larry. "Humanitarian Aid in a World of Politics." *Lutheran Partners* 5, no. 2 (March–April 1989): 12–16.

Minear, Larry. "Humanitarian Intervention in a New World Order." Pp. 113–22 in *NGOs and Refugees: Reflections at the Turn of the Century,* ed. Morten Kjaerum, Klaus Slavensky, and Finn Slumstrup. Copenhagen: Danish Centre for Human Rights, 1993.

Minear, Larry. "Learning to Learn." *Program in Touch: News and Views from CARE and the NGO Community* (summer 1998): 15–21.

Minear, Larry. "New Opportunities and Dilemmas for Independent Agencies." *Conrad Grebel Review: A Journal of Christian Inquiry* 13, no. 3 (fall 1995): 335–46.

Minear, Larry. "Partnerships in the Protection of Refugees and Other People at Risk: Emerging Issues and Work in Progress." *New Issues in Refugee Research.* Working Paper no. 13. Geneva: UNHCR Centre for Documentation and Research, 1999.

Minear, Larry. "Reflections on Development Policy: A View from the Private Voluntary Sector." Pp. 13–39 in *Private Voluntary Organizations as Agents of Development,* ed. Robert F. Gorman. Boulder, Colo., and London: Westview, 1984.

Minear, Larry. "Terms of Engagement with Human Need." *Ecumenical Review* 24, no. 1 (January 1990): 4–16.

Training Materials

Books

Humanitarian Principles and Operational Dilemmas in War Zones, Disaster Management Training Programme. Madison, Wisc.: Disaster Management Training Programme, undated. A separate Trainer's Guide is also available.

Minear, Larry, and Thomas G. Weiss. *Humanitarian Action in Times of War: A Handbook for Practitioners.* Boulder, Colo.: Lynne Rienner, 1993. In Spanish: *Acción Humanitaria en Tiempos de Guerra.* Boulder, Colo.: Lynne Rienner, 1993. In French: *Action Humanitaire en Temps de Guerre.* Boulder, Colo.: Lynne Rienner, 1993.

The News Media and Humanitarian Action. Disaster Management Training Programme. Madison, Wisc.: Disaster Management Training Programme, 1997. A separate Trainer's Guide is also available.

Research Monographs

Deng, Francis M., and Larry Minear. *The Challenges of Famine Relief: Emergency Operations in the Sudan.* Washington, D.C.: Brookings Institute, 1992.

Hansen, Greg. *Humanitarian Action in the Caucasus: A Guide for Practitioners.* Occasional Paper 32. Providence: Watson Institute, 1998. *Gumanitarnye Dejstviq na Kavkaze: Spravohnik dlq Praktiheskovo Rabotnika.* Moscow: Watson Institute, 1999.

Minear, Larry, U. B. P. Chelliah, Jeff Crisp, John Mackinlay, and Thomas G. Weiss. *United Nations Coordination of the International Humanitarian Response to the Gulf Crisis, 1990–1992.* Occasional Paper 13. Providence: Watson Institute, 1992.

Minear, Larry, Colin Scott, and Thomas G. Weiss. *The News Media, Civil War, and Humanitarian Action.* Boulder, Colo.: Lynne Rienner, 1996.

Minear, Larry, and Thomas G. Weiss. *Humanitarian Action in Times of War: A Handbook for Practitioners.* Boulder, Colo.: Lynne Rienner, 1993.

Minear, Larry, and Thomas G. Weiss. *Mercy under Fire: War and the Global Humanitarian Community.* Boulder, Colo.: Westview Press, 1995.

O'Neill, William G. *A Humanitarian Practitioner's Guide to International Human Rights Law.* Occasional Paper 34. Providence: Watson Institute, 1999.

United Nations Volunteers. Introduction and Conclusion by Larry Minear and Thomas G. Weiss. *Volunteers against Conflict.* Tokyo: United Nations Press, 1996.

Weiss, Thomas G., and Larry Minear, eds. *Humanitarianism across Borders: Sustaining Civilians in Times of War.* Boulder, Colo.: Lynne Rienner, 1993.

CD-ROM

Humanitarian Action in Conflicts: A Compendium of Publications, 1991–2000. To order CD-ROM, please contact *hwproject.tufts.edu.*

Appendix 3

Financial Contributors

HUMANITARIANISM AND WAR PROJECT DONORS	PHASE
GOVERNMENTS	
Australia	2,4
Canada	3,4
France	1
Netherlands	OLS,1,2,3
Sweden	OLS,3,4
Switzerland	4
United Kingdom	1,2,3
United States	1,2,3
INTERGOVERNMENTAL ORGANIZATIONS	
European Community Humanitarian Office (ECHO)	2,3
International Organization for Migration	2,3
OCHA/UNDHA/UNDRO	1,2,3,4
OECD	2
UNDP	OLS,1,2
UNHCR	1,3
UNICEF	OLS, 1,2,3
UNITAR	3
UN Special Emergency Program for the Horn of Africa	1
UN Staff College	3
UN University	2,3
UN Volunteers	2
WFP	OLS,1,3,4
WHO	3

OLS: Precursor Study on Operational Lifeline Sudan (1989–90)
Phase 1: 1991–93
Phase 2: 1994–96
Phase 3: 1997–2000
Phase 4: 2000 ff.

HUMANITARIANISM AND WAR PROJECT DONORS	PHASE
NGOs	
American Red Cross	2,3
Canadian Council for International Cooperation	OLS
CARE Canada	4
CARE U.S.	3
Catholic Relief Services	1,2
Church World Service	OLS
Danish Red Cross Society	2
Danish Refugee Council	1,2,3
Finnish Red Cross Society	2,4
Fourth Freedom Forum	3
Icelandic Red Cross Society	2
IFRC	1,3
International Council of Voluntary Agencies	OLS
International Orthodox Christian Charities	2
International Rescue Committee	2
Lutheran World Federation	OLS,1,2,3,4
Lutheran World Relief	OLS,1,2,3
Mennonite Central Committee (Can)	3,4
Mennonite Central Committee (US)	OLS,1,2,3,4
Mercy Corps International	3
Norwegian Refugee Council	1,2
Oxfam-UK	1
Oxfam-US	4
Save the Children-UK	1
Save the Children-US	2,3,4
Swedish Red Cross Society	2,4
Trócaire	2,4
World Vision Canada	4
World Vision U.S.	2,3
FOUNDATIONS	
Aga Khan Foundation Canada	4
Arias Foundation	1
Ford Foundation	3,4
MacArthur Foundation	3
McKnight Foundation	2,3
Andrew W. Mellon Foundation	3,4
Pew Charitable Trusts	1,2
Rockefeller Foundation	1
U.S. Institute of Peace	2

Appendix 4

Project-Related Personnel

CONSULTANTS, AUTHORS, AND COAUTHORS
OF RESEARCH AND PUBLICATIONS

Tabyiegen A. Aboum
Mary B. Anderson
Mohammed Ayoob
Edwige Balutansky
Judy A. Benjamin
Fred H. Cate
Joel R. Charney
U. B. P. Chelliah
Eshetu Chole
Jarat Chopra
Jeffrey Clark
Roberta Cohen
Cindy Collins
David Cortright
Neta C. Crawford
Jeff Crisp
Frederick C. Cuny
Jaleh Dashti-Gibson
Hedwig Deconick
Frances M. Deng
Julia Devin
Antonio Donini
Christina Equizábal
Åge Eknes

Jacques Fomerand
Mark Frohardt
Dennis Gallagher
Edward Girardet
Iain Guest
Philippe Guillot
John C. Hammock
Greg Hansen
Eric W. Hoskins
Don Hubert
James C. Ingram
Ephraim Isaac
James O. C. Jonah
Karen Kenny
Randolph C. Kent
David Lewis
Steven Livingston
George A. Lopez
Stephen C. Lubkemann
S. Neil MacFarlane
John Mackinlay
Robert Maguire
Koste Manibe
Julie A. Mertus

Larry Minear
Abdul Mohammed
Andrew Natsios
Samantha Nutt
William G. O'Neill
Amir Pasic
Diane Paul
Lionel Rosenblatt
Robert I. Rotberg
Colin Scott
Jennefer Sebstad
Robert Seely
John Shattuck
Stephen Shenfield
Peter Shiras
Ian Smillie
Gayle E. Smith
Peter Sollis
Marc Sommers
Ted A. van Baarda
Michael Veuthey
Julie Wagler
Thomas G. Weiss
Sarah Zaidi

OTHER INDIVIDUALS AND INSTITUTIONAL COLLABORATORS

During the four phases of the Humanitarianism and War Project, many people have provided assistance in carrying out country-specific research, reading draft manuscripts, providing specialized social science and geographical expertise, offering contacts in various country settings, and translating publications. Special thanks are conveyed here to Nora Dudwick, Olga Fadina, Laura Holgate, Eugenia Jenkins, Arthur Keys, Hazel McFerson, Cheryl Morden, Joy Olson, Bill Rau, Alex Their, and Giles Whitcomb.

In addition, the project has benefited from collaboration with a wide variety of institutions. Special recognition is extended to Dennis Gallagher who, as executive director of the Refugee Policy Group, provided institutional support for the Humanitarianism and War Project during the years 1991–94. On specific studies, we have collaborated with the Arias Foundation of San Jose, Costa Rica; the Fourth Freedom Forum; the Humanitarian Law Consultancy; the International Centre for Conflict and Negotiation in Tbilisi, Georgia; the International Human Rights Trust, the Joan B. Kroc Institute for Peace Studies at the University of Notre Dame; the Local Capacities for Peace Project of the Collaborative for Development Action; the United Nations University; and the World Peace Foundation. Institutional financial contributors are listed in appendix 3.

PROJECT STAFF

Estrella Alves, staff assistant, 2000–2001

Andy Blackadar, project manager, 1997–1999

Jennifer Gatto, staff assistant, 2001–present

Margareta Levitsky, staff assistant, 1996–2000

Sarah E. Lum, staff assistant, 1992–1993

Suzanne Miller, project coordinator, 1993–1997

Larry Minear, codirector, 1991–1998; director, 1998–present

Judy Ombura, staff assistant, 1992–1994

John Patten, research assistant, 2000–2001

Laura Sadovnikoff, project manager, 1999–2000

Kevin Von See Dahl, research assistant, 1998–1999

Thomas G. Weiss, codirector, 1991–1998

Notes

1. The Setting and the Research

1. For an elaboration of these points, see the chapter on "Humanitarian Action in the Post–Cold War Era," in Mark Frohardt, Diane Paul, and Larry Minear, *Protecting Human Rights: The Challenges to Humanitarian Organizations*, Occasional Paper 35 (Providence: Watson Institute, 1999). References to this subject that have come to our attention since publication of Occasional Paper 35 include Yahya Sadowski, *The Myth of Global Chaos* (Washington, D.C.: Brookings Institution, 1998), and J. R. Bowen, "The Myth of Global Ethnic Conflict," *Journal of Democracy* 7, no. 4 (October 1996): 3–14.

2. The formulation, quoted in Occasional Paper 35, 18–19, is excerpted from correspondence from Michael Renner, a researcher at the Worldwatch Institute in Washington, D.C.

3. Frohardt, Paul, and Minear, *Protecting Human Rights,* 13.

4. See, for example, the annual report of the National Defense Council Foundation of Alexandria, Va. ("Study Finds Decline in Number of Countries Engaged in Conflicts in 2001," Carolyn Skorneck, Associated Press, Washington, D.C., December 23, 2001).

5. Frohardt, Paul, and Minear, *Protecting Human Rights,* 16.

6. Flows of "emergency and distress relief" increased from $766 million in 1989 to $4.365 billion in 1999, of total official development assistance in those years of $46.399 billion and $56.378 billion respectively. (The 1989 figure is based on a two-year average with 1988 and does not include emergency food aid.) OECD/DAC, *Development Cooperation 2000 Report* (Paris), Table 2, 180–81.

7. Frohardt, Paul, and Minear, *Protecting Human Rights,* 28.

8. Larry Minear, "Introduction to Case Studies," in *Humanitarian Action and Peace-keeping Operations: Debriefing and Lessons* (London, the Hague, Boston: Kluwer Law International, 1997), 63–64. The volume reprints other papers offered at an international conference in Singapore, cosponsored by the Institute of Policy Studies of Singapore, UNITAR, and the National Institute for Research Advancement of Japan, and summarizes the discussions and recommendations.

9. Larry Minear, "Introduction to Case Studies," 64.

10. Cristina Eguizábal, David Lewis, Larry Minear, Peter Sollis, and Thomas G. Weiss, *Humanitarian Challenges in Central America: Learning Lessons of Recent Armed Conflict,* Occasional Paper 14 (Providence: Watson Institute, 1993), 19, 73.

11. Neil MacFarlane, *Politics and Humanitarian Action,* Occasional Paper 41 (Providence: Watson Institute, 2000).

12. Don Hubert, *The Landmine Ban: A Case Study in Humanitarian Advocacy,* Occasional Paper 42 (Providence: Watson Institute, 2000).

13. Francis M. Deng and Larry Minear, *The Challenges of Famine Relief: Emergency Operations in the Sudan* (Washington, D.C.: Brookings Institution, 1992), 134–35.

14. Thomas G. Weiss and Larry Minear, eds., *Humanitarianism across Borders: Sustaining Civilians in Times of War* (Boulder, Colo.: Lynne Rienner, 1993), 60.

15. Barbara Crossette, "U.S. Finding Alliances on Rights are Tangled," *New York Times,* April 8, 2001, 7.

16. Jackson Diehl, "Chechnya Discounted," *Washington Post,* June 11, 2001, A19.

17. For further discussion, see Mohammed Ayoob, "The New-Old Disorder in the Third World," in *The United Nations and Civil Wars,* ed. Thomas G. Weiss (Boulder, Colo.: Lynne Rienner, 1995), 13–30. Also, in the same volume, Larry Minear, "The Humanitarian Enterprise," 89–106.

18. Frohardt, Paul, and Minear, *Protecting Human Rights,* 8.

19. ALNAP, *Humanitarian Action: Learning from Evaluation* (London: ALNAP, 2001), 14–17, updated in conversation with ALNAP staff.

20. *A Critical Review of Operation Lifeline Sudan: A Report to the Aid Agencies.* The book, *Humanitarianism under Siege: A Critical Review of Operation Lifeline Sudan* (Trenton, N.J.: Red Sea Press, 1991), was circulated by UNICEF Director James P. Grant at the conference convened in New York in August 1990 to approve the text of the newly negotiated Convention on the Rights of the Child.

21. For a more detailed description of the debriefings held on the advocacy study, see the project's Status Reports 36 and 37 at *hwproject.tufts.edu.*

22. For additional details, see Greg Hansen and Larry Minear, "Waiting for Peace: Perspectives from Action-Oriented Research on the Humanitarian Impasse in the Caucasus," *Disasters* 23, no. 3 (September 1999): 257–70.

23. Deng and Minear, *The Challenges of Famine Relief.* The drought-induced famine of 1983–86 is compared and contrasted with the conflict-related famine of 1987–91.

2. Coordination

1. See Larry Minear, "Foreword," in Marc Sommers, *The Dynamics of Coordination,* Occasional Paper 40 (Providence: Watson Institute, 1992), v.

2. Larry Minear, U. B. P. Chelliah, Jeff Crisp, John Mackinlay, and Thomas G. Weiss, *United Nations Coordination of the International Response to the Gulf Crisis, 1990–1992,* Occasional Paper 13 (Providence: Watson Institute, 1992), 3.

3. Antonio Donini, *The Policies of Mercy: UN Coordination in Afghanistan, Mozambique, and Rwanda,* Occasional Paper 22 (Providence: Watson Institute, 1996).

4. Marc Sommers, *The Dynamics of Coordination,* Occasional Paper 40 (Providence: Watson Institute, 2000).

5. See, for example, Larry Minear, "Learning the Lessons of Coordination," in *A Framework for Survival: Health, Human Rights, and Humanitarian Assistance*

in Conflicts and Disasters, ed. Kevin M. Cahill, rev. ed. (New York and London: Routledge, 1999), 298–316.

6. Sommers, *Dynamics of Coordination,* 56.

7. Ibid., 5.

8. Ibid., 99.

9. Higher expenditures on coordination during the past decade are widely assumed to have resulted in more effective programming. The data, however, remains fragmentary. New research might document the extent to which more resources are now indeed invested in coordination, and whether they have resulted in more effective humanitarian activities.

10. For a description, see Donini, *The Policies of Mercy,* 26–41, a section entitled "A New Approach to Coordination."

11. Donini, *The Policies of Mercy,* 15 and 122.

12. Larry Minear, Ted van Baarda, and Marc Sommers, *NATO and Humanitarian Action in the Kosovo Crisis,* Occasional Paper 36 (Providence: Watson Institute, 2000), 37.

13. Sommers, *Dynamics of Coordination,* 100.

14. Sue Lautze, Bruce D. Jones, and Mark Duffield, *Strategic Humanitarian Coordination in the Great Lakes Region, 1996–1997: An Independent Assessment* (New York: IASC, 1998), para. 118.

15. Antonio Donini, the analyst who authored the three-country comparison, suggested as a motto for effective UN coordination "adapt or die." *The Policies of Mercy,* 126.

16. S. Neil MacFarlane and Larry Minear, *Humanitarian Action and Politics: The Case of Nagorno-Karabakh,* Occasional Paper 25 (Providence: Watson Institute, 1997), 45–46, 56–58.

17. International Federation of Red Cross and Red Crescent Societies, *World Disasters Report 1994* (Geneva: IFRC, 1995), 67.

18. For a discussion of the role of the media in influencing aid and government policy in the Rwanda crisis, see Larry Minear, Colin Scott, and Thomas G. Weiss, *The News Media, Civil War, and Humanitarian Action* (Boulder, Colo., and London: Lynne Rienner, 1996), 62–67.

19. "Women Return to Work for WFP in Afghanistan," Reuters, November 20, 2001.

20. In June 2001, WFP suspended for a time, but later reinstated, its food aid activities in response to a demand that Afghan women be barred from the teams conducting a survey of nutritional needs.

21. For a more extended discussion, see Julie A. Mertus, *War's Offensive on Women: The Humanitarian Challenge in Bosnia, Kosovo, and Afghanistan* (Bloomfield, Conn.: Kumarian Press, 2000), 52–69. The material quoted is by Judy A. Benjamin and found on page 62.

22. Development Initiatives, *Global Humanitarian Assistance 2000* (Geneva: Inter-Agency Standing Committee, 2000), 49.

23. Nancy Lindborg, vice president of Mercy Corps International and vice-chair

of the InterAction Disaster Response Committee, e-mail correspondence to Marc Sommers, January 31, 2001.

24. Another analysis concludes that the "Big Eight" federations of NGOs control roughly half of the resources available to the international humanitarian enterprise. About $500 million of the $8 billion available annually is programmed by CARE, World Vision International, Oxfam, MSF, Save the Children, Eurostep, Coopération internationale pour le développement et la solidarité (CIDSE), and the Association of Protestant Development Organizations in Europe (APDOVE). See P. J. Simmons, "Learning to Live with NGOs," in *Foreign Policy* (fall 1998): 92. (Note: The figure of $8 billion is higher than the OECD/DAC figure cited in the previous chapter.)

25. Development Initiatives, *Global Humanitarian Assistance*, 47.

26. Amir Shah, "Taliban Allege Plot to Convert," Associated Press, August 13, 2001.

27. Our study of UN efforts to integrate human rights noted the observation of several of those interviewed that OHCHR "misses key [interagency] meetings, lacks consistency of representation needed to follow a particular issue, and is represented by staff lacking authority to discuss policy." Karen Kenny, *When Needs Are Rights: An Overview of UN Efforts to Integrate Human Rights in Humanitarian Action*, Occasional Paper 38 (Providence: Watson Institute, 2000), 65.

28. A study commissioned by OCHA and released in mid-2001 offers a detailed review of obstacles to coordination and institutional options. See Nicola Reindorp and Peter Wiles, *Humanitarian Coordination: Lessons from Recent Field Experience* (London: Overseas Development Institute, 2001). Annex 2 provides a useful Matrix of Coordination Arrangements used in several dozen recent major emergencies. I served as a peer reviewer for the study.

29. John Borton, "Doing Study 3 of the Joint Evaluation of Emergency Assistance to Rwanda: The Team Leader's Perspective," in *Evaluating International Humanitarian Action: Reflections from Practitioners*, ed. Adrian Wood, Raymond Apthorpe, and John Borton (London and New York: Zed Books and ALNAP, 2001), 91. The term proved inflammatory.

30. The situation is complicated by the fact that the humanitarian coordinator in a given country reports to the emergency relief coordinator in New York, the resident coordinator to the UNDP administrator in New York.

31. Kofi Annan, "Note from the Secretary-General: Guidance on the Relations between Representatives of the Secretary-General, Resident Coordinators, and Humanitarian Coordinators," December 11, 2000. Despite some skepticism among outside analysts, Secretariat staff credit the note with having established a positive framework for coordinating UN humanitarian activities in complex emergencies.

32. In early 1992 when UNHCR was given lead responsibility in Bosnia, DHA was just becoming established.

33. Office for the Coordination of Humanitarian Affairs, Terms of Reference, "The Future of Humanitarian Coordination," 2.

34. "Report of the Panel on Peace Operations," A/55/305-S/2000/809, August 20, 2000. The secretary-general's recommendations are contained in "Report of the Secretary-General," A/55/502, October 2000.

35. Development Initiatives, *Global Humanitarian Assistance*, 90.

36. Ibid., 25. The doubling of humanitarian assistance during the decade cited here contrasts with the OECD figure cited in chapter 1.

37. Some of these differences (for example, in policies and strategies vis-à-vis the UN and NGOs) emerged and were processed in a series of dialogues facilitated by the H & W Project in 1999–2000 between the EU and the U.S. government.

38. MacFarlane and Minear, *Humanitarian Action and Politics: The Case of Nagorno-Karabakh*, 45–46, 56–58.

39. For an account of the discussion, see NGO Policy Dialogue 6, "NATO and NGOs in the Kosovo Crisis," on the project's Web site, *hwproject.tufts.edu* (December 13, 1999).

40. For an overview of the Sphere Project, the NGO/Red Cross Code of Conduct, and other statements of humanitarian principles, see Box 5.2, "Initiatives to Improve Quality," in Development Initiatives, *Global Humanitarian Assistance 2000*, 86.

41. Sommers, *Dynamics of Coordination*, vii.

42. Ibid., 104.

43. Ibid., x.

44. Donini, *The Policies of Mercy*, 113.

45. Greg Hansen, *Humanitarian Action in the Caucasus: A Guide for Practitioners*, Occasional Paper 32 (Providence: Watson Institute, 1998), 48. Issues of the interface between the humanitarian community and political and diplomatic actors are addressed in chapter 5 of the present volume.

46. In February 2000, eleven NGOs opted to leave the Sudan rather than sign a memorandum of agreement with the humanitarian wing of the insurgency. See "3/4 of NGO Operations in OLS Shut Down in Part of South Sudan," *Talk Back: The Newsletter of the ICVA* 2, no. 2 (March 2000).

47. Sommers, *Dynamics of Coordination*, 5.

3. Human Rights

1. Larry Minear and Thomas G. Weiss, *Mercy under Fire: War and the Global Humanitarian Community* (Boulder, San Francisco, and Oxford: Westview Press, 1995), 107–8. For a review of U.S.-Ethiopian relations at the time of the famine, see Jack Shepherd, "A Fragile American-Ethiopian Bridge," *New York Times*, October 31, 1985, A27.

2. See, for example, Claude Bruderlein, "People's Security as a New Measure of Global Stability," *International Review of the Red Cross* 83, no. 842 (June 2001): 353–66. Bruderlein argues that classical distinctions between civilian and military assets and the traditional assumption that nations will observe and promote humanitarian norms and principles no longer hold.

3. The conference, convened by UNHCR, was titled, "Strengthening Collaboration with Humanitarian and Human Rights NGOs in Support of the International Refugee Protection System."

4. For a review of the NGO discussions, see Larry Minear, *Helping People in an Age of Conflict: Toward a New Professionalism in U.S. Voluntary Humanitarian Assistance* (New York and Washington, D.C.: InterAction, 1988), 69.

5. The evolution of sovereignty during these years is discussed in greater detail in chapter 5.

6. Cherne was chief executive of the International Rescue Committee from 1951 onward and later chair of its board until 1991. He also served as an advisor on defense and security policy to a succession of U.S. administrations. Michael T. Kaufman, "Leo Cherne, Leader of Agency for Refugees, Is Dead at 86," *New York Times,* January 14, 1998, A18.

7. See Robert Maguire et al., *Haiti Held Hostage: International Responses to the Quest for Nationhood, 1986–1996* (Providence: Watson Institute, 1996), 42. A similar incident involving Oxfam-UK in Ethiopia during the 1984–85 famine is described in Larry Minear and Thomas G. Weiss, *Mercy under Fire: War and the Global Humanitarian Community* (Boulder, San Francisco, Oxford: Westview, 1995), 122.

8. The connections between humanitarian activities and conflict are explored in chapter 6.

9. "The Politics of Human Rights," *The Economist* (August 18–24, 2001): 9.

10. Bruderlein, "People's Security," 365.

11. The Statute of Amnesty International, as amended by the 25th International Council, meeting in Dakar, Senegal, August 17–25, 2001, is available at *http://web.amnesty.org.*

12. Amnesty International, International Council Meeting: "An Agenda for Human Rights in the 21st Century," press release (August 28, 2001).

13. "The Politics of Human Rights," *The Economist.*

14. Some advocates have urged human rights groups to diversify their tool kit further still. Beyond the naming of problems, "Perhaps it is high time for human rights organizations to put more into the development of real problem-solving tactics that they themselves can implement," writes Liam Mahony. "And perhaps it is time to start loosening up some of the mandate and neutrality concerns that have prevented [them] from capitalizing on the growing possibilities of mounting powerful joint efforts with other civil society forces." *Military Intervention in Human Rights Crises: Responses and Dilemmas for the Human Rights Movement* (Geneva: International Council on Human Rights Policy, 2001), 21.

15. Michael McClintock, "Tensions between Assistance and Protection: A Human Rights Perspective," in *Humanitarian Action: A Transatlantic Agenda for Operations and Research,* ed. Larry Minear and Thomas G. Weiss, Occasional Paper 39 (Providence: Watson Institute, 1999), 26.

16. Greg Hansen, *Humanitarian Action in the Caucasus: A Guide for Practitioners,* Occasional Paper 32 (Providence: Watson Institute, 1998), 54.

17. Ibid.

18. For a more extended discussion of the concept of humanitarianism in its strict and broader senses, see Minear and Weiss, *Mercy under Fire,* 18–22.

19. In Deborah Eade and Ernst Ligteringen, *Debating Development* [Development in Practice Reader] (London: Oxfam-GB, 2001), 287–91.

20. Gilbert Loescher, book review, *Journal of Refugee Studies* 9, no. 2 (1996): 221–22.

21. Willliam Demars, book review, *Mershon International Studies Review* 40 (1996): 83. The NGO discussions in the mid-1980s referenced in note 4 above also focused almost exclusively on relief delivery in the politicized Cold War terrain, with little attention to the underlying human rights issues.

22. Mark Frohardt, Diane Paul, and Larry Minear, *Protecting Human Rights: The Challenge to Humanitarian Organizations,* Occasional Paper 35 (Providence: Watson Institute, 1999), 44–45.

23. Julie A. Mertus, *War's Offensive on Women: The Humanitarian Challenge in Bosnia, Kosovo, and Afghanistan* (Bloomfield, Conn.: Kumarian Press, 2000).

24. During the years 1996–2000, the ICRC convened a series of four workshops on the topic of protection. See Jacques de Maio, ed., *The Challenges of Complementarity* (Geneva: ICRC, 2000).

25. S. Neil MacFarlane, Larry Minear, and Stephen D. Shenfield, *Armed Conflict in Georgia: A Case Study in Humanitarian Action and Peacekeeping,* Occasional Paper 21 (Providence: Watson Institute, 1996), 78.

26. Jeffrey Clark, Roberta Cohen, Dennis Gallagher, Iain Guest, Larry Minear, and Thomas G. Weiss, *Humanitarian Action in the Former Yugoslavia: The U.N.'s Role, 1991–1993,* Occasional Paper 18 (Providence: Watson Institute, 1994), 68.

27. Ibid., 64.

28. Ogata Sadako, "Ten Years Devoted to Protecting Refugees," *Japan Echo* (August 2001): 45.

29. Benny Ben Otim, "Caught in the Crossfire: Dilemmas of Human Rights Protection in Former Yugoslavia, in United Nations Volunteers," in *Volunteers against Conflict* (Tokyo, New York, and Paris: United Nations University Press, 1996), 123.

30. Clark et al., *Humanitarian Action in the Former Yugoslavia,* 68.

31. International Council of Voluntary Agencies, "Meeting Note" (January 18, 2001), 1.

32. Karen Kenny, *When Needs Are Rights: An Overview of UN Efforts to Integrate Human Rights in Humanitarian Action,* Occasional Paper 38 (Providence: Watson Institute, 2000).

33. Mentioned earlier, the UNHCR conference was held in New York, March 11–12, 1999. For its background paper, see Larry Minear, "Partnership in the Protection of Refugees and Other People at Risk: Emerging Issues and Work in Progress," New Issues in Refugee Research: Working Paper No. 13 (Geneva: UNHCR Centre for Documentation and Research, July 1999).

34. Andrew Jones, "A Rights Approach and Responsibility Analysis," in *Promoting Rights and Responsibilities,* CARE U.S. newsletter, October 2000, 7.

35. Uwe Korus, quoted in "Staff Reflections: Adopting a Rights-Based Approach, in *Promoting Rights and Responsibilities,* CARE U.S. newsletter, February 2001, 7.

36. "Righting Wrongs: Human Rights," *The Economist* (August 18–24, 2001): 19.

37. The human rights interface was the subject of one of the project's series of dialogues with North American NGO officials. See NGO Policy Dialogue III, May 14, 1998, "Protecting Human Rights in Complex Emergencies" (*hwproject.tufts.edu*)

38. For a more extended discussion, see Larry Minear and Thomas G. Weiss,

eds., *Humanitarian Action: A Transatlantic Agenda for Operations and Research,* Occasional Paper 39 (Providence: Watson Institute, 2000)

39. A fuller review of the tension between neutrality and political engagement is contained in chapter 5.

40. William O'Neill, *A Humanitarian Practitioner's Guide to International Human Rights Law,* Occasional Paper 34 (Providence: Watson Institute, 1999), 59.

41. Mertus, *War's Offensive on Women,* 67–68.

42. Advocacy activities by aid groups are reviewed in chapter 5.

43. Elizabeth Ferris, "Notes on UNHCR's Global Consultations on International Protection," World Council of Churches, Geneva, March 16, 2001.

44. Minear and Weiss, eds., *Humanitarian Action: A Transatlantic Agenda,* 39.

45. Such intrusions of politics into humanitarian action are examined in chapter 5.

46. Minear and Weiss, eds., *Humanitarian Action: A Transatlantic Agenda,* 36.

47. O'Neill, *A Humanitarian Practitioner's Guide to International Human Rights Law,* 53.

48. Minear and Weiss, eds., *Humanitarian Action: A Transatlantic Agenda,* 5–6.

49. O'Neill, *A Humanitarian Practitioner's Guide to International Human Rights Law,* 58.

50. Its author, William G. O'Neill, is himself a human rights lawyer and participant in a number of UN and NGO human rights operations.

51. For the application of the concept of fundamentalism in this sense see Minear and Weiss, eds., *Humanitarian Action: A Transatlantic Agenda,* 5–6.

52. One suggestion for further research is to examine whether human rights–based aid programming was more effective and cost-effective than traditional aid efforts. Minear and Weiss, eds., *Humanitarian Action: A Transatlantic Agenda,* 9.

4. Strengthening Local Capacity

1. Larry Minear, U. B. P. Chelliah, Jeff Crisp, John Mackinlay, and Thomas G. Weiss, *United Nations Coordination of the International Humanitarian Response to the Gulf Crisis, 1990–1992,* Occasional Paper 13 (Providence: Watson Institute, 1992), 23.

2. Arjuna Parakrama, "Humanitarian Assistance to War Victims in Sri Lanka," in *Patronage or Partnership,* ed. Ian Smillie (Bloomfield, Conn.: Kumarian Press, 2001), 120.

3. Ibid., 116.

4. Peter Morgan, "Capacity Development — An Introduction," quoted in Ian Smillie, "Capacity Building and the Humanitarian Enterprise," in *Patronage or Partnership,* ed. Smillie, 9.

5. Greg Hansen, *Humanitarian Action in the Caucasus: A Guide for Practitioners,* Occasional Paper 32 (Providence: Watson Institute, 1998), 51.

6. Ephraim Isaac, "Humanitarianism across Religions and Cultures," in *Human-*

itarianism across Borders: Sustaining Civilians in Times of War, ed. Thomas G. Weiss and Larry Minear (Boulder, Colo.: Lynne Rienner, 1993), 14.

7. Ibid., 18.

8. Kathy Mangones, "Alternative Food Aid Strategies and Local Capacity Building in Haiti," in *Patronage or Partnership,* ed. Smillie, 53. The vibrancy of Haitian civil society is also noted in Robert Maguire, Edwige Balutansky, Jacques Fomerand, Larry Minear, William G. O'Neill, Thomas G. Weiss, and Sarah Zaidi, *Haiti Held Hostage: International Responses to the Quest for Nationhood,* Occasional Paper 23 (Providence: Watson Institute, 1996).

9. Mike Leffert, "Women's Organizations in Guatemalan Refugee and Returnee Populations," in *Patronage or Partnership,* ed. Smillie, 135.

10. Ibid., 135, 150–52.

11. Minear et al., *United Nations Coordination,* 27–28.

12. See S. Neil MacFarlane, Larry Minear, and Stephen D. Shenfield, *Armed Conflict in Georgia: A Case Study in Humanitarian Action and Peacekeeping,* Occasional Paper 21 (Providence: Watson Institute, 1996).

13. Kathy Mangones, "Alternative Food Aid Strategies and Local Capacity Building in Haiti," in *Patronage or Partnership,* ed. Smillie, 70. *Soldes* are traditional solidarity loan associations; *eskwads* are one of many forms of traditional agricultural work groups, bringing together farmers for tasks such as planting and harvesting.

14. Ian Smillie and Goran Todorovic, "Reconstructing Bosnia, Constructing Civil Society," in *Patronage or Partnership,* ed. Smillie, 45.

15. Ibid.

16. Antonio Donini, *The Policies of Mercy: UN Coordination in Afghanistan, Mozambique, and Rwanda,* Occasional Paper 22 (Providence: Watson Institute, 1996), 79.

17. See Stephen C. Lubkemann, "Rebuilding Local Capacities in Mozambique," in *Patronage or Partnership,* ed. Smillie, 79. A recent British government study observes that "Mozambique's successful emergence from conflict has been in no small part due to its success in relegitimizing the state in the eyes of the population. This was done through a strong commitment to reestablishing and delivering basic services, thereby demonstrating the value of national government." See Cabinet Sub-Committee on Conflict Prevention in Africa, *The Causes of Conflict in Africa,* 2001, para. 52.

18. The make-up of the board of governors of the American Red Cross is described in Deborah Sontag's "Who Brought Bernadine Healy Down? The Red Cross: A Disaster Story without Any Heroes," *New York Times Magazine,* December 23, 2001, 36. Healy was fired from her position as president of the American Red Cross in the wake of the organization's response to the terrorist attacks of September 11, 2001.

19. Minear et al., *United Nations Coordination,* 24.

20. Tabyiegen A. Aboum, Eshetu Chole, Koste Manibe, Larry Minear, Abdul Mohammed, Jennefer Sebstad, and Thomas G. Weiss, *A Critical Review of Operation*

Lifeline Sudan: A Report to the Aid Agencies (Providence: Humanitarianism and War Project, 1990), 51–52.

21. For a detailed review of the experience, see Kathy Mangones, "Alternative Food Aid Strategies and Local Capacity Building in Haiti," in *Patronage or Partnership,* Smillie, ed., 51–76.

22. Ibid., 66.

23. Hansen, *Humanitarian Action in the Caucasus: A Guide for Practitioners.*

24. Greg Hansen and Larry Minear, "Waiting for Peace: Perspectives from Action-Oriented Research on the Humanitarian Impasse in the Caucasus," *Disasters* 23, no. 3 (September 1999): 265.

25. For additional details, see Hansen and Minear, "Waiting for Peace," 264.

26. Barry Bearak, "Accused Aid Workers Face Islamic Judges in Afghanistan," *New York Times,* September 9, 2001, 3.

27. Scott Baldauf, "Workers' Release Heralds an Aid-Friendly Afghanistan," *Christian Science Monitor,* November 16, 2001.

28. Larry Minear, "Partnerships in Protection: An Overview of Emerging Issues and Work in Progress," UNHCR Centre for Documentation and Research, Geneva, 1999, 7–8.

29. George Devendorf, director, Global Emergency Operations, Mercy Corps International, telephone interview, September 13, 2001.

30. Lubkemann, "Rebuilding Local Capacities in Mozambique," in *Patronage or Partnership,* ed. Smillie, 103, 116.

31. Development Initiatives, *Global Humanitarian Assistance 2000* (Geneva: Inter-Agency Standing Committee, 2000), 85.

32. Sue Lautze of the Feinstein International Famine Center, letter to author, July 25, 2001.

33. Parakrama, "Humanitarian Assistance to War Victims in Sri Lanka," in *Patronage or Partnership,* ed. Smillie, 118, 122.

34. Mary B. Anderson, ed., *Options for Aid in Conflict: Lessons from Field Experience, Local Capacities for Peace Project* (Cambridge, Mass.: Collaborative for Development Action, 2000), 49–50.

35. Francis M. Deng and Larry Minear, *The Challenges of Famine Relief: Emergency Operations in the Sudan* (Washington, D.C.: Brookings Institution, 1992), 129. The drought-induced famine of 1983–86 is compared and contrasted with the conflict-related famine of 1987–91. The skills needed to undergird the recommended approach are discussed in chapter 8.

5. Humanitarian Politics

1. S. Neil MacFarlane, letter to author, July 15, 2001.

2. S. Neil MacFarlane and Thomas G. Weiss, "Political Interest and Humanitarian Action," *Security Studies* 10, no. 1 (autumn 2000), 142.

3. Larry Minear, foreword in S. Neil MacFarlane, *Politics and Humanitarian Action,* Occasional Paper 41 (Providence: Watson Institute, 2000), vi.

4. Letter to author, July 15, 2001.

5. Jean Pictet, *The Fundamental Principles of the Red Cross* (Geneva: Henry Dunant Institute, 1979), 56. See also David P. Forsythe, *Humanitarian Politics: The International Committee of the Red Cross* (Baltimore: Johns Hopkins University Press, 1977).

6. The quotations are excerpted from a more extended discussion in Larry Minear, "The Theory and Practice of Neutrality: Some Thoughts on the Tensions," *International Review of the Red Cross* 81, no. 833 (March 1999): 63–71.

7. Urs Boegli, interview by author, Washington, D.C., October 24, 2001.

8. For a review of UNHCR's approach to these issues, see David P. Forsythe, "UNHCR's Mandate: The Politics of Being Non-Political," working paper, UNHCR, Geneva, 2001).

9. Larry Minear and Thomas G. Weiss, *Humanitarian Action in Times of War: A Handbook for Practitioners* (Boulder, Colo.: Lynne Rienner, 1993), 23.

10. John Swenson, Testimony before the House Select Committee on Hunger, September 25, 1992, 134.

11. Sally Engle Merry, "Mennonite Peacebuilding and Conflict Transformation: A Cultural Analysis," in *From the Ground Up: Mennonite Contributions to International Peacebuilding,* ed. Cynthia Sampson and John Paul Lederach (New York: Oxford University Press, 2000), 213. Peace Brigades also uses the solidarity paradigm.

12. Thomas Getman, *Newsletter from Israel* 53, January 13, 2001.

13. For a more extended discussion of various paradigms, see Larry Minear, "Terms of Engagement with Human Need," *The Ecumenical Review* 24, no. 1 (January 1990): 4–16.

14. Thomas G. Weiss, "Principle, Politics, and Humanitarian Action," *Ethics and International Affairs* 13 (1999): 1–21.

15. Hugo Slim, "Sharing a Universal Ethic: The Principle of Humanity in War," *The International Journal of Human Rights* 2, no. 4 (winter 1998): 28–48. Slim also offers some useful definitions of humanitarian action itself. See "Military Intervention to Protect Human Rights: The Humanitarian Agency Perspective," International Council on Human Rights Policy, Geneva, 2001), 4ff.

16. Mark Duffield, *Global Governance and the New Wars: The Merging of Development and Security* (London and New York: Zed Books, 2001), 75. See in particular chapter 4, "The New Humanitarianism."

17. Larry Minear, "The Morality of Sanctions," in *Hard Choices,* ed. Jonathan Moore (Lanham, Md., and Oxford, England: Rowman & Littlefield, 1998), 233.

18. Ted A. van Baarda, "The Involvement of the Security Council in Maintaining International Humanitarian Law," *Netherlands Quarterly of Human Rights* 12, no. 2 (1994): 137–52. The quotation is taken from page 138.

19. Development Initiatives, *Global Humanitarian Assistance 2000* (Geneva: IASC, 2000), 54.

20. Maurice Torrelli, "From Humanitarian Assistance to 'Intervention on Humanitarian Grounds,'" *International Review of the Red Cross,* May–June 1992, reprinted in House Select Committee on Hunger, 102d Cong., 2d sess., 1992, 100.

21. U.S. policy discouraged use of the term "genocide," which would have

required the United States and other signatories of the genocide convention to take re-medial action. One analyst describes how "the Forbidden G-word" was consciously avoided for sixty-seven days. (Helen Fein, "Rwanda 1994: What the US Knew and Why It Stood By," Institute for the Study of Genocide; undated.) A subsequent UN re-port criticized the Security Council's decision not to respond positively to the request from General Roméo Dallaire in Rwanda.

22. While enhancing the security of some Rwandan civilians, the French initiative also had negative political consequences for humanitarian interests on the ground. See chapter 5 in Larry Minear and Philippe Guillot, *Soldiers to the Rescue: Human-itarian Lessons from Rwanda* (Paris: Organization for Economic Cooperation and Development, 1996).

23. For a fuller discussion of these examples, see Larry Minear, "Introduction to Case Studies," in *Humanitarian Action and Peace-Keeping Operations: Debrief-ing and Lessons. Report and Recommendations of the International Conference, Singapore, February 1997,* ed. Nassrine Azimi (London, The Hague, and Boston: Kluwer Law International, 1997), 47–48, and Robert Maguire, Edwige Balutansky, Jacques Fomerand, Larry Minear, William G. O'Neill, Thomas G. Weiss, and Sarah Zaidi, *Haiti Held Hostage: International Responses to the Quest for Nationhood, 1986–1996,* Occasional Paper 23 (Providence: Watson Institute, 1996).

24. During the years 1994–97, the project produced separate studies on *Armed Conflict in Georgia: A Case Study in Humanitarian Action and Peacekeeping* (1995), *Humanitarian Action and Politics: The Case of Nagorno-Karabakh* (1997), and *War and Humanitarian Action in Chechnya* (1997).

25. The setting for humanitarian action in "post-Soviet space" is described in the preface to the Georgia study. S. Neil MacFarlane, Larry Minear, and Stephen Shenfield, *Armed Conflict in Georgia: A Case Study in Humanitarian Action and Peacekeeping,* Occasional Paper 21 (Providence: Watson Institute, 1996), v.

26. UN Department of Humanitarian Affairs, "United Nations Consolidated Inter-Agency Appeal for Persons Displaced as a Result of the Emergency Situation in Chechnya" and Report on Activities in 1995, April 1996. By contrast, OCHA's *Hu-manitarian Action in the North Caucasus Information Bulletin* (December 16–31, 2001) mentions activities supported by WFP within Chechnya through four NGOs as well as among IDPs from Chechnya in the neighboring republics.

27. Greg Hansen and Robert Seely, *War and Humanitarian Action in Chechnya,* Occasional Paper 26 (Providence: Watson Institute, 1996), 53.

28. Agence France-Presse, "Russia Protests UN Report on Chechnya Human Rights Violations," March 4, 2001.

29. Reuters, "Russia Rights Envoy Raps U.N. Robinson on Chechnya," April 3, 2001.

30. Steven Mufson, "American Foreign Policy Suddenly Shifts Course: From Chechnya to China, New Priorities Rule," *International Herald Tribune,* Septem-ber 28, 2001, 3.

31. For a more detailed discussion, see Greg Hansen, *Humanitarian Action in the Caucasus: A Guide for Practitioners, Occasional Paper* 32 (Providence: Watson Institute, 1998), 65.

32. Larry Minear and Thomas G. Weiss, "Getting the Relationship Right," in *Humanitarian Politics* (New York: Foreign Policy Association, 1995), 32–51. The quotation is taken from page 32.

33. Ibid., 50–51.

34. United Nations Report of the Secretary-General, *New International Humanitarian Order,* General Assembly Document A/40/348, October 9, 1985, 36. Quoted in Larry Minear, Thomas G. Weiss, and Kurt M. Campbell, *Humanitarianism and War: Learning the Lessons from Recent Armed Conflicts,* Occasional Paper 8 (Providence: Watson Institute, 1991).

35. For a discussion of the consultation's findings and recommendations on a new international agreement, see Minear, Weiss and Campbell, *Humanitarianism and War,* 20–22.

36. 1999 UN Secretary-General's Bulletin on Observance by United Nations Forces of International Humanitarian Law, UN doc. ST/SGB/1999/13 (*www.un.org/peace/stsgb_19_12.pdf.*) Positive change has also taken place at the level of regional organizations. See, for example, the OSCE's Code of Conduct on Political-Military Aspects of Security.

37. United Nations Resolutions 1265 (1999) and 1296 (2000).

38. S/2001/331, paras. 30–37.

39. See Don Hubert, *The Landmine Ban: A Case Study in Humanitarian Advocacy,* Occasional Paper 42 (Providence: Watson Institute, 2000).

40. Ibid., 12.

41. Landmine Monitor, *Landmine Monitor Report 2000: Toward a Mine-Free World* (Washington, D.C.: Human Rights Watch, 2000), quoted in Marc Lindenberg and Coralie Bryant, *Going Global* (Bloomfield, Conn.: Kumarian Books, 2001), 199.

42. See preface by S. Neil MacFarlane in Hubert, *The Landmine Ban,* xi.

43. Secretary of State Madeline Albright and Secretary of Defense William Cohen announced the decision with great fanfare on October 31, 1997 (State Department Press Briefing on Landmine Policy, October 31, 1997; see also State Department fact sheet, Humanitarian Demining Program, May 20, 1998).

44. Hubert, *The Landmine Ban,* 1–2.

45. Ibid., 40.

46. Our study identifies the elements that contributed to the success of the criminal court and child soldiers initiatives as well as weaknesses in the current parallel effort to ban small arms transfers.

47. In the absence of agreement, at the July 2001 conference, on an international plan of action to restrict illicit trade in small arms, advocacy efforts are seeking to reframe the agenda in more clearly humanitarian terms and to restart momentum toward a convention banning small arms transfers. For a discussion of the provisions of international law regarding refugees and IDPs, see William G. O'Neill, *A Humanitarian Practitioner's Guide to International Human Rights Law,* Occasional Paper 34 (Providence: Watson Institute, 1999), 39–43.

48. The statement is taken from a report by Francis Deng to the April 1998 session of the UN Human Rights Commission introducing the guiding principles, quoted in ibid., 42.

49. Hubert, *The Landmine Ban,* 67.

50. Frances Deng and Kofi Asomani, Joint Statement on Afghanistan, November 1, 2001.

51. For a discussion of NGO interaction with the Council, see also Lindenberg and Bryant, *Going Global,* 197–98. OCHA and the Global Policy Forum have orchestrated meetings between the council and NGOs. During the year 2000, the Forum (*globalpolicy@globalpolicy.org*) organized more than thirty meetings for NGOs with Security Council ambassadors. While informal NGO briefings of the Security Council represent a new development, the ICRC for years has provided regular briefings to the council's chairman.

52. Disproportionalities in aid allocations among crises are examined in chapter 7.

53. The quotation is taken from the commission's volume of background research and bibliography, *The Responsibility to Protect* (International Commission on Intervention and State Sovereignty, December 2001), 6.

54. Francis M. Deng and Larry Minear, *The Challenges of Famine Relief: Emergency Operations in the Sudan* (Washington, D.C.: Brookings Institution, 1992), 134–35.

55. Development Initiatives, *Global Humanitarian Assistance 2000,* 69.

56. See Adam Roberts, "NATO's 'Humanitarian War' over Kosovo," in Larry Minear, Ted van Baarda, and Marc Sommers, *NATO and Humanitarian Action in the Kosovo Crisis,* Occasional Paper 36 (Providence: Watson Institute, 2000), 121.

57. For an extended discussion, see Larry Minear et al., *Humanitarianism under Siege* (Trenton, N.J.: Red Sea Press, 1991), 104.

58. See ibid., 102–3. In response to a question early in the 1990s by the author, John Garang, leader of the Sudan Peoples Liberation Movement, acknowledged that while to the best of his knowledge his troops did not have a copy of the Geneva Conventions in their field library, they would be open to an ICRC field tutorial on their legal obligations.

59. Marc Sommers, *The Dynamics of Coordination,* Occasional Paper 40 (Providence: Watson Institute, 2000), 59.

60. Antonio Donini, *The Policies of Mercy: UN Coordination in Afghanistan, Mozambique, and Rwanda,* Occasional Paper 22 (Providence: Watson Institute, 1996), 77, 79.

61. Natsios has served as a U.S. National Guard official in northern Iraq, head of USAID's Office of Foreign Disaster Assistance, an executive of the NGO World Vision, and, currently, administrator of the U.S. Agency for International Development. He is quoted in Neil MacFarlane, *Politics and Humanitarian Action,* Occasional Paper 41 (Providence: Watson Institute, 2000), 1.

62. The quotation is from Maurice Torrelli, "From Humanitarian Assistance to 'Intervention on Humanitarian Grounds,'" *International Review of the Red Cross* (May–June 1992), reprinted in hearing before the House Select Committee on Hunger, 102d Cong., 2d sess., 1992, 232.

63. A/Res/46-182, December 17, 1991.

64. For a discussion of the balance between sovereignty and human rights, see

Larry Minear, "Humanitarian Intervention in a New World Order," Overseas Development Council, *Policy Focus*, no. 1 (1992): 3.

65. International Commission on Intervention and State Sovereignty, "State Sovereignty," in *The Responsibility to Protect*, 8.

66. See Minear et al., *Humanitarianism under Siege*, 99.

67. The findings of our studies on Central America, particularly El Salvador, and on Haiti offer instructive examples of such difficulties. The politically driven timetable of international involvement undercut the necessarily slower processes of social and economic reconstruction.

68. The issue of humanitarian action fueling conflicts is reviewed in chapter 8.

69. S. Neil MacFarlane, *Humanitarian Action: The Conflict Connection*, Occasional Paper 43 (Providence: Watson Institute, 2000), 40.

70. MacFarlane, *Politics and Humanitarian Action*, 79.

71. Larry Minear et al., *Toward More Humane and Effective Sanctions Management: Enhancing the Capacity of the United Nations System* (Providence: Watson Institute, 1998) Occasional Paper 31, 73.

6. Coercive Humanitarianism

1. Following his retirement, General Zinni served in late 2001 and early 2002 as special U.S. mediator in the worsening conflict between Israelis and Palestinians.

2. Our colleague Ted van Baarda has pointed out that "the Charter of the United Nations has no express provision empowering the Security Council to uphold international humanitarian law." Humanitarian issues are subsumed by state practice under human rights issues, which are the province of the General Assembly, the Economic and Social Council, the Trusteeship Council, and their subsidiary organs. Theodore A. van Baarda, "The Involvement of the Security Council in Maintaining International Humanitarian Law," *Netherlands Quarterly of Human Rights* 12, no. 2 (1994): 143.

3. UN Charter, Articles 1, 11, and 39–51.

4. United Nations, "Secretary-General Presents His Annual Report to the General Assembly," Press Release SG.SM.7136, September 20, 1999.

5. For a detailed and nuanced review of the varying views of relief and rights agencies toward engaging the military in conflicts, see International Council on Human Rights Policy, "NGO Responses to Military Interventions in Human Rights Crises," draft report, September 2001 (*www.international-council.org*).

6. See, for example, Bernard Kouchner and Mario Bettati, *Le Devoir d'ingérence* (Paris: Denoël, 1987), and Bernard Kouchner, *Le Malheur des autres* (Paris: Odile Jacob, 1991).

7. Yves Sandoz, "'*Droit* or *devoir d'ingérence*' and the Right to Assistance: The Issues Involved," an *International Red Cross Review* article reprinted in "Humanitarian Intervention: A Review of Theory and Practice," U.S. House of Representatives Select Committee on Hunger, 102d Cong., 2d sess., 1992, 29.

8. van Baarda, "The Involvement of the Security Council," 144.

9. Sadako Ogata, statement (Conference on Humanitarian Response and the Prevention of Deadly Conflict convened by the Carnegie Commission on the Prevention

of Deadly Conflict and UNHCR, Geneva, February 1997); quoted in Thomas G. Weiss and Cindy Collins, *Humanitarian Challenges and Intervention: World Politics and the Dilemmas* (Boulder, Colo.: Westview Press, 1996), 159.

10. The quotation is from a statement by ICRC President Jakob Kellenberger, quoted in Stefan Borkert, "Nahe an den Opfer sein," *Thurgau* [Switzerland] *Tagblatt* (May 17, 2001): 55.

11. Yves Sandoz, "'*Droit*' or *devoir d'ingérence*' and the right to assistance: the issues involved," an *International Red Cross Review* article reprinted in "Humanitarian Intervention: A Review of Theory and Practice," 30 [Hearing held September 25, 1992].

12. Larry Minear, Jeffrey Clark, Roberta Cohen, Dennis Gallagher, Iain Guest, and Thomas G. Weiss, *Humanitarian Action in the Former Yugoslavia: The U.N.'s Role, 1991–1993*, Occasional Paper 18 (Providence: Watson Institute, 1994), 86.

13. Larry Minear and Thomas G. Weiss, *Mercy under Fire* (Boulder, Colo.: Westview Press, 1995), 123–24.

14. International Council on Human Rights Policy, "NGO Responses to Military Interventions in Human Rights Crises," paras. 59–64.

15. Larry Minear and Philippe Guillot, *Soldiers to the Rescue: Humanitarian Lessons from Rwanda* (Paris: Organization for Economic Cooperation and Development, 1996), 37.

16. Weiss and Collins, *Humanitarian Challenges and Intervention*, 159–82.

17. Thomas G. Weiss, letter to author, September 14, 2001.

18. Weiss and Collins, *Humanitarian Challenges and Intervention*, chapter 6, "Policies of Militarized Humanitarian Intervention," 159–82.

19. Analyst Hugo Slim makes a similar point, noting that "government bodies, commercial companies and military forces can operate as humanitarian agencies if they pursue humanitarian activities as prescribed in international law in an impartial manner. But there is nevertheless an important distinction between an organisation that is essentially (as a whole or in a significant part of itself) concerned with humanitarian work and an organisation which is primarily concerned with other objectives but is in part operating in a humanitarian fashion." "Military Intervention to Protect Human Rights: The Humanitarian Agency Perspective," International Council of Human Rights Policy, Geneva, 2001, 5.

20. See Larry Minear, Ted van Baarda, and Marc Sommers, *NATO and Humanitarian Action in the Kosovo Crisis*, Occasional Paper 36 (Providence: Watson Institute, 2000), 4, 97.

21. Ibid., *NATO and Humanitarian Action*, 117.

22. Larry Minear and Philippe Guillot, *Soldiers to the Rescue: Humanitarian Lessons from Rwanda* (Paris: Organization for Economic Cooperation and Development, 1996). Five chapters examine the various configurations of international troops engaged in the Rwanda crisis; two chapters examine the global policy issues involved.

23. Ibid., *Soldiers to the Rescue*, 150.

24. Ibid., 119.

25. Ibid., 123.

26. Charles Bierbauer, foreword, in Larry Minear, Colin Scott, and Thomas G. Weiss, *The News Media, Civil War, and Humanitarian Action* (Boulder, Colo.: Lynne Rienner, 1996), viii.

27. Minear and Guillot, *Soldiers to the Rescue*, 116.

28. Ibid., 140.

29. See, for example, UN Department of Humanitarian Affairs, "The Oslo Guidelines on the Use of Military and Civil Defence Assets in Disaster Relief," May 1994.

30. An exception is MSF-US, which withdrew from InterAction's Disaster Relief Committee in 2001 to protest the ongoing dialogue between the NGO professional association and US, NATO, and UN military and peacekeeping contingents.

31. See, for example, "Guidelines for InterAction Staff Relations with Military Forces Engaged in, or Training for, Peacekeeping and Disaster Response" (Washington, D.C.: InterAction, n.d.).

32. For a discussion of using military assets as an exercise in global stewardship, see Minear and Guillot, *Soldiers to the Rescue*, 47–48, 161–63.

33. *NATO Military Policy on Civil-Military Co-operation*, MCC/411/1, 1, 4.

34. Ed Schenkenberg, "Civil-Military Cooperation in the Wake of Kosovo: A Humanitarian Perspective," in *CIMIC Civil-Military Co-operation: Lessons Learned and Models for the Future*, Report from the Danish Institute of Public Affairs Conference in Copenhagen, September 1–2, 2000, ed. Peter Viggo Jakobsen (Copenhagen: DUPI, 2000), 124.

35. NATO, "NATO Civil-Military Co-operation (CIMIC) Doctrine," Allied Joint Publication-9, study draft 4 (November 2001).

36. See Minear, van Baarda, and Sommers, *NATO and Humanitarian Action*, 26–33.

37. Michael Elmquist, "CIMIC in East Timor," a report to OCHA (December 1999): 9.

38. Greg Hansen, "Report to the Minorities Alliance Working Group of Humanitarian Agencies," November 20, 2000, 11–12.

39. Larry Minear, U. B. P. Chelliah, Jeff Crisp, John Mackinlay, and Thomas G. Weiss, *United Nations Coordination of the International Humanitarian Response to the Gulf Crisis, 1990–1992*, Occasional Paper 13 (Providence: Watson Institute, 1992), 11.

40. For a discussion of the ZCSC, see Mark Frohardt, Diane Paul, and Larry Minear, *Protecting Human Rights: The Challenge to Humanitarian Organizations*, Occasional Paper 35 (Providence: Watson Institute, 1999), 70.

41. Growing out of its experience in the Rwanda crisis and elsewhere, UNHCR has proposed a "ladder of options," including soft, medium, and hard measures, to enhance refugee camp security. See Sadako Ogata, statement to the UN Security Council, November 10, 1998. Also Nicolas Bwakira, introductory remarks to the Open-Ended Ad Hoc Working Group on the Causes of Conflict and the Promotion of Durable Peace and Sustainable Development in Africa.

42. For example, a workshop on the use of private security companies by humanitarian agencies, held at Tufts University in April 2001, reviewed issues that

aid groups need to address in reaching decisions. See International Alert and Feinstein International Famine Center, "The Politicisation of Humanitarian Action and Staff Security: The Use of Private Security Companies by Humanitarian Agencies" (London and Medford, Mass., 2001).

43. Tony Vaux, "Private Security Companies and Humanitarian Agencies," background paper for the conference described in note 42.

44. Bernd McConnell had earlier served in the U.S. Air Force as director of the Balkan Task Force of the under secretary of defense for policy, and as deputy assistant secretary of defense for African Affairs.

45. David Cortright and George A. Lopez, *The Sanctions Decade: Assessing UN Strategies in the 1990s* (Boulder, Colo., and London: Lynne Rienner, 2000), 1–2.

46. Ibid., 2.

47. See in particular United Nations Charter, Chapter VII, Articles 41–42.

48. The Fourth Freedom Forum and the Joan B. Kroc Institute for International Peace Studies at the University of Notre Dame.

49. Larry Minear, David Cortright, Julia Wagler, George A. Lopez, and Thomas G. Weiss, *Toward More Humane and Effective Sanctions Management: Enhancing the Capacity of the United Nations System*, Occasional Paper 31 (Providence: Watson Institute, 1998).

50. See Larry Minear et al., *United Nations Coordination of the International Humanitarian Response to the Gulf Crisis;* Minear et al., *Humanitarian Action in the Former Yugoslavia;* Robert Maguire (team leader), Edwige Balutansky, Jacques Fomerand, Larry Minear, William O'Neill, Thomas G. Weiss, and Sarah Zaidi, *Haiti Held Hostage: International Responses to the Quest for Nationhood, 1986–1996,* Occasional Paper 23 (Providence: Watson Institute, 1996); and Eric Hoskins and Samantha Nutt, *The Humanitarian Impacts of Economic Sanctions on Burundi,* Occasional Paper 29 (Providence: Watson Institute, 1997).

51. For a more detailed discussion, see Thomas G. Weiss, David Cortright, George A. Lopez, and Larry Minear, eds., *Political Gain and Civilian Pain: Humanitarian Impacts of Economic Sanctions* (Lanham, Md., and Oxford, England: Rowman & Littlefield, 1998). The experience in South Africa is reviewed in a chapter by Neta C. Crawford, "The Humanitarian Consequences of Sanctioning South Africa: A Preliminary Assessment," 57–90.

52. For a further discussion, see Larry Minear, "The Morality of Sanctions," in *Hard Choices: Moral Dilemmas in Humanitarian Intervention,* ed. Jonathan Moore (Lanham, Md., Boulder, Colo., New York, and Oxford: Rowman & Littlefield, 1998), 229–50.

53. Minear et al., *Humanitarian Action in the Former Yugoslavia,* 94.

54. Minear et al., *United Nations Coordination of the International Humanitarian Response to the Gulf Crisis, 1990–1992,* 22.

55. Minear et al., *Humanitarian Action in the Former Yugoslavia.*

56. Maguire et al., *Haiti Held Hostage,* 47, 49.

57. Minear et al., *Toward More Humane and Effective Sanctions Management,* vi–vii.

58. Ibid., v.

59. United Nations Security Council Resolution 1054, April 26, 1996.

60. United Nations Security Council Resolution 1070, August 16, 1996.

61. Ted van Baarda, letter to the author, June 22, 2001.

62. Minear et al., *Toward More Humane and Effective Sanctions Management*, 73.

63. For a detailed review of the evolution and implications of military humanitarianism, see David Chandler, "The Road to Military Humanitarianism: How the Human Rights NGOs Shaped a New Humanitarian Agenda," *Human Rights Quarterly* 23 (2001): 678–700.

64. Minear, van Baarda, and Sommers, *NATO and Humanitarian Action*, 114.

65. International Council on Human Rights Policy, "NGO Responses to Military Interventions in Human Rights Crises," draft report, September 2001 (*www.international-council.org*)," 17ff.

66. U.S. NGOs have experienced difficulty in agreeing on ground rules for their discussions with military forces. These are clarified in "Guidelines for InterAction Staff Relations with Military Forces Engaged in, or Training for, Peacekeeping and Disaster Response" (Washington, D.C.: InterAction, n.d.).

67. Minear and Guillot, *Soldiers to the Rescue*, 164.

7. Humanitarian Architecture

1. House Select Committee on Hunger, "Humanitarian Intervention: A Review of Theory and Practice," 102d Cong., 2d sess., 1992, 3.

2. The earlier hearing by the House Select Committee on Hunger on July 29, 1991, was entitled "Decade of Disasters: The United Nations' Response." The statement offered by Larry Minear, "A Strengthened Humanitarian System for the Post–Cold War Era," is reprinted in Larry Minear, Thomas G. Weiss, and Kurt M. Campbell, eds., *Humanitarianism and War: Learning the Lessons from Recent Armed Conflicts,* Occasional Paper 8 (Providence: Watson Institute, 1991), 29–49.

3. House Select Committee on Hunger, "Humanitarian Intervention: A Review of Theory and Practice," 102d Cong., 2d sess., 1992, 148.

4. For a more extended discussion of the concept of humanitarian action, see Larry Minear and Thomas G. Weiss, *Mercy under Fire* (Boulder, Colo.: Westview Press, 1995), 18–22.

5. The court's decision is referenced in ibid., 18–19.

6. Larry Minear and Philippe Guillot, *Soldiers to the Rescue: Humanitarian Lessons from Rwanda* (Paris: Organization for Economic Cooperation and Development, 1996), 16.

7. Jonathan Moore, ed., *Hard Choices: Moral Dilemmas in Humanitarian Intervention* (Lanham, Md., Boulder, Colo., New York, and Oxford: Rowman & Littlefield, 1998), 2.

8. Dallaire made the observation in a keynote speech to a workshop cosponsored by CARE Canada and the Humanitarianism and War Project in Ottawa, April 24, 2001.

9. Tabyiegen A. Aboum, Eshetu Chole, Koste Manibe, Larry Minear, Abdul Mohammed, Jennefer Sebstad, and Thomas G. Weiss, *A Critical Review of Operation*

Lifeline Sudan: A Report to the Aid Agencies (Washington, D.C.: Refugee Policy Group, 1990), 41–43.

10. See notes 1 and 2 in this chapter.

11. Nicola Reindorp and Peter Wiles, *Humanitarian Coordination: Lessons from Recent Field Experience* (London: Overseas Development Institute, 2001), 50.

12. James Ingram, "The Future Architecture for International Humanitarian Assistance," in *Humanitarianism across Borders: Sustaining Civilians in Times of War,* ed. Thomas G. Weiss and Larry Minear (Boulder, Colo.: Lynne Rienner, 1993), 183.

13. Aboum et al., *A Critical Review of Operation Lifeline Sudan*, 33.

14. S. Neil MacFarlane and Larry Minear, *Humanitarian Action and Politics: The Case of Nagorno-Karabakh,* Occasional Paper 25 (Providence: Watson Institute, 1997), 107.

15. See Ingram, "The Future Architecture" in *Humanitarianism across Borders,* ed. Weiss and Minear, 183, 187.

16. In the interim since the tabling of Ingram's proposal in 1993, the ICRC has taken steps to enlist a more multinational array of staff, giving the organization a more global complexion.

17. See Larry Minear, "The Evolving Humanitarian Enterprise," in *The United Nations and Civil Wars,* ed. Thomas G. Weiss (Boulder, Colo.: Lynne Rienner, 1995), 103.

18. Development Initiatives, *Global Humanitarian Assistance 2000* (Geneva: United Nations, 2000), 14.

19. Ibid., 63.

20. Ibid., 65.

21. Donor consultations held at Montreaux, Switzerland, in March 2000 and March 2001 have reviewed the CAP process and made a number of recommendations.

22. For an elaboration, see Stephen C. Lubkemann, "Rebuilding Local Capacities in Mozambique: The National Health System and Civil Society," in *Patronage or Partnership: Local Capacity Building in Humanitarian Crises,* ed. Ian Smillie (Bloomfield, Conn.: Kumarian Press, 2001), 77–106.

23. John Kirby, Chris Howorth, Phil O'Keefe, and Andrew Collins, "A Survey of Evaluation Experience in Complex Emergencies," *International Journal of Human Rights* 5, no. 2 (2001): 114–29.

24. Mary B. Anderson, "Aid: A Mixed Blessing," in *Debating Development: A Development in Practice Reader,* ed. Deborah Eade and Ernst Ligteringen (London: Oxfam-GB, 2001), 294.

25. For a discussion of the increased capacity of Southern NGOs and their pressure on the traditional North-South division of labor, see Marc Lindenberg and Coralie Bryant, *Going Global* (Bloomfield, Conn.: Kumarian Books, 2001), particularly chapter 5, "Emerging Global Organizational Structures," 155–72.

26. Earl Wall, CARE West Bank–Gaza, quoted in "Staff Reflections: Adopting a Rights-Based Approach: Initial Experiences," in *Promoting Rights and Responsibilities,* CARE newsletter, February 2001, 7.

27. WARIPNET is described at *www.lchr.org/ticker/irp/htm*. The paper prepared

for discussions involving the UNHCR Executive Committee in October 2000 is available at *www.lchr.org/conference/ResponseSolutions.htm*. The Lawyers Committee also participates in an innovative initiative by the Social Sciences Research Council, pairing academic researchers and humanitarian and human rights organizations engaged in West Africa.

28. The difficulties imposed upon humanitarian action by situating it within a complex of policies and activities are also examined by Mark Duffield, *Global Governance and the New Wars: The Merging of Development and Security* (London and New York: Zed Books, 2001).

29. United Nations, Department of Humanitarian Affairs, "Protection of Humanitarian Mandates in Conflict Situations," April 13, 1994, 1, 2, 4, and Annex 1.

30. Ibid., 2, 8.

31. See, for example, Larry Minear (team leader), Jeffrey Clark, Roberta Cohen, Dennis Gallagher, Iain Guest, and Thomas G. Weiss, *Humanitarian Action in the Former Yugoslavia: The U.N.'s Role, 1991–1993*, Occasional Paper 18 (Providence: Watson Institute, 1994), particularly the sections on "Dealing with Belligerents Who Defy International Humanitarian Law," 78–83; "Determining the Appropriate Uses of the Military," 83–92; and "Protecting the Integrity of Humanitarian Action," 92–103.

32. United Nations, Note from the Secretary-General, "Guidance on the Relations between Representatives of the Secretary-General, Resident Coordinators, and Humanitarian Coordinators," December 11, 2000. In the same year, a panel headed by Ambassador Lakhdar Brahimi made a comprehensive set of recommendations regarding the reform of UN peacekeeping operations. They did not, however, address in any detail the structural issues of relationships with humanitarian activities.

33. Ogata Sadako, "Ten Years Devoted to Protecting Refugees," *Japan Echo*, August 2001, 44. Tensions within the UN were further highlighted when Madame Ogata rejected an offer from a UN commander of military protection for an aid convoy leaving Sarajevo, only to be overruled by the UN secretary-general.

34. Minear, "The Evolving Humanitarian Enterprise," 98.

35. One recent effort to review the issues was a conference convened by OCHA on "The Relationship between Humanitarian Action and Peacebuilding," held at the Centre for Humanitarian Dialogue in Geneva, January 23, 2001. The group was divided on the extent to which humanitarian activities at the country level should be viewed as integral to UN peace-building efforts.

36. OCHA work plan for 2002 includes continuing work on these "interface" issues.

37. For an example of the orchestration of such input, see the work of the New York–based NGO, Global Policy Forum (*www.globalpolicyforum.org*), mentioned in chapter 5.

38. Minear et al., *A Critical Review of Operation Lifeline Sudan*, 43. Also, Minear, "A Strengthened Humanitarian System for the Post–Cold War Era," in *Humanitarianism and War*, ed. Minear, Weiss, and Campbell, 42–43.

39. Kofi Annan, Address to the United Nations General Assembly presenting his Annual Report, Press Release SG/SM/7136, September 20, 1999.

40. Michael Elmquist, "CIMIC in East Timor," a report to OCHA, December 1999, 9.

41. NATO Civil-Military Cooperation (CIMIC) Doctrine, Allied Joint Publication 9, Study Draft 4, Section 202.1, Principles Governing the Military Direction of CIMIC, November 2001.

42. NATO Military Policy on Civil-Military Co-operation, EAPC/PFP(PCG)N, Annex 1, para. 9, (2001)004.

43. Ibid., Annex 1, paras. 10 and 11e.

44. Larry Minear, Ted van Baarda, and Marc Sommers, *NATO and Humanitarian Action in the Kosovo Crisis,* Occasional Paper 36 (Providence: Watson Institute, 2000), 117–19. The secretary-general's report on the situation in Bosnia-Herzegovina was S./24540, dated September 10, 1992, para. 8ff.

45. The InterAction position is found in "Guidelines for InterAction Staff Relations with Military Forces Engaged in, or Training for, Peacekeeping and Disaster Response." The guidelines authorize InterAction staff to promote four objectives in its dialogue with the military, including "to persuade governments to accept NGO views on what constitutes appropriate use of military assets in disaster response." Those views themselves are not identified.

46. "Issue of the Month: Military Finds the 'Right' Forum for Moving Ahead on Humanitarian Aid," ICVA newsletter *Talkback* 3, no. 1 (February 28, 2001).

47. This proposal resurfaced in our review of the Kosovo crisis. Minear, van Baarda, and Sommers, *NATO and Humanitarian Action in the Kosovo Crisis,* 119–20.

48. Larry Minear, David Cortright, Julia Wagler, George A. Lopez, and Thomas G. Weiss, *Toward More Humane and Effective Sanctions Management: Enhancing the Capacity of the United Nations System,* Occasional Paper 31 (Providence: Watson Institute, 1998), 74–75. While the Security Council has yet to make such a policy affirmation, the UN system has adopted other recommendations that encouraged greater consistency in the area of humanitarian exemptions to sanctions regimes.

49. See ibid., 63–70.

50. United Nations, Note by the President of the Security Council, S/2000/319, April 17, 2000.

51. The Fourth Freedom Forum and the International Peace Academy are currently reviewing recent changes.

52. Minear et al., *Toward More Humane and Effective Sanctions Management,* 23–54.

53. United Nations, Report of the Secretary-General on the Humanitarian Implications of the Measures Imposed by Security Council Resolutions 1267 (1999) and 1333 (2000) on Afghanistan, S/2001/241, para. 30.

54. Ibid., para. 17.

55. Ibid., para. 30.

56. "Afghanistan: Continuing to Apply Bandaids," in *Talkback,* newsletter of the ICVA, 3, no. 1 (February 28, 2001). In January 2002 with the interim administration in place in Kabul, the Security Council adjusted the sanctions, lifting the ban on air

travel but continuing to freeze Al Qaeda and Taliban assets (UNWire, January 17, 2002).

57. James P. Grant, "What It Means to Be Human: The Challenge of Respecting Children's Rights in the 1990s," remarks to the UN Commission on Human Rights, Geneva, March 8, 1994, delivered by UNICEF Deputy Director Stephen Lewis.

58. See Larry Minear, Colin Scott, and Thomas G. Weiss, *The News Media, Civil War, and Humanitarian Action* (Boulder, Colo., and London: Lynne Rienner, 1996), 1.

59. The comment, attributed to the secretary-general by his spokesperson Sylvanna Foa, is quoted in ibid., 4.

60. Ibid., 55.

61. Ibid., 54.

62. Quoted in ibid., 55.

63. Ibid., 56–57.

64. Minear et al., *Humanitarian Action in the Former Yugoslavia*, 133.

65. Robert Maguire (team leader), Edwige Balutansky, Jacques Fomerand, Larry Minear, William O'Neill, Thomas G. Weiss, and Sarah Zaidi, *Haiti Held Hostage: International Responses to the Quest for Nationhood, 1986–1996*, Occasional Paper 23 (Providence: Watson Institute, 1996), 108.

8. Equipping the Enterprise

1. Quoted in Hugo Slim, "The Continuing Metamorphosis of the Humanitarian Practitioner: Some New Colours for an Endangered Chameleon," *Disasters* 19, no. 2 (1995): 110.

2. For an elaboration of the heightened difficulties of complex emergencies as contrasted with natural disasters, see Francis M. Deng and Larry Minear, *The Challenges of Famine Relief: Emergency Operations in the Sudan* (Washington, D.C.: Brookings Institution, 1992).

3. Slim, "The Continuing Metamorphosis," 111.

4. Peter Walker, IFRC Head of Regional Delegation, Bangkok, letter to author, January 10, 2002.

5. As noted earlier, however, donor agencies are increasingly dependent on NGOs to implement their programs.

6. Evidence seems to show, on the one hand, a proliferation of NGOs while, on the other, an increasing share of international relief efforts being handled by a small number of large private agencies.

7. Slim, "The Continuing Metamorphosis," 121–22.

8. Philip White and Lionel Cliffe, "Matching Response to Context in Complex Political Emergencies," *Disasters* 24, no. 4 (December 2000): 326.

9. Cristina Eguizábal, David Lewis, Larry Minear, Peter Sollis, and Thomas G. Weiss, *Humanitarian Challenges in Central America: Learning the Lessons of Recent Armed Conflicts,* Occasional Paper 14 (Providence: Watson Institute, 1993), 31.

10. John Oxenham and Robert Chambers, "Organising Education and Training for Rural Development: Problems and Challenges," in *Patronage or Partnership:*

Local Capacity Building in Humanitarian Crises, ed. Ian Smillie (Bloomfield, Conn.: Kumarian Press, 2001), 9.

11. Smillie, ed., *Patronage or Partnership,* 11. Smillie references the work on capacities and vulnerabilities analysis of Mary B. Anderson and Peter Woodrow.

12. Arjuna Parakrama, "Means without End: Humanitarian Assistance in Sri Lanka," in *Patronage or Partnership,* ed. Smillie, 121.

13. Sean Lowrie, "Sphere at the End of Phase II," *Humanitarian Exchange,* no. 17 (October 2000): 11.

14. For a more extended discussion of accountability issues, see *Humanitarian Exchange: The Magazine of the Humanitarian Practice Network,* October 2000, 1, 11–25. Also see the special issue on accountability of the *Forced Migration Review* (Refugee Studies Center and Norwegian Refugee Council), August 2000, 4–23.

15. For an extended discussion, see S. Neil MacFarlane, *Humanitarian Action: The Conflict Connection,* Occasional Paper 43 (Providence: Watson Institute, 2001), 1–12.

16. Barbara Hendrie, ed., with Ataul Karim (Team Leader), Mark Duffield, Susanne Jaspars, Aldo Benini, Joanna Macrae, Mark Bradbury, Douglas Johnson, and George Larbi, *Operation Lifeline Sudan: A Review* (July 1996).

17. See, for example, Larry Minear, "Time to Pull the Plug on Operation Lifeline Sudan?" *Crosslines Global Report* (March–April 1997): 59–60. An editorial in the *New York Times* observed that the Sudan's eighteen-year civil war had "perversely transformed many international efforts to provide humanitarian assistance into fuel for further fighting." See "Redemption of Sudanese Slaves," *New York Times,* April 27, 2001.

18. See MacFarlane, *Humanitarian Action: The Conflict Connection.*

19. For an elaboration of the connections, see Philippe Le Billon (with Joanna Macrae, Nick Leader, and Roger East), *The Political Economy of War: What Relief Agencies Need to Know,* Network Paper 33 (London: Humanitarian Practice Network, 2000). Also Gayle E. Smith, "Relief Operations and Military Strategy," in *Humanitarianism across Borders: Sustaining Civilians in Times of War,* ed. Thomas G. Weiss and Larry Minear (Boulder, Colo., and London: Lynne Rienner, 1993), 97–124. Smith argues that "relief practitioners should study military strategy and then plan their interventions to prevent the intersection between conflict and relief work from exacerbating the plight of civilians" (97).

20. See MacFarlane, *Humanitarian Action: The Conflict Connection,* viii. A recent British government interdepartmental study ranks "misplaced humanitarian assistance" among the *tertiary* causes of conflict in Africa. See Cabinet Sub-Committee on Conflict Prevention in Africa, "The Causes of Conflict in Africa," 2001, para. 50.

21. Mary B. Anderson, *Do No Harm: Supporting Local Capacities for Peace through Aid* (Cambridge, Mass.: The Collaborative for Development Action, 1996), and Mary B. Anderson, *Do No Harm: How Aid Can Support Peace — or War* (Boulder, Colo., and London: Lynne Rienner, 1999).

22. Anderson, *Do No Harm* (1999), 1–2.

23. Peace and Relief Seminar Conference Report, "Do No Harm," Oxford

Brookes University, October 28, 1998. See also Mark Duffield, "Response to Mary Anderson," September 2, 1998.

24. Peace and Relief Seminar Conference Report.

25. MacFarlane, *Humanitarian Action: The Conflict Connection,* 49.

26. Ibid., 62.

27. Eguizábal et al., *Humanitarian Challenges in Central America,* 75–76.

28. S. Neil MacFarlane and Larry Minear, *Humanitarian Action and Politics: The Case of Nagorno-Karabakh,* Occasional Paper 25 (Providence: Watson Institute, 1997), 106.

29. For an analysis of the pros and cons of placing humanitarian activities within the broader context of conflict resolution and development, see Mark Duffield, *Global Governance and the New Wars: The Merging of Development and Security* (London and New York: Zed Books, 2001). The issue of the connections between humanitarian action and the political sphere are also treated in chapters 5 and 7 of the present volume.

30. Stephen C. Lubkemann, Larry Minear, and Thomas G. Weiss, eds., *Humanitarian Action: Social Science Connections,* Occasional Paper 37 (Providence: Watson Institute, 2000).

31. Larry Minear, "Learning to Learn," *Program in Touch: News from CARE and the NGO Community,* no. 8 (summer 1998).

32. Ibid., 21.

33. Larry Minear and Thomas G. Weiss, *Humanitarian Action in Times of War: A Handbook for Practitioners* (Boulder, Colo., and London: Lynne Rienner, 1993), 37.

34. Lubkemann et al., *Humanitarian Action: Social Science Connections,* 15–17.

35. MSF press release, April 9, 1999, dateline Skopje, quoting MSF director general Lex Winkler. See also Larry Minear, Ted van Baarda, and Marc Sommers, *NATO and Humanitarian Action in the Kosovo Crisis,* Occasional Paper 36 (Providence: Watson Institute, 2000), 14–15. While MSF's statement was clear and timely, there were apparently some divergences among staff on the views expressed.

36. Lubkemann et al., *Humanitarian Action: Social Science Connections,* 29.

37. Chapter 3 mentioned a similarly hopeful conclusion, also based on limited data, regarding whether human rights–based programming has increased the effectiveness of humanitarian activities. See also Larry Minear and Thomas G. Weiss, eds., *Humanitarian Action: A Transatlantic Agenda for Operations and Research,* Occasional Paper 39 (Providence: Watson Institute, 2000), 9.

38. Julie A. Mertus, *War's Offensive on Women: The Humanitarian Challenge in Bosnia, Kosovo, and Afghanistan* (Bloomfield, Conn.: Kumarian Press, 2000), 120.

39. Ibid., 103. The material quoted is from Robert Casson and Associates, *Does Aid Work?* 2d ed. (Oxford: Clarendon Press, 1994), 92.

40. Susanne Schmeidl, "The Quest for Accuracy in the Estimation of Forced Migration," in *Humanitarian Action: Social Science Connections,* ed. Lubkemann, Minear, and Weiss, 155.

41. Jeff Crisp, "Who Has Counted the Refugees? UNHCR and the Politics of

Numbers," in *Humanitarian Action: Social Science Connections,* ed. Lubkemann, Minear, and Weiss, 62.

42. Marc Sommers, "On the Margins, in the Mainstream: Urban Refugees in Africa," in *Humanitarian Action: Social Science Connections,* ed. Lubkemann, Minear, and Weiss, 89.

43. Stephen C. Lubkemann, "Socio-Cultural Factors Shaping Mozambican Repatriation Process," in *Humanitarian Action: Social Science Connections,* ed. Lubkemann, Minear, and Weiss, 91.

44. For an elaboration of some of the parallels, see Jeff Crisp, "Thinking outside the Box: Evaluation and Humanitarian Action," *Forced Migration Review,* no. 8 (August 2000): 4–7.

45. Eguizábal et al., *Humanitarian Challenges in Central America,* 31.

46. Niels Dabelstein, "Evaluating the International Humanitarian System: Rationale, Process, and Management of the Joint Evaluation of the International Response to the Rwanda Genocide," *Disasters* 20, no. 4 (1996): 287. The lessons-learning process is the subject of chapter 9.

47. In the situation described in chapter 5 regarding a request from NGOs to U.S. government authorities for the deployment of additional military forces to Somalia, a number of agency executives took positions different from the frontline staff and/or did not consult them.

48. The U.S.-based International Rescue Committee is one NGO with such a reputation.

49. MacFarlane and Minear, *Humanitarian Action and Politics: The Case of Nagorno-Karabakh,* 108–9.

9. The Dynamics of Institutional Change

1. "UN Rejects Rwanda Charges," *International Peacekeeping News,* no. 2–01, March–April 1996.

2. "Report of the Independent Inquiry into the Actions of the United Nations during the 1994 Genocide in Rwanda," December 15, 1999.

3. Secretary-General Kofi Annan, "Statement on Receiving the Report of the Independent Inquiry into the Actions of the United Nations during the 1994 Genocide in Rwanda," December 16, 1999.

4. ALNAP, "Improved Performance through Improved Learning," Annual Review 2002, forthcoming.

5. Larry Minear, Colin Scott, and Thomas G. Weiss, *The News Media, Civil War, and Humanitarian Action* (Boulder, Colo.: Lynne Rienner, 1996), 57–58.

6. Ibid., 79–98.

7. Development Initiatives, *Global Humanitarian Assistance 2000* (Geneva: IASC, 2000), 88.

8. Julie A. Mertus, *War's Offensive on Women: The Humanitarian Challenge in Bosnia, Kosovo, and Afghanistan* (Bloomfield, Conn.: Kumarian Press, 2000), 119.

9. Nicola Reindorp and Peter Wiles, *Humanitarian Coordination: Lessons from Recent Field Experience* (London: Overseas Development Institute, 2001). I served as a peer reviewer for the study.

10. For an earlier examination by OCHA of these issues, see "Humanitarian Co-ordination: Lessons Learned," Report of a Review Seminar, Stockholm, April 3–4, 1998 (New York: OCHA, 1998).

11. For an unpacking of the four cultural impediments to learning, see Larry Min-ear, "Making the Humanitarian System Work Better," in *A Framework for Survival: Health, Human Rights, and Humanitarian Assistance in Conflicts and Disasters*, ed. Kevin M. Cahill (New York and London: Routledge, 1999), 309–14. The OCHA study on coordination referred to in the previous note identifies structural, institu-tional, and management obstacles to change. See Reindorp and Wiles, *Humanitarian Coordination*, iii, 8–19.

12. Hearing before the House Select Committee on Hunger, 102d Cong., 2d sess., 1992, 67, 75.

13. One review of evaluations with definite impacts on agency functioning men-tions one by the U.K.'s Overseas Development Administration on the southern African drought, one by DANIDA on its own policies, and an independent study commissioned by UNHCR on its response to the Kosovo crisis. See ALNAP, "Improved Performance through Improved Learning."

14. See, for example, Roberta Cohen and Francis M. Deng, *Masses in Flight: The Global Crisis of Internal Displacement* (Washington, D.C.: Brookings Institution, 1998), and Roberta Cohen and Francis M. Deng, eds., *The Forsaken People: Case Studies of the Internally Displaced* (Washington, D.C.: Brookings Institution, 1998).

15. Don Hubert, *The Landmine Ban: A Case Study in Humanitarian Advocacy*, Occasional Paper 42 (Providence: Watson Institute, 2000), 13.

16. Reindorp and Wiles, *Humanitarian Coordination*, 50.

17. Niels Dabelstein, "Evaluating the International Humanitarian System: Ration-ale, Process and Management of the Joint Evaluation of the International Response to the Rwanda Genocide," *Disasters* 20, no. 4 (1996): 292.

18. Larry Minear, U. B. P. Chelliah, Jeff Crisp, John Mackinlay, and Thomas G. Weiss, *United Nations Coordination of the International Humanitarian Response to the Gulf Crisis, 1990–1992*, Occasional Paper 13 (Providence: Watson Institute, 1992), 39.

19. For a listing of several studies conducted by individual agencies and their impacts, see John Kirby, Chris Howorth, Phil O'Keefe, and Andrew Collins, "A Survey of Evaluation Experience in Complex Emergencies," *International Journal of Human Rights* 5, no. 2 (2001): 114–29.

20. Steering Committee of the Joint Evaluation of Emergency Assistance to Rwanda, *International Response to Conflict and Genocide: Lessons from the Rwanda Experience* (Copenhagen: Steering Committee, 1996), 5 vols. The chairman of the evaluation's steering committee, Niels Dabelstein of DANIDA, commented in 1996 that "only the UN Secretariat has attempted to discredit the evaluation through aggressive and inaccurate press statements." Dabelstein, "Evaluating the International Humanitarian System," 282.

21. John Borton, "Doing Study 3 of the Joint Evaluation of Emergency Assistance to Rwanda: The Team Leader's Perspective," in *Evaluating International Humani-*

tarian Action: Reflections from Practitioners, ed. Adrian Wood, Raymond Apthorpe, and John Borton (London and New York: Zed Books and ALNAP, 2001), 99.

22. Joint Evaluation Follow-Up Monitoring and Facilitation Network (JEFF), "The Joint Evaluation of Emergency Assistance to Rwanda: A Review of Follow-Up and Impact One Year after Publication," Stockholm, SIDA, February 2, 1997; and "The Joint Evaluation of Emergency Assistance to Rwanda: A Review of Follow-Up and Impact Fifteen Months after Publication," Stockholm, SIDA, June 12, 1997.

23. Abby Stoddard, "Background Paper on Issues in Humanitarian Aid," Center for International Cooperation, New York University, 1999, quoted in Development Initiatives, *Global Humanitarian Assistance 2000,* 88.

24. Dabelstein, "Evaluating the International Humanitarian System," 288, 294.

25. Borton, "Doing Study 3," 99.

26. "Only the UN Secretariat has attempted to discredit the evaluation through aggressive and inaccurate press statements." Dabelstein, "Evaluating the International Humanitarian System," 291. The study also came under considerable pressure at certain points from the French government and UNHCR.

27. See Box 5.3 in Development Initiatives, *Global Humanitarian Assistance 2000,* 88. The Feinstein International Famine Center, of which the Humanitarianism and War Project is part, is an institutional member of ALNAP.

28. ALNAP, "Improved Performance through Improved Learning." Another promising institutional offshoot of the Rwanda study is the Humanitarian Ombudsman Project, an initiative begun in 1998 by a consortium of UK-based NGOs. The undertaking morphed into the Humanitarian Accountability Project, which began a pilot project in 2000 (*www.oneworld.org/ombudsman/todate/htm*).

29. Giles M. Whitcomb, "Humanitarianism and War Project: Review of Phases 1 and 2, Implications for Phase 3," November 19, 1996, 6.

30. S. Neil MacFarlane and Larry Minear, *Humanitarian Action and Politics: The Case of Nagorno-Karabakh,* Occasional Paper 25 (Providence: Watson Institute, 1997), v.

31. Robert O. Krikorian, book review, in *Journal for the Society of Armenian Studies* 9 (1996, 1997): 189–97.

32. Larry Minear, in *Journal for the Society of Armenian Studies* 10 (1998, 1999): 189–91.

33. For a discussion of some of the ethical issues in research, see Jonathan Goodhand, "Research in Conflict Zones: Ethics and Accountability," *Forced Migration Review,* no. 8 (August 2000). See *www.fmreview.org/fmr083.htm.*

34. For a discussion of traditional and newer evaluation categories, see ETC UK, "Making Evaluation More Effective in Humanitarian Assistance," a consultancy report for ALNAP, 2001.

35. Larry Minear, *Helping People in an Age of Conflict: Toward a New Professionalism in U.S. Voluntary Humanitarian Assistance* (New York and Washington, D.C.: InterAction, 1988), 74.

36. The project is launching a study of the political economy of humanitarian action in May 2002. For updated information see *hwproject.tufts.edu.*

37. Minear, van Baarda, and Sommers, *NATO and Humanitarian Action in the Kosovo Crisis,* 114.

38. Dabelstein, "Evaluating the International Humanitarian System," 282.

39. Adrian Wood, Raymond Apthorpe, and John Borton, "Conclusions," in Wood, Apthorpe, and Borton, *Evaluating International Humanitarian Action: Reflection from Practitioners,* 209.

40. Ibid., 211.

41. Joanna Macrae, "Studying Up, Down, and Sideways," in *Humanitarian Action,* ed. Minear and Weiss, 52–53. For a more extended discussion, see also "Understanding Forced Migration: Rethinking Collaborative Arrangements," in *Humanitarian Action: Social Science Connections,* ed. Lubkemann, Minear, and Weiss, 1–32.

42. Minear, van Baarda, and Sommers, *NATO and Humanitarian Action in the Kosovo Crisis,* 12.

43. Larry Minear, "Report of a Consultation of Experts," Brown University, April 1991, in Larry Minear, Thomas G. Weiss, and Kurt M. Campbell, *Humanitarianism and War: Learning the Lessons from Recent Armed Conflicts,* Occasional Paper 8 (Providence: Watson Institute, 1991), 11.

44. Larry Minear, Jeffrey Clark, Roberta Cohen, Dennis Gallagher, Iain Guest, and Thomas G. Weiss, *Humanitarian Action in the Former Yugoslavia: The U.N.'s Role, 1991–1993,* Occasional Paper 18 (Providence: Watson Institute, 1994), 2.

45. Antonio Donini, *The Policies of Mercy: UN Coordination in Afghanistan, Mozambique, and Rwanda,* Occasional Paper 22 (Providence: Watson Institute, 1996), 113.

46. Tabyiegen A. Aboum, Eshetu Chole, Koste Manibe, Larry Minear, Abdul Mohammed, Jennefer Sebstad, and Thomas G. Weiss, *A Critical Review of Operation Lifeline Sudan: A Report to the Aid Agencies* (Washington, D.C.: Refugee Policy Group, 1990), 54.

47. Larry Minear, "The Humanitarian and Military Interface: Reflections on the Rwanda Experience," *Hunger Notes* (summer 1996): 23.

Epilogue

1. Richard Tomkins, "Fortitude in a Fearful New World," *Financial Times,* September 29–30, 2001, 2.

2. Zalmay Khalilzad, who served as a special State Department advisor on the Iran-Iraq War and the Soviet war in Afghanistan, has been appointed special assistant to the president and senior director for Gulf, Southwest Asia and other regional issues at the National Security Council (press release, Office of the White House Press Secretary, May 23, 2001). Otto Reich, who served in a number of State Department posts during 1980s with responsibilities for Latin America and the Caribbean, has been appointed assistant secretary of state for western hemisphere affairs (Office of the White House Press Secretary, March 22, 2001). John Negroponte, who served as ambassador to Honduras from 1981 to 1985, has been appointed representative of the United States to the United Nations (press release, Office of the White House Press Secretary, March 6, 2001).

3. Larry Minear, "After the Bombings: Terrorism vs. Humanitarianism," *Providence Sunday Journal,* August 30, 1998.

4. David M. Shribman, "US Tackling Terrorists, but Slow to Explore Their Roots," *Boston Globe,* January 15, 2002, A12.

5. John Donnelly, "Heavy Lifting Seen in Afghans' Hands," *Boston Globe,* November 28, 2001.

6. Meeting of the Afghan Reconstruction Steering Group, "Chairmen's Summary of Conclusions," Brussels, December 20–21, 2001.

7. IRIN interview with UNICEF head Carol Bellamy, Islamabad, December 6, 2001.

8. Senior UN official based in Islamabad, private communication with the author, December 2, 2001.

9. Both the Kosovo and Kabul positions were suggested in discussions in the project's NGO Policy Dialogue series. In Kosovo such a position was created by the Save the Children Alliance. In Afghanistan the idea was not implemented.

10. Agence France-Presse, "US Military Food Airdrops Condemned as 'Catastrophe,'" October 15, 2001.

11. Office for the Coordination of Humanitarian Efforts, "UN Officials Concerned with Internal Displacement Call for Immediate Humanitarian Access to the Displaced and Other Vulnerable Groups in Afghanistan," press statement, Geneva, November 16, 2001.

12. Integrated Regional Information Network (IRIN), "Reconstruction Requires Strong Afghan Perspective," Islamabad, November 27, 2001.

13. Nieko Nishimizu, vice president of the South Asia region for the World Bank, quoted in John Donnelly, "Heavy Lifting Seen in Afghans' Hands," *Boston Globe,* November 28, 2001.

14. Stephen C. Lubkemann, "Rebuilding Local Capacities in Mozambique," in *Patronage or Partnership,* ed. Ian Smillie (Bloomfield, Conn.: Kumarian Press, 2001), 79. A recent British government study observes that "Mozambique's successful emergence from conflict has been in no small part due to its success in relegitimizing the state in the eyes of the population. This was done through a strong commitment to reestablishing and delivering basic services, thereby demonstrating the value of national government." See Cabinet Sub-Committee on Conflict Prevention in Africa, "The Causes of Conflict in Africa," 2001, para. 52.

15. See Larry Minear, "Report to the Headquarters Colloquium on the InterAgency Strategic Framework Mission to Afghanistan," September 1997, *hwproject.tufts.edu.*

16. David E. Lockwood, UNDP's deputy regional director for Asia and the Pacific, at an international conference in Islamabad in November 2001. Quoted in Donnelly, "Heavy Lifting."

17. Neil Swidey, "Devils of Mercy," *Boston Sunday Globe,* January 13, 2002, E3.

18. Ibid.

19. Antonio Donini, *The Policies of Mercy: UN Coordination in Afghanistan, Mozambique, and Rwanda,* Occasional Paper 22 (Providence: Watson Institute, 1996).

20. This tabulation of civilian Afghan deaths comes from University of New Hampshire professor Marc Herold, based on published news accounts. See *http://pubpages.unh.edu/~Mwherold/*.

21. Remarks by the president to State Department employees, Washington, D.C., October 4, 2001.

22. Graham T. Allison, "Bombing Afghanistan with Food: War's Second Front," *Boston Globe,* October 14, 2001.

23. Ed Schenkenberg, op-ed, *De Volkskrant,* October 8, 2001.

24. InterAction, Letter to President George W. Bush, September 19, 2001, signed by Mary E. McClymont, President and CEO, and Nancy A. Aossey, Chairman of the Board.

25. InterAction, Letter to President George W. Bush, October 1, 2001, signed by Mary E. McClymont, President and CEO, and Nancy A. Aossey, Chairman of the Board.

26. The November 1 statement was signed by officials from Lutheran World Relief, the American Friends Service Committee, the Mennonite Central Committee, Church World Service, and Presbyterian Disaster Assistance.

27. Statement made in Ottawa, September 26, 2001, by groups including Oxfam, World Vision, the Mennonite Central Committee, and the Canadian Red Cross.

28. "Working to Solve the Crisis in Afghanistan," a statement by NGOs, October 5, 2001, Afghanistan.

29. Interview with the author, January 16, 2002.

30. Larry Minear, Ted van Baarda, and Marc Sommers, *NATO and Humanitarian Action in the Kosovo Crisis* (Providence: Watson Institute, 2000), 63–64.

31. Ibid., 67–68.

32. Ibid., 52.

33. James Carroll, "US Moves Fuel Bellicosity Elsewhere," *Boston Globe,* January 15, 2002, A19.

34. Minear, "Report to the Headquarters Colloquium on the InterAgency Strategic Framework Mission to Afghanistan." *hwproject.tufts.edu.*

35. Mark Duffield, Patricia Gossman, and Nicholas Leader, *Review of the Strategic Framework for Afghanistan,* report commissioned by the Strategic Monitoring Unit, Afghanistan, final draft, October 2001, 29–30.

36. Carlotta Gall, "Pleas for Food, Help, and a Way Out," *New York Times,* January 20, 2002, 13. The reporter quotes a UNICEF official as saying, "The U.S. Army . . . say they could cover the whole camp, and we asked them to be ready."

37. See, for example, Beth Daley, "Aid Workers Said to Steal Afghan Food: Seen Joining Warlords in Diverting Tons," *Boston Globe,* January 8, 2002, A1, 8. See also Aziz Ahmad Rahmand, professor of modern history at Kabul University, quoted in Alfon Luna, "Aid Agencies Are New Colonial Rulers of Afghanistan, Academics Say," Agence France-Presse, January 10, 2002.

38. ETC UK, "Making Evaluation More Effective in Humanitarian Assistance," consultancy report for ALNAP, 2001.

39. InterAction, Letter to U.S. National Security Adviser Condoleezza Rice, April 2, 2002 (*www.interaction.org*).

40. The effort was led by John Borton of ALNAP and the Overseas Development Institute, joined by six colleagues, including myself. For the text of the study, paraphrased slightly here, see *www.alnap.org*.

41. Stephen Smith and Sandy Tolan, "The Roots of Resentment: America, Great Britain, and the Arab World," *American Radioworks,* December 23, 2001.

42. Ibid.

Abbreviations

ALNAP	The Active Learning Network for Accountability and Performance in Humanitarian Action
AP	Associated Press
APDOVE	Association of Protestant Development Organizations in Europe
BBC	British Broadcasting Corporation
CAP	Consolidated Appeals Process (UN)
CECI	Centre canadien d'étude et de la cooperation internationale
CIDA	Canadian International Development Agency
CIDSE	Coopération internationale pour le développement et la solidarité
CIMIC	Civil-military cooperation
DAC	Development Assistance Committee (OECD)
DHA	Department of Humanitarian Affairs (UN)
ECHA	Executive Committee for Humanitarian Affairs (UN)
ECHO	European Community Humanitarian Office
ECOSOC	Economic and Social Council (UN)
EU	European Union
FINNIDA	Finnish Cooperation [government bilateral assistance agency]
H & W	The Humanitarianism and War Project
HACU	Humanitarian Assistance Coordination Unit (UN/Sierra Leone)
HURIST	Human Rights Strengthening Program (UNDP)
IANSA	International Action Network on Small Arms

IASC	Inter-Agency Standing Committee
ICISS	International Commission on Intervention and State Sovereignty
ICRC	International Committee of the Red Cross
ICVA	International Council of Voluntary Agencies
IDP	Internally displaced person
IFRC	International Federations of the Red Cross and Red Crescent Societies
INTERFET	International Force for East Timor
KFOR	Kosovo Force (NATO)
LCPP	Local Capacities for Peace Project
MSF	Médecins sans Frontières (Doctors Without Borders)
MONUA	United Nations Mission in Angola
NATO	North Atlantic Treaty Organization
NGO	Nongovernmental organization
OCHA	Office for the Coordination of Humanitarian Affairs (UN)
ODA	Official Development Assistance
OECD	Organization for Economic Cooperation and Development
OEOA	Office of Emergency Assistance in Africa (UN)
OFDA	Office for Foreign Disaster Assistance (U.S.)
OHCHR	Office of the High Commissioner for Human Rights (UN)
OLS	Operation Lifeline Sudan
ONUSAL	UN Observer Group in El Salvador
OSCE	Organization for Security and Cooperation in Europe
P5	Permanent Five Members of the Security Council (UN)
RUF	Revolutionary United Front (Sierra Leone)
SCC	Sudan Council of Churches
SHIRBRIG	UN Standby Forces High Readiness Brigade
SPLA	Sudan People's Liberation Army
UN	United Nations

UNICEF	United Nations Children's Fund
UNDP	United Nations Development Programme
UNGCI	United Nations Guard Contingent in Iraq
UNHCR	United Nations High Commissioner for Refugees
UNMIK	United Nations Mission in Kosovo
UNOMSIL	United Nations Observer Mission in Sierra Leone
UNPROFOR	UN Protection Force (Former Yugoslavia)
UNREO	United Nations Rwanda Emergency Operation
UNRWA	United Nations Relief Works Administration
UNTAC	United Nations Transnational Authority in Cambodia
USAID	United States Agency for International Development
VOICE	Voluntary Organisations in Cooperation in Emergencies
WARIPNET	West African NGO Refugee and Internally Displaced Persons Network
WFP	World Food Program (UN)
WHO	World Health Organizations (UN)
ZCSC	Zairian Camp Security Contingent

Index

About the Authors

Photo of Larry Minear by Mark Morelli © 2002

Larry Minear directs the Humanitarianism and War Project at the Feinstein International Famine Center in Tufts University's Friedman School of Nutrition Science and Policy, where he is on the faculty. He has worked on humanitarian and development issues since 1972, serving as staff member to two NGOs, Lutheran World Relief and Church World Service, and as consultant to NGOs, governments, and UN organizations. He has a bachelor's degree from Yale University and masters degrees from Yale and Harvard. He has conducted research in many humanitarian emergencies and has written extensively for specialized and general audiences.

His books in the humanitarian field, whether by himself or with various coauthors, include *Helping People in an Age of Conflict: Toward a New Professionalism in U.S. Voluntary Humanitarian Assistance* (1988), *The Challenges of Famine Relief: Emergency Operations in the Sudan* (1992), *Humanitarian Action in Times of War: A Handbook for Practitioners* (1993), *Mercy under Fire: War and the Global Humanitarian Community* (1995), *Humanitarian Politics* (1995), *Soldiers to the Rescue: Humanitarian Lessons from Rwanda* (1996), and *Political Gain and Civilian Pain: The Humanitarian Impacts of Economic Sanctions* (1997). These books, along with various Occasional Papers and articles, are among the publications listed in appendix 2.

Jan Eliasson is currently Sweden's ambassador to the United States. Earlier assignments have included six years as Sweden's deputy secretary of state and service as Sweden's ambassador to the United Nations in New York during the years 1988–92. Mr. Eliasson was vice president of the UN Economic and Social Council and chair of the U.N. General Assembly's working group on emergency relief, in which capacity he negotiated the terms of UN resolution 46/182 on humanitarian coordination. In 1992, he was appointed the UN's first under-secretary-general for humanitarian affairs, a post created as a result of the resolution. He has been actively engaged in international humanitarian assistance and conflict resolution efforts in Nagorno-Karabakh, the Balkans, Sudan, Mozambique, and Somalia. Mr. Eliasson is author or coauthor of numerous books and articles and a frequent lecturer on foreign policy and diplomacy.

John C. Hammock is associate professor of international humanitarian aid at the Fletcher School of Law and Diplomacy and Alexander N. McFarlane Professor of Nutrition at the Tufts University Gerald J. and Dorothy R. Friedman School of Nutrition Science and Policy at Tufts University. Founder in 1996 of the Feinstein International Famine Center at Tufts, he headed the center through August 2001. Previously he directed two NGOs, ACCION International (1973–80) and Oxfam America (1984–95). His current research interests involve ethics and values in international humanitarian aid, Central American development, and Latinos in the United States. His writings include *Coping with Crisis, Coping with Aid: Capacity Building, Coping Mechanisms, and Dependency* (1997).

# Also from Kumarian Press...

International Development

Advocacy for Social Justice: A Global Action and Reflection Guide
David Cohen, Rosa de la Vega and Gabrielle Watson

Patronage or Partnership: Local Capacity Building in Humanitarian Crises
Edited by Ian Smillie for the Humanitarianism and War Project

Sustainable Livelihoods: Building on the Wealth of the Poor
Kristin Helmore and Naresh Singh

Transcending Neoliberalism: Community-Based Development in Latin America
Edited by Henry Veltmeyer and Anthony O'Malley

War's Offensive on Women:
The Humanitarian Challenge in Bosnia, Kosovo and Afghanistan
Julie A. Mertus for the Humanitarianism and War Project

Conflict Resolution, Environment, Gender Studies, Global Issues, Globalization, Microfinance, Political Economy

Bound: Living in the Globalized World
Scott Sernau

Capitalism and Justice: Envisioning Social and Economic Fairness
John Isbister

Exploring the Gaps: Vital Links Between Trade, Environment and Culture
James R. Lee

The Hidden Assembly Line:
Gender Dynamics of Subcontracted Work in a Global Economy
Edited by Radhika Balakrishnan

Inequity in the Global Village: Recycled Rhetoric and Disposable People
Jan Knippers Black

Mainstreaming Microfinance:
How Lending to the Poor Began, Grew and Came of Age in Bolivia
Elisabeth Rhyne

Managing Policy Reform:
Concepts & Tools for Decision-Makers in Developing & Transitioning Countries
Derick W. Brinkerhoff and Benjamin L. Crosby

Where Corruption Lives
Gerald Caiden, O.P. Dwivedi and Joseph Jabbra

Visit Kumarian Press at **www.kpbooks.com** or
call **toll-free 800.289.2664** for a complete catalog.

Kumarian Press, located in Bloomfield, Connecticut, is a forward-looking, scholarly press that promotes active international engagement and an awareness of global connectedness.